Cartier to Frontenac

Cartier to Frontenac

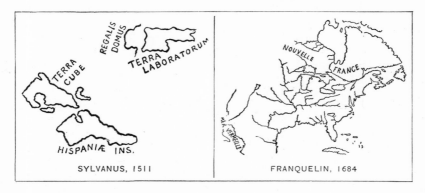

SYLVANUS, 1511   FRANQUELIN, 1684

GEOGRAPHICAL DISCOVERY IN THE INTERIOR

OF

NORTH AMERICA

IN ITS HISTORICAL RELATIONS

1534—1700

*WITH FULL CARTOGRAPHICAL ILLUSTRA-
TIONS FROM CONTEMPORARY SOURCES*

BY

JUSTIN WINSOR

COOPER SQUARE PUBLISHERS, INC.
NEW YORK
1970

F 1030
W 78

Originally Published 1894
Published by Cooper Square Publishers, Inc.
59 Fourth Avenue, New York, N. Y. 10003
Standard Book Number 8154-0323-2
Library of Congress Catalog Card No. 79-114670

Printed in the United States of America
by Noble Offset Printers, Inc., New York, N. Y. 10003

To JAMES B. ANGELL, LL. D.,

PRESIDENT OF THE UNIVERSITY OF MICHIGAN.

———

DEAR DOCTOR : —

Your fortune took you from the seaboard of New England to the valley of the St. Lawrence, and on the banks of that lake where Champlain first invoked the enmity of the Iroquois, you took your place among those who preside over our American colleges. Thence you went to a distant verge of that same valley, and near the path which La Salle followed in the boldest action of his life, you have developed the greatest university which we have beyond the mountains.

No one knows better than yourself how the great valley which the American people shares with others on the north, and the greater valley of the interior which is all ours, and which almost becomes one with the other at various points, carry the streams of national life back and forth between the gulf which Cartier opened and that other gulf which Columbus failed to comprehend. This book cannot be more fitly inscribed than to you, by an adopted son of your university, and your friend,

Justin Winsor

HARVARD UNIVERSITY,
September, 1893.

CONTENTS AND ILLUSTRATIONS.

CHAPTER I.

CHAPTER II.

CHAPTER III.

CHAPTER IV.

A STUDY OF GEOGRAPHICAL DISCOVERY IN THE INTERIOR OF NORTH AMERICA.

CHAPTER I.

FROM COLUMBUS TO CARTIER.

1492–1534.

It was not long after the discovery of Columbus before it became evident to some, at least, that the great Discoverer had not found any part of the world neighboring to Cathay,

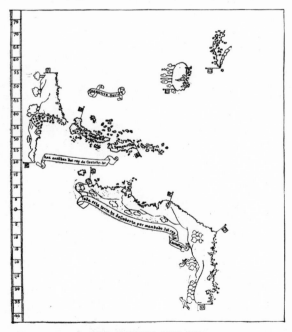

THE CANERIO MAP, 1503.
[From the Sketch in Ruge's *Kartographie von Amerika*.]

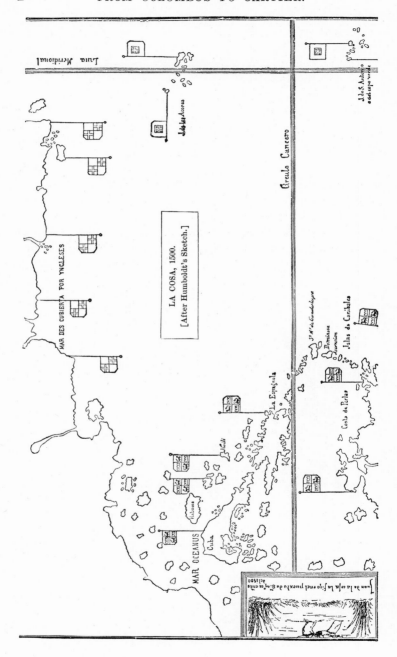

LA COSA, 1500.

[After Humboldt's Sketch.]

however remotely connected with the Orient of Marco Polo the
new regions might prove to be. After the return of
Columbus in 1493, it is apparent that Peter Martyr
hesitated to believe that Asia had been reached. It was quite
clear that Columbus, on his second voyage, himself felt uncertain of his proximity to Asia, since, to preserve his credit with
the Spanish sovereigns, he forced his companions, against the
will of more than half of them, and on penalty of personal
violence if they recanted, to make oath that Cuba was an Asiatic
peninsula. He even took steps later to prevent one of the re-
calcitrant victims going back to Spain, for fear his representations would unsettle the royal faith that the fabled Orient
had been reached. When his pilot, Juan de la Cosa, who was
one of those forced to perjure themselves, found himself free to
make Cuba an island in his map of 1500, the fact that he put
no Asiatic names on the coast of a continent west of Cuba has

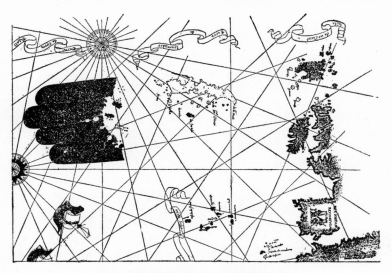

PART OF CHART NO. II. IN KUNSTMANN.
[Also in *Bull. de Géog. Hist. et Descriptive*, 1886, pl. iv.]

been held to show that the doubt of its being Asia had already
possessed that seaman's mind. The makers of the Cantino
and Canerio maps in 1502 and 1503 respectively, in putting in
a coast for Asia distinct from this continent which La Cosa had

delineated, establish the point that as early as the first years
of the sixteenth century the cartographers whose works have
come down to us had satisfied themselves that areas of land of
continental proportions had blocked further progress to the
west. The geographical question then uppermost was thus
reduced to this: Was this barrier a new continent, or had the
islands which it was supposed would be found in the path to
Asia proved to be larger than was imagined? It was Columbus's purpose in his fourth voyage to find an opening in this
barrier through which to reach the territories of the Asiatic potentates, and then to continue the circumnavigation of the earth.
It may, then, well be questioned if the statement ordinarily
made, that Columbus in 1506 died in ignorance of the true
geographical conditions pertaining to a new continent, is true,
whatever may have been his profession in the matter. There
is, as we have seen, good ground for the belief that he did
not mean the Spanish sovereigns to be awakened from a delusion in which he deemed it for his interests that they should
remain.

When Balboa, twenty years after Columbus's discovery, made
Balboa and
Magellan.
it more palpable that south of the Isthmus of Panama there was a substantial barrier to western progress, and when ten years later Magellan pierced this southern
barrier at its Antarctic extremity, it still remained a problem
to find out the true character of the northern barrier to such a
progress, and to find a place to enter the land, along a northern
parallel, far enough to reach the historic India.

There were two waterways by which this northern land could
The two
great North
American
waterways.
have been explored far inland; but for forty years
after the landfall of Columbus, it is not safe to af-
firm positively that any one had attempted to follow
their channels. A local pride among the rugged sea-folk of the
north of France has nevertheless presented claims for our consideration that one at least of these passages had been tried at
different times early in the sixteenth century. Similar claims
have been made for Portuguese mariners a little later, and before the attempt of Cartier. Hakluyt even mentions that the
English had known at this early date something of the St. Lawrence region; but it is safe to say that no such record is known
to-day. These great waterways lay within the two great valleys

of the yet uncomprehended continent of the north, — the Mississippi and the St. Lawrence, — which at the west were so closely connected that tidal waves arising in Lake Michigan sometimes overflowed the dividing ridge.   The early explorers of the Great Lakes are known to have passed, during the spring freshets, in their canoes from one valley to the other, by that route which enables the modern Chicago to discharge its sewage into the Gulf of Mexico instead of the Gulf of St. Lawrence.

The striking experiences of the Spaniards at the south served to draw their attention from a due examination of the north-

REINEL CHART, 1503.

[After the Sketch in Kretschmer's *Atlas*, ix.[2]]

ern shores of the Gulf of Mexico; so that Pineda in 1519, in finding a great river flowing from the north, which we now identify with the Mississippi, was not prompted to enter it in search of gold, "because it is too far from the tropics," as the Spanish cosmographer Ribero afterwards expressed it in a legend on his map of 1529.   Moreover, this metal was not associated in their minds with such low regions as this river apparently drained; and the white and turbid flow of its waters well out into the gulf, as La Salle later noticed, seems to have raised no conception of the vast area of its tributary watershed. Almost two centuries were to pass before its channel was to be

fairly recognized as a great continental waterway; and then
the explorations which divulged its extent were from the north
and down the stream.

The voyages of the Cabots and the Cortereals had been the
Aims of Eng-
land and
Portugal. outcome of a national rivalry which had sought for
England and Portugal some advantage in the north
to counterbalance that of Spain in the south. It will
be remembered that the line of demarcation moved westerly
by the treaty of Tordesillas had thrown, it was supposed, these

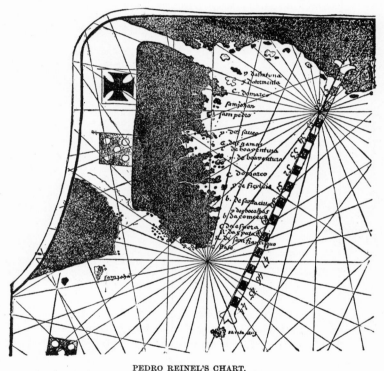

PEDRO REINEL'S CHART.
[From Fac-similes in Kunstmann, and in *Bull. de Géog. Hist. et Descriptive*, 1886, pl. iii.]

northern regions beyond the reach of Spain. Whether the
Cabots had discovered at the north a gulf to correspond with
the Mexican gulf at the south, and had found an expanse of
water which had already coursed another great continental valley, and by which it was practicable to go a long distance

towards the west, must probably remain uncertain. Investigation in critical hands has produced a divided opinion. Just what the Portuguese, who soon followed the English into these waters, did, is also not quite certain ; and though it can hardly be proved that the Cortereals entered the great northern gulf, it seems to be evident from a Portuguese portolano of 1504,

FROM A PORTUGUESE MAPPEMONDE, 1502.
[An Extract from the Fac-simile in E. T. Hamy's Paper, in the *Bull. de Géog. Hist. et Descriptive*, 1886, p. 147 and pl. ii.   It is sometimes called "The King Map."]

which Kunstmann has reproduced, that at this time they had not developed the entrances to this gulf north and west of Newfoundland ; while it is clear by the Reinel chart of 1505 that they had discovered but had not penetrated these passages.

The student in Europe who curiously watched the progress of geographical development beyond the sea during the sixteenth century naturally followed the revelations   *Ptolemy.* in the successive editions of the *Geographia* of Ptolemy, with the new maps of recent progress made to supplement those long familiar as pertaining to the Old World. The man who made the map for the Roman Ptolemy of 1507–8 is believed to have been a companion of Cabot in these northern   Ruysch's voyages ; and this work of Johann Ruysch is the   map, 1507–8. earliest engraved map which we have showing the new discover-

ies.   This map is interesting as making more apparent than La
Cosa, seven or eight years before, had done, that these new
discoveries might have been in part along the coast of Asia,
but not altogether so.   There is no sign in it of the landlocked
region where now we place the Gulf of Mexico; and in this
respect it is a strong disproof of the alleged voyage of Vespu-
cius in 1497; but it may give the beginning of a continental
area which was soon to develop, adjacent to the West Indies,
into what we call North America.   But at the north Ruysch
places the discoveries of the English and Portuguese unmistak-

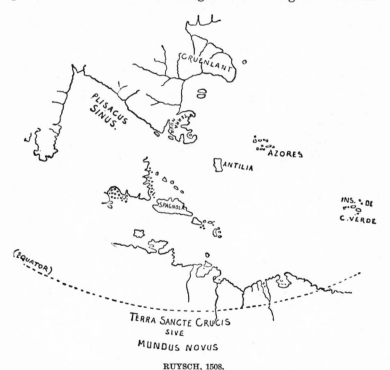

RUYSCH, 1508.

[From the earliest engraved Map showing the discoveries in the west, in the Ptolemy of 1508
(Rome).]

ably on the upper Asiatic coast; and while he does not dissever
Newfoundland from the mainland, he goes some way towards
doing it.

So we may say that in 1507, one working in Rome with the

available material which had been gathered from the Atlantic
seaports had not yet reached a conception of this great watery
portal of a continent which lies back of Newfoundland.
That there could not have been knowledge of this obscure
gulf in some of the seaports of northern and western France

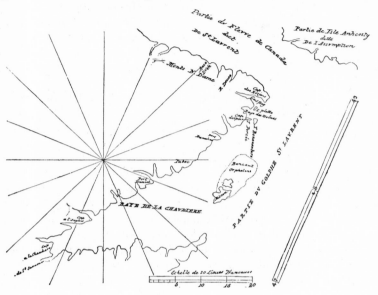

JEAN DENYS (*alleged Map*), 1506.
[Reduced from a Tracing furnished from the Archives at Ottawa.]

may indeed admit of doubt; and perhaps some day a dated
chart may reveal the fact. We need not confidently trust the
professions of Michel and other advocates of the Basques
Basques, and believe that a century before Cabot their and Normans.
hardy fishermen had discovered the banks of Newfoundland, and had even penetrated into the bays and inlets of

the adjacent coasts.   There seems, however, little doubt that very early in the sixteenth century fishing equipments for these regions were made by the Normans, as Bréard chronicles them in his *Documents relatifs à la Normand.*

In the very year when the Ruysch map became known in Europe (1508), it is claimed by Desmarquets and other Diep-

Aubert.
Denys. pese, solicitous for the credit of their seaport, that Thomas Aubert went eighty leagues up the St. Law-rence River.   If this be true, the great northern portal was entered then for the first time, so far as we have any record ; but such pretensions, even with the support of Ramusio, hardly rest on indisputable documents.   We learn from Charlevoix — too late an authority to be assuring — that Jean Denys had made a chart of the Gulf of St. Lawrence two years earlier (1506) ; but the evidence to prove it is wanting.   This map is said to have been formerly preserved in the Paris Archives, but is not found there or elsewhere at this day.   What passes for a copy of it, treasured at Ottawa, shows names of a palpa-bly later period.   If the original could be discovered, it might be found, possibly, that this nomenclature has been added by a more recent hand.   There does not seem to be anything in the configuration of its shore lines that might not have been achieved in 1506 by an active navigator.   If the outlines freed from the names are genuine, it would show that there had thus early been explorations to the west of Newfoundland, which might account for the otherwise surprising delineation of the " Golfo Quadrado," or Square Gulf, which appeared on the

Sylvanus,
1511. mappemonde of Sylvanus in his edition of Ptolemy in 1511.   This represents in mid-ocean in the north Atlantic a large island, little resembling Newfoundland, how-ever, with a landlocked gulf to the west of it, shut in by a coast which in the north and south parts bends so as nearly to touch the island.   That it is intended for Newfoundland and the neighboring parts admits of no question ; for the strange interior coast is considered to be the region of the Cortereal discoveries, since there is upon it a Latinized rendering of that name, *Regalis Domus.*   Some explorations developing such a gulf, whether Denys's or those of others, must have already taken place, then, before 1511.   There is some evidence in Navarrete's documents (iii. 42) that the Spaniard, Juan de

Agramonte, had been engaged in 1511 to go to the Newfoundland region; but we are ignorant of the sequel. After this
date, for a score of years and more, this landlocked water of
Sylvanus absolutely disappears from all the maps which have
come down to us, — nothing remaining but indications of
entrances to the gulf by the Straits of Belle Isle and by the
southern passage. It is noticeable that Gomara, describing this

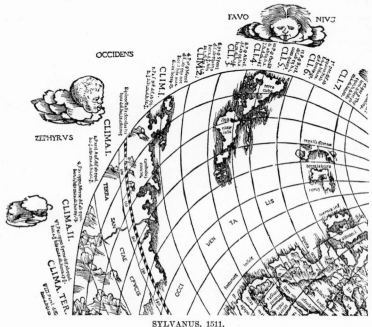

SYLVANUS, 1511.
[From the Ptolemy of 1511.]

water so late as 1555, speaks of it in the same way, as the
" Square Gulf."

France was now to find rivalry in these waters in the renewed
efforts of the Portuguese. The French had established a fishing-station in Bradore Bay, just within the Straits of Belle
Isle, which they called Brest. This was early in the century,
but its precise date is difficult to determine. Showing some of
the activity of the Portuguese, we have a chart of that Fagundes,
people, of not far from 1520, which indicates that 1520.
they had looked within the gulf both at the north and at the

south, but not far enough to discover its open and extensive channels. If we are to believe the interpretation which some have put upon a voyage ascribed to Joăm Alvarez Fagundes at this time, the Portuguese had attained far more knowledge of this inner gulf than this anonymous chart indicates. Indeed, a map, made in 1563 by Lazaro Luiz, has been put forward as indicating just what Fagundes had done; and this clearly gives him the credit of unveiling the hydrography of the gulf, so that his results might be considered to exceed in accuracy those of Cartier in his first voyage. This map of Luiz makes the shores of the gulf complete, except a portion of the inner coast of Newfoundland, and even gives the St. Lawrence River for a long distance from its mouth. Being made forty years and more after Fagundes, the draftsman had the temptation to embody later results ; and the map naturally starts the question of how much

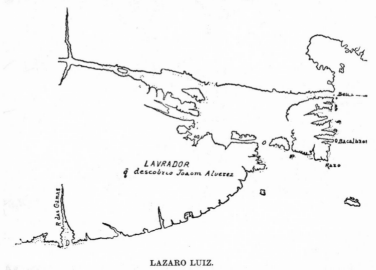

LAZARO LUIZ.

[A Sketch of the Map in Bettencourt's *Descobrimentos dos Portuguezes* (Lisbon, 1881–82).]

of this posterior knowledge was embodied in it. Since Bettencourt in his *Descobrimentos dos Portuguezes* brought forward this map, in 1881–82, its pretensions in this respect have been studied, and often questioned ; but Dr. Patterson, a recent Nova Scotian writer, has advocated its claims; and Harrisse in his last book, *The Discovery of North America*, has committed him-

self to a belief in the Fagundes explorations. The unquestioned facts are these : Ancient documents mention the voyage
as being for the purpose of establishing a fishing-station. The
Portuguese king had also promised Fagundes control by patent
of the regions which in this tentative voyage he should discover. On Fagundes's return he reported what he
had found; and in accordance with his report, his Fagundes's report, 1521.
king, March 13, 1521, granted to him these lands,
supposed to be a new discovery. This patent describes them,
presumably in accordance with Fagundes's report; and it is
this description, taken in conjunction with the Luiz map, which
must enable us to say where Fagundes had been.

The language of the patent, not as clear as we might wish,
says that the coast which he had found lay north of those
known to the Spaniards and south of that visited by Cortereal,
which would put it between Newfoundland and perhaps the
Chesapeake, or possibly a region a little farther north than the
Chesapeake. The assigned country includes, as the patent
says, the Bay of Auguada, which contains three islands ; a
stretch of coast where are other islands, which Fagundes had
named St. John, St. Peter, St. Ann, St. Anthony, and an
archipelago, also named by him the Eleven Thousand Virgins ;
an island " close to the bank," which he called Santa Cruz, and
a second island called St. Ann. The patent closes with granting all these islands and lands to their discoverer.

On a coast so crowded with islands and bays as that of
Maine and New Brunswick, — apparently the " firm land " of
the description, — we need more details than the patent gives
us to determine beyond dispute the geographical correspondences of these names. The inscription "Lavrador q̄ descobrio
Joaom Alverez [Fagundes] " is on the Luiz map, placed on the
peninsula formed by the St. Lawrence Gulf and the Atlantic.
This, in the opinion of Harrisse, requires the Baya d' Auguada,
which is described as having a northeast and southwest extension, to be none other than the St. Lawrence Gulf. That writer
is convinced that the bay was named the Watering Bay, because Fagundes must have gone through it to the outlet of its
great river to fill his water-casks. He also allows that the
three islands of this bay may possibly have been Prince Edward, Anticosti, and Orleans ; since these islands in the Luiz

map are all colored yellow, like a Portuguese escutcheon placed
on the map.   This, however, would have carried Fagundes up
the St. Lawrence River farther than Harrisse is inclined to believe; and he would rather substitute for the island of Orleans
the Magdalen group or some peninsula of the gulf mistaken for
an island.   Harrisse also applies rather neatly what may be
termed the " liturgical " test in respect to all the names mentioned in the patent; and he finds that the corresponding saints'
days in the Roman calendar run from June 21 to October 21.
This would seem to indicate that it was in the summer and
autumn, probably in 1520, when these names were applied, in
accordance with a habit, common with explorers in those days,
of naming landmarks after the saint on whose day they were
discovered.   Another proof of the voyage, also worked out by
the same writer, is that names which appear on no map ante-
dating this patent are later found for this coast on the maps
known by the name of Maiollo (1527), Verrazano (1529), Viegas (1534), Harleyan (1542), Cabot (1544), Freire (1546),
and Descelliers (1550).

This is the nature of the evidence which makes Harrisse give
Fagundes's   a map, tracking the progress of Fagundes from the
track.   time he passed near the islands of St. Pierre and
Miquelon.   By this it would appear that he coasted north the
west shore of Newfoundland, and at the Straits of Belle Isle
turned and followed the Labrador coast well within the St.
Lawrence River, and then returning, skirted the New Brunswick coast, that of Prince Edward Island, Cape Breton, and
Nova Scotia to the entrance of the Bay of Fundy, where he
bore away seaward, and returned to Portugal.   Few, we suspect, will accept this route of Fagundes as proved.   Most will
be content to acknowledge the fact of an acquaintance with the
gulf and its neighboring waters rather than such an extent of
the acquaintance.

The advocates of these Portuguese anticipations of Cartier
point to the melons and cucumbers which that navigator found
among the natives of the gulf region as indicating that Europeans had left the seeds of such fruits among them.   They also
think that Cartier's own recitals leave the impression that the
Indians of the St. Lawrence had become used to European
contact before his advent.   It is known, however, that the In-

dians of the interior had long been used to resort to the shores of the gulf and its vicinity during the summer season ; and it is not unlikely that by this habit, as well as by a common custom of intertribal communication, the ways of Europeans were not unknown in the interior.

A belief in a comparatively short stretch of unknown sea sep-

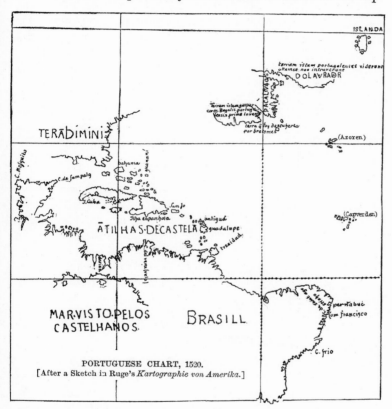

PORTUGUESE CHART, 1520.
[After a Sketch in Ruge's *Kartographie von Amerika.*]

arating the Azores from Cathay had been no small inducement to Columbus to make his hazardous voyage. Now that the land to the west had proved so far a barrier to a farther westward way, it was in turn no small inducement to those prompted to pierce this barrier to believe that the land which confronted them was even narrower than the

The continental barrier.

ocean had been thought to be. Balboa had proved how narrow the land was at Panama, and Cortes had shown that it
was not wide in Mexico.   How wide was it farther north?

Columbus had suspected that South America was of continental extent, because of the great volume of water which the
Orinoco poured into the Gulf of Paria.   Ships when out of
sight of land had filled their water-casks from the water poured
out by the Amazon, which told of an immense inland drainage.
None of the early navigators remarked upon anything of the
kind at the north.   The flow of the Mississippi did not seem
to impress them as indicating an enormous valley towards its
source.   The early maps given to portraying its supposed sys-

COPPO, 1528.
[After Kretschmer.]

tem of drainage represent it as very scant.   On the eastern seaboard of the northern continent the Alleghany range rendered
it impossible for any river to have a very large volume of water.
It was only when one got as far north as the St. Lawrence Gulf,
and even into its inner reaches, that evidence such as had been
indicative on the coast of South America could have suggested
a vast continental area at the north.   Therefore, before this
revelation was made in the St. Lawrence River, it is not strange
that there were current views against the continental character
of the region lying north of the Mexican gulf and west of the
country discovered by Cabot and the Cortereals.   Some would

believe that it was no continent at all, but only an immense
archipelago, filled with passages, if they could only be found.
Coppo had mapped it in this way in 1528. Others had followed
Oviedo in supposing that the land at the north, at one place at
least, was as narrow as it was at Panama; for this historian, in
1526, in his *Sumario*, had first given published indication of
what was for many years following known as the Sea of Verrazano. This expanse of water was imagined to fill the space

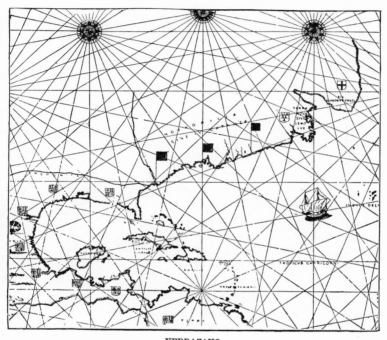

VERRAZANO.
[A part of Brevoort's Fac-simile.]

now known to be occupied by the two great valleys of the
upper Mississippi and the Great Lakes; while its easternmost
waves nearly broke through the land, to mingle its waters with
the Atlantic somewhere along the eastern seaboard of the present United States.

The supposition of this mysterious sea arose from an interpretation of Verrazano's experiences on the coast in Verrazano,
1524, which constitute the first decided and official 1524.

manifestation of French activity in the new regions. This navigator is supposed to have become acquainted with the coast from Spanish Florida to the seaboard of Maine; and his explorations were held in later times to be the basis of the French claim to territory in the New World. Freville, in his *Mémoire* on the commerce of Rouen, prints a paper by Admiral Chabot, which shows that for a while it had been the intention of Francis I. to follow up this voyage of Verrazano. The political exigencies in which that French king found himself involved had caused delays; and his attention was not again seriously given to such efforts until he commissioned Cartier, ten years later. During this decade Verrazano's notion of this sea beyond the barrier had become the belief of a school of geographers; and the believers in it found it not difficult to count the chances good of reaching it by a strait at some point along the Atlantic coast.

There have been two maps brought into prominence of late years, which reflect this belief. One is the map of Hieronomo da Verrazano, preserved in the College of the Propaganda at Rome, made by his brother not long after the voyage of that navigator. His chart shows this sea as a great watery wedge lying athwart the interior of the undeveloped North America, and pointing with its apex to a narrow strip of land somewhere in the latitude of Carolina. Indeed, one might suppose that the sailor brother of the cartographer had described to him a stretch of sea with an obscure distance, as he saw it above the dunes in the neighborhood of Cape Hatteras; while the cartographer himself had given his fancy play in extending it to the west. The other map has been brought within ten years to help elucidate this transient faith in such a western sea. This second chart had long been known in the Ambrosian Library at Milan as the work of the Visconte Maggiolo (Maiollo); but its full import had not been suspected, since it bore the apparent date of 1587. The Abbé Ceriani had discovered its true date to be 1527, and that somebody had changed, in sport or in mischief, the figure 2 into 8. Signor Desimoni, the archivist of Genoa, who was at this time working on the Verrazano problem, happening in the library, was struck with the coast lines and legends on the map as being similar to those of the Propaganda map, with which he was

Maps of the Verrazano Sea.

familiar; and he first brought the Maggiolo map to the attention of students in 1882.

The Sea of Verrazano is much the same in the two maps, and

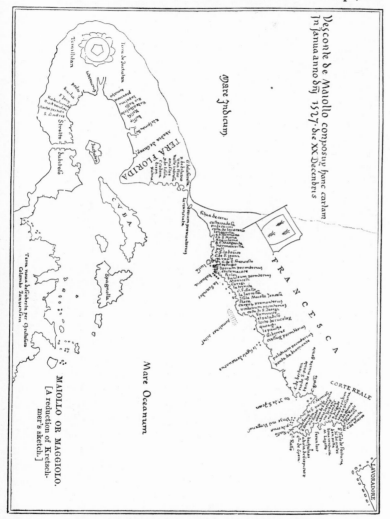

their delineations of this oceanic delusion marked for a good
many years yet to come a prevailing opinion as to the kind of
goal the searchers for a western passage were striving to reach.

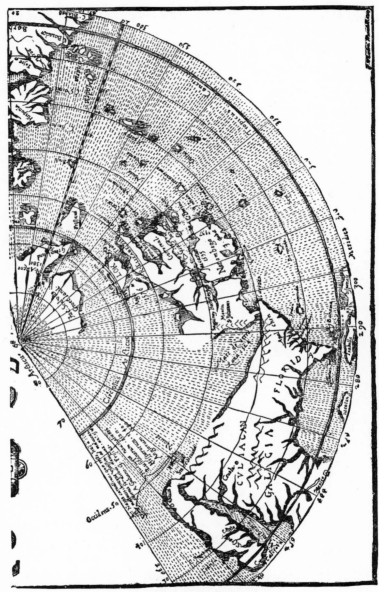

MICHAEL LOK, 1582.

The same sea is found in the well-known English map of Michael Lok, published by Hakluyt so late as 1582, — or nearly forty years after the close of the series of explorations which Cartier conducted.

While it is probable that such supposed conditions as this Sea of Verrazano supplied were a considerable incentive to Francis I. to renew his interest in explorations, the problem was complicated by another view which an eminent German geographer had espoused, and which had already been engaging attention for some ten years. The conditions of political and social life which Cortes had found in Mexico had revived the old hope that Cathay had at last been found; and the reports of the conquerors which were sent to Europe, with all their exaggerations, were welcomed as far more nearly conforming to the descriptions of Marco Polo than anything which had been discovered among the West Indies or on the South American coasts. If the region, then, which Cortes had subdued was in truth Asia, the ocean which Magellan had crossed made an independent continent of South America only; while the northern spaces, instead of being an archipelago or a continental barrier, must be simply an eastern extension of Asia, and its coast must border on the north Atlantic.

It is known from the text of a little geographical treatise (1533) which has survived, that Schöner, a famous globe-maker of Germany, had made a terrestrial sphere in 1523; but it has not probably come down to us. Some gores which were discovered a few years ago have been held by Henry Stevens and others to belong to this globe; but they delineate North America as a distinct continent, just as it was delineated in other globes by Schöner of an earlier date, which are well known. It is denied, however, by Nordenskiöld, that these gores can be of so early a date as 1523, and he places them more than twenty years later. Harrisse has later still examined the claim, and contends that the gores cannot possibly be those by Schöner of this date, because it seems apparent from his treatise that the globe of 1523 must have been made in accordance with the theory of an Asiatic extension for North America. If this was so, — and Harrisse's reasons are not without effect, — this theory of an Asiatic extension in North America is traced to Schöner as its originator,

Schöner's Asiatic theory.

so far as is known.   If it is a matter of contention as respects
Schöner, it is certain as regards a little figure of a globe made
by Franciscus Monachus in 1526, which unmistakably repre-
Franciscus sents North America as a part of Asia.   This the-
Monachus. ory got a firm advocate in Orontius Finæus in 1531,
who, however, so far departed from the view held by Franciscus as to unite South America to the northern continent by the
Isthmus of Panama, while the other had placed a strait to the
north of that connection.   This theory was made prominent in
so well known a treatise as the *Novus Orbis* of Grynæus,

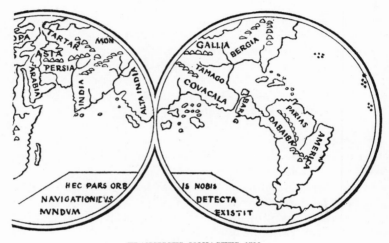

FRANCISCUS MONACHUS, 1526.
[After Sketch in Kretschmer's *Atlas.*]

where the map of Orontius appeared; and at intervals through
that century and into the next, other expressions of this view
appeared in prominent maps.

If Cartier or his royal master had entertained the expectation that his expedition might penetrate into the heart of northern Asia when it started for the gulf back of Newfoundland, it
is altogether probable that its equipment would not have been
undertaken.   It is far more likely that the faith which the earlier expedition of Verrazano had developed in the narrowness
of the northern continent prevailed at Paris and St. Malo when
Cartier started on his fateful voyage.

CHAPTER II.

CARTIER, ROBERVAL, AND ALLEFONSCE.

1534–1542.

THE story of the personal career of Cartier, separate from his American explorations, is not an extended one. Mod- _{Sources.} ern writers have in the main gone back to the *Mé-moire* which Charles Cunat prepared for a general biographical account of the Breton race. Here Hoefer went for details used in his great dictionary, and D'Avezac and Ramé for what they have said in editing the documents pertaining to Cartier's career. Harrisse in his *Cabots* has done something to elucidate the bibliography of the subject; but the most important critical examination of Cartier's life is made in François Joüon des Longrais's *Jacques Cartier* (Paris, 1888). The researches of this writer were too late for the use of Dr. De Costa in the *Narrative and Critical History of America* (vol. iv.), but have been followed by three recent prize essayists on the theme : Joseph Pope (Ottawa, 1890), in English; Hiram B. Stephens (Montreal, 1890), also in English; and N. E. Dionne (Quebec, 1889), in French.

Longrais's inquiries show Cartier to have been an older man by three years than had been supposed, or a man of forty-three instead of forty, when he sailed from St. Malo, April 20, 1534, with the aim of raising the French arms, as an act of posses-sion, in the neighborhood of the Square Gulf of Sylvanus. Norman, Breton, and Basque had been frequenters of its shores for many years. These mariners were to find it hereafter within the jurisdiction of their common monarch.

Just what constituted Cartier's fitness to carry out the behests of the French king is only apparent as an inference _{Cartier's early career.} from the fact that Admiral Chabot, eager companion of Francis, and sharing his ambition and confidence, hit upon

Cartier as the instrument to place France on an equality with her maritime rivals. Some of the contemporary records call Cartier a corsair, which means that he had roved the seas to despoil the enemies of France. There is a probability that he had voyaged at one time to Brazil. When he was married, in 1519, he had risen high enough in his profession to be called a master pilot.

We know that when Cartier shipped his crew, a voyage of His voyage, discovery had fewer attractions than the better paying 1534. occupations of fishing and trading on the Newfoundland coasts. They preserve at St. Malo to-day a list of those finally brought to sign the ships' papers, which were made out in Cartier's own hand. He superintended the equipment of his two vessels of sixty tons each, and when all his men were piped to duty they numbered sixty-one souls.

That Cartier was bound for the land lying beyond the Newfoundland banks, and for the water which that island inclosed, conveyed, very likely, varying notions to the crews of the fishing craft then afloat in this Norman harbor. We have no knowledge that Cartier started with any charts; but he could hardly have been denied the help of the rough sketches of the coasts, which many a fisherman, habituated to the region, could have made for him. If such charts embodied information which they had shared with the Portuguese, whom they were accustomed to meet on those fishing-grounds, we may look to the chart of Viegas of this same year (1534), which has come down to us, as indicating, perhaps, the notions then prevalent respecting this inner sea at the back of Newfoundland. This chart certainly shows but an inadequate conception of its great expanse, and makes the gulf open to the sea at the south, and not at the north. Cartier's course in his voyage hardly accords with such a belief on his part.

It was a rugged port, this St. Malo, with its crowded pe- St. Malo. ninsular town, jutting out to form a harbor, in and out of which thirty or forty feet of water rushed with the tide, leaving the vessels at the ebb keeled upon the ribbed sand. The place had a reputation for hardy seamen, and Jacques Cartier was then its boast, and has been ever since. When his vessels, that April day, righted with the flood and their booms creaked to the vigorous pull of their crews, and the gazing idlers along the shore waved their farewells to St. Malo's maritime hero, it was doomed that he should give the great interior of a new continent to an aspiring rival of Spain, Portugal, and England.

GASPAR VIEGAS.
[After a Sketch in Kohl's *Discovery of Maine*.]

Cartier experienced rough weather as he made the coast of Newfoundland, in the neighborhood of Cape Bonavista (May 10), and he was obliged to seek a harbor to make repairs. Kohl, in his *Discovery of Maine*, thinks that if Cartier had known of the southern entrance to the gulf, with its seventy-five miles of breadth, he would now have sought it. After he had completed his repairs he did, in fact, turn north and not south, and on May 27 he was at the

At Newfoundland, May 10, 1534.

opening of the Straits of Belle Isle. This was a region familiar
to the fishermen, although one would not suspect it from the
Viegas chart, and in the harbors of the Labrador coast within
the passage their ships had been long accustomed to find ref-
uge in bad weather. It was somewhere here that Cartier met
a ship from La Rochelle. He saw also some of the natives of
the region. The country seemed to him to be forbidding, so

In the gulf.   he turned his prows south, and tracked the inner coast
of Newfoundland till near the point opposite Cape
Breton. Cartier was thus the earliest to define this coast, and
if the explorations of Fagundes are allowed, that Portuguese
navigator seems not to have outlined this repellant shore. Cartier now steered westerly and, passing the Magdalene Islands,
reached the shore of Prince Edward Island; whence, heading

July, 1534.   north (July 2), he made the Bay of Chaleur, a name
which he now gave to that inlet in recognition of the
great heat which he experienced (July 8). Still proceeding
northward, he struck the coast of Anticosti Island, and, rounding its eastern point, followed its northern shore almost to its
western head. Here the ships turned and, skirting backward
the dreary shores of Labrador, finally emerged into the ocean
by the strait which had led them in, and bore away for France.

There are landmarks along this passage through the gulf
which earlier visitors had perhaps named. Others still bear the
designations which Cartier bestowed. His own account and
these geographical traces make pretty clear the general direction
which he took; but in parts the record is obscure as to details,
and there is much difference of opinion among investigators,

His track.   particularly as to his track across the gulf from Newfoundland to Prince Edward Island and the mainland
of New Brunswick. Kohl, De Costa, Ganong, Bourinot, and
others have exercised their ingenuity upon the problem. It
seems probable that familiarity with these waters and a close
study of Cartier's text are safer for an inquiry than the deduc-
tions of the European cartographers, even of the earlier time.
The study, however, is curious rather than important.

Just where the coast of Gaspé juts to sever the gulf from its
great affluent, Cartier erected a cross and took possession of
the country for his king. It was at this point that he entrapped
two Indians, who were to serve him as interpreters during his

next voyage, for they were natives of a region high up the
St. Lawrence, who had come down for the fishing season. It
was on the passage from this point to Anticosti, in which he
struck across the great tide rolling from the St. Lawrence, that
he seems to have been unconscious of missing the portal that
opened two thousand miles of waterway through the interior of
the continent. When he went to the north of Anticosti and
reached its western end, he failed to discover that he had nearly
circumnavigated an island, and was again at a lesser portal of
the great river.

Cartier was nearly two months and a half in making this
circuit of the gulf. He passed out to sea on August
15, and early in September he reëntered the harbor of
St. Malo. He could report little success in discovering a passage to Cathay, but he had done more, perhaps, to
map the gulf than any of his predecessors, and he had laid the
foundations of its future cartography. So the expedition was
not altogether futile, and he returned with some enthusiasm
left, — enough at least to throw spirit into his story, and reas-
sure his superiors that the prospect was still hopeful.

One would like to think that, in following the events of this
voyage, he had beyond a doubt been depending on a recital by
Cartier himself. If Ramé, a recent editor of the documents, is
not deceived, they preserve at St. Malo the actual register of
his companions, to which reference has already been made. A
similar authentication can hardly be held to attach to
that one of several manuscripts, professing to tell the
story of this initial voyage of Canadian discovery, upon which
we are most inclined to depend. It was placed first before the
public in 1867, and if there is here and there a demur to its
being Cartier's own text, it can at least be trusted better than
any other. We trace other contemporary accounts in the main
back to the narrative in Ramusio; but no one of all these is
so distinctly phrased that the student can be quite sure in all
details of Cartier's course when once he had entered the gulf.

Within two months after Cartier's return to St. Malo, he had
interested the vice-admiral, Charles de Mouy, in a new voyage,
and the king had been induced to sign a commission at the end

[margin note:] Back in St. Malo, September, 1534.

[margin note:] Narrative of the voyage.

of October (1534) giving Cartier authority to make further explorations.   He was told to take fifteen months for the trial.
He was allowed three vessels, the " Grande Hermine," of perhaps a hundred and twenty tons, which carried his flag; the " Petite Hermine," of sixty tons, under Macé Jalobert; and a small galley, the " Emerillon," of forty tons, of which Guillaume le Breton Bastille had the command.

Voyage of 1535.

Cartier mustered for this cruise a company of one hundred and ten persons, of whom we know the names of eighty-four. This crew was not altogether a worthy one, for the dangerous plan of impressing criminals had been followed.   It is a little incongruous with such a following to find the commander writing to his sovereign that he looked upon his enterprise as one likely to open new fields for Christian endeavor.   The looker-on must have beheld a motley crowd when Cartier led his men to church on Whit-Sunday (May 16, 1535) to make confession and receive the benediction of the bishop.

Three days later the little fleet sailed.   The season was boisterous, and they had not made land when the vessels were scattered in a gale.   The little harbor of Blanc Sablon, well within the Straits of Belle Isle on the Labrador side, had been made the rendezvous.   Cartier reached it first, late in July, and his other ships were not long behind.

Sails, May 19, 1535.

July.

After three days he led the way westward along the Labrador coast, and passed into the channel between Anticosti and the main.   Here on the northern shore he entered a harbor and named it the Bay of St. Lawrence, — the first appearance of a name (Sainct Laurens) in this region, which was in time to be extended to the great gulf and to the river which feeds it.   On August 14, he sailed still westward, with spouting whales about his track.   He seems now first to have comprehended from the two Indians whom he had kidnapped during the previous year, and who had picked up enough French to be communicative, that the southern shore of this channel belonged to an island which divided the great passage to the interior.   Cartier was thus enabled to mark on his chart the westernmost end of this island, which he called Assumption (August 15).   Passing on, he found himself at last in the great river, with hopes brightening at the prospect of its great volume of water proving to be the long-sought passage to the Orient.

August.

As he passed from one shore to the other, on his westward way, Cartier noted distant mountains to the south, and saw the two banks of the river gradually drawing together. He questioned his Indians, and learned that as he went on farther the water would begin to freshen. It was not a welcome thought; and as behind him there was a stretch of the northern shore of the river, which he had missed in crossing to the south, he went back on his course in the hope that he had thus overlooked the main salt-water passage. His quest was futile, and by the 24th he had doubled on this backward track and was once more stemming the current of the great river. On September 1, he was opposite the mouth of the Saguenay. He met here some natives in canoes, who were emboldened by the voices of Cartier's Indians to come alongside and parley.

September.

Cartier left the Saguenay without exploring it, and continued up the main stream to the Isle aux Coudres. Here he remained some days, beguiled with the sports of the natives as they caught the white whales. A religious service was held on Sunday (September 7), though he seems to have had no priest to conduct it. Another stretch up the river brought him to a conference with Donnacona, the leading chieftain of the region, who told Cartier that he dwelt in Stadacona, a place still higher up. The savage received the strangers with words which, so far as the Frenchmen could interpret them, were becoming and friendly.

At last the ships reached what is now known as the Island of Orleans, just below the basin of Quebec. Cartier saw vines festooning the trees, and called it the Island of Bacchus. Anchoring his vessels here, he proceeded in boats to find a good wintering place, and discovered a spot to his liking just up the stream which, flowing into the St. Lawrence, forms the headland of Quebec, — the modern St. Charles River. In the northern parts of the modern town, outside the walls, and where the streets cover the lowlands south of the St. Charles, there is a peninsula formed by a loop of the stream. Opposite the head of this curve, north of the St. Charles, lay the Indian village of Stadacona, the home of the savage chieftain. Adjacent to it a small rivulet came from the north, and at this point it seemed to Cartier that his ships could be

Stadacona.

moored in security, and easily protected. So upon September
14 the vessels were brought from below and warped into position. It is the general belief that this little stream is the
modern Lairet, and as the result of an agitation beginning as
far back as 1835, and seeking also to honor the memory of the
Jesuits, who in 1625 built their abode on the same site, there
was erected a monument here in 1889 to commemorate the sojourn of Cartier, — not, however, without some protest from
such as believed that the exact spot was at the confluence of
the St. Michel, a little farther up the St. Charles. The fact
that remains of a vessel were found in 1843 at the mouth of
the St. Michel has been held by the advocates of that spot as
showing Cartier to have abandoned the " Petite Hermine "
there, presumably near his fort; but on the other hand it is
strenuously denied that the hulk there found could be as old
as the early part of the sixteenth century. De Caze and Dionne, two of the later Canadian antiquaries, have taken issue
on the problem.

Cartier's two native interpreters, finding themselves now
among friends, communicated to Donnacona the intention of
Cartier to leave his vessels at this spot and go himself higher
up the St. Lawrence to a place called Hochelaga. The Indian
chieftain much preferred to snatch the opportunity of barter
for the Frenchmen's trinkets, instead of letting it fall into the
hands of a rival at Hochelaga, — or at least such an interpretation of Donnacona's discontent at Cartier's proposal seems
the most reasonable. The savage's opposition to Cartier's purpose of ascending the river, not a little urged on by the atti-
tude of the interpreters, seemed likely, for a while, to embroil
all parties in a hostile outbreak. Though this was avoided
and a sort of friendly pact was formed, Donnacona resigned
himself to the thought very slowly, and not till after he had
tried the effect of artifice to enforce his powers of persuasion.
He made some of his people dress and caper like devils, as if
they were messengers sent from Cudragmy, the local deity of
Hochelaga, to persuade the French not to venture on the hazard
of the trip.

There is a portrait of Cartier in the town hall of St. Malo
which the townspeople cherish. It has often been engraved,

and the fearless leader has been confidently seen in it. Parkman, who saw it in 1881, found it recent in origin and a questionable likeness. It looks, however, like a man of courage,
whom it would take much to intimidate, and he stands in con-
templation, as if he might have been caught at this moment
as his mind strengthened with a determination to ascend the
river in spite of obstacles.

So, leaving the body of his followers in good plight to resist
attack, Cartier took the " Emerillon " and two boats, with fifty
men for an escort, and on September 19 pulled out September
into the St. Lawrence and began to breast the current. 19, 1535.
Something of the autumnal joy conspicuous in the foliage
buoyed the spirits of the adventurers, and they went on successfully. On the 28th, they reached a place where the river
expanded into a lake, and in recognition of his sovereign, he
named it the Lake of Angoulême, which recalls the birthplace
of Francis I. As the river narrowed again, the currents became too strong to force the " Emerillon " against them ; so she
was left behind, while Cartier and a body of picked men went
on in two boats. On October 2, he drew his boats up beside
a piece of level land, out of the current here known as St.
Mary's, and found that he was about three miles be- October.
low Hochelaga. The news of his coming soon spread, Hochelaga.
and the natives in large numbers gathered on the shore, offering food and manifesting delight.

Accompanied by five of his principal officers and with a detail of twenty men, Cartier went the next day to the Indian
town, and was graciously received by the chieftain of these savage hordes. The intruders found the settlement situated near
the base of a high hill, and surrounded by cultivated fields.
Cartier and his companions were led to a gate in a circular palisaded village. Along this palisade they found on the inner
side a gallery from which missives could be hurled at assailants,
and piles of stones lay ready for use. There is a bird's-eye
view of this town in Ramusio. It neither corresponds very ex-
actly with Cartier's description, nor is it wholly comprehensible
in itself.

We know that nearly seventy years later Champlain found
people and town alike wanting, and another race possessing the
land. Who the people were that Cartier met is a question upon

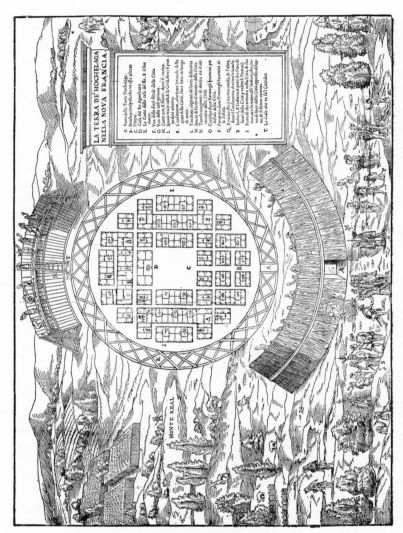

RAMUSIO'S HOCHELAGA.

which there has been some difference of opinion. The decision rests mainly upon the ethnic relations of the scant vocabulary which Cartier picked up and recorded. Dawson has held that the words in Cartier's list have Algonquin roots. The Abbé Faillon holds them to be Huron, and the weight of opinion seems to sustain the abbé. The Hurons had given place to Algonquins in the time of Champlain, as we shall later see.

When Cartier was conducted within the gate of this Huron village, he found a public square, round which the huts of its inhabitants were grouped. In this space he was welcomed by men, women, and children, with signs of emotion and confidence. The white strangers were evidently looked upon as superior beings, capable of healing by the hand, for the palsied were brought to be touched. The chieftain of the savages was borne into the throng upon the shoulders of men, and he offered a shrunken limb to be stroked. In recognition of the potency of the Frenchman's charm, the Indian lifted his wreath of authority from his own head and placed it upon the brow of his visitor. Cartier, in fulfillment of the missionary spirit which he had avowed to the French king, began to repeat the Gospel of St. John. Then, making the sign of a cross, he uttered a prayer, and afterwards read the Passion of Christ. It was mere necromancy to the astonished savages. There was something they could better understand when the French leader caused a distribution of trinkets. Hatchets and knives were passed out to the dusky applicants amid a flourish of trumpets. In view of the forebodings of Donnacona, it was not the most prudent of actions to distribute such dangerous largesses.

Cartier's eyes must all the while have wandered away to the conspicuous lookout which the neighboring eminence afforded. He tells us of its imposing character, when he says that he gave it the name of Mont Royale. The capital town, which the traveler finds to-day on the site of Hochelaga, is a reminder of the first European who surveyed the site of Montreal. As Cartier gazed from the summit of this hill, — for his new-found friends soon conducted him thither, — he scanned the hazy distance, in which on the one hand the St. Lawrence and on the other the Ottawa lost themselves, and we can well imagine that he asked, " Which way must I go to seek Cathay ? "

There needed an earlier start in the season than was possible now, to solve this pregnant question. October, with its short

October,
1535. days, was already advancing, and it was not prudent to tarry longer with his new-found friends. There was provision yet to make for the winter in Stadacona. So exchanging courtesies with the savages, he pushed off his boats

LESCARBOT'S HOCHELAGA.

and started down the river with the current. He reached his

Havre de
Sainte Croix. galley on October 4, and on the 11th he was once more in the Havre de Sainte Croix, as his station on the St. Charles had already been named. During his three weeks' absence, his men had worked to some advantage. They had completed a fort and had mounted some guns, and other preparation had been made for the winter; but his peace with Donnacona had still to be strengthened. He cultivated the friendship of the savages by going freely from one native hut to another. In this he did not fail to see that they sometimes overcame their enemies, for they had a habit of decorating their walls with scalps. He found, too, they had provident habits, for winter was not at hand without their having laid in stores of supplies. He fancied, too, they were docile enough to receive Christian teaching, and he was sorry he had not a priest with him to administer the rites of the Church. He told them that he would come again, and bring with him holy men, who could render them such service.

The winter had hardly come on in its severity before a pestilence like scurvy broke out among the natives. It soon spread to the French fort. At one time there were but ten sound Frenchmen to minister to the sick, and twenty-five of the company died. They tried to appease what they thought an offended Deity by erecting crosses. Weak and well alike prostrated themselves in the snow before these holy symbols. They sought content for the mind in penitential hymns, and they supported each other with mutual vows.

Sickness.

All this, however, seemed to less purpose — if we may believe their own accounts — than a concoction of which they drank freely, after the habit of the natives. It was probably made from the bark of the white pine (*ameda*). "If all the physicians of Montpelier and Louvain had administered all the drugs of Alexandria, the effect would not have been so good in a year as the draughts of ameda caused in six days." So runs their record, — and it is very likely.

As the spring came on, this little company of Frenchmen recovered its tone. On May 3 they set up a new cross, with more jubilation than before, and put upon it a legend that noted formal possession of the country for the French crown: FRANCISCUS PRIMUS, DEI GRATIA FRANCORUM REX REGNAT. The first act of sovereignty exercised by the representative of that absent monarch was to lure the local chieftain into a snare, and to carry him and other savages on board the ships. The act was resented by

*1536.
Spring.*

Donnacona seized.

Donnacona's people, and they offered ransoms. The majesty of France could not condescend to bargain, and the savages were put off with a promise of having their chieftain restored to them the next year.

The French had received special kindnesses from the people of a neighboring village, and in their weakened condition, finding it necessary for want of a crew to abandon one of their vessels, they gave the Petite " Hermine " to this people, in order that they might profit by the metal spikes in the hulk. If the vessel which was found in 1843 — as already stated — had shown that the fastenings had been removed from her timbers, there would be more ground for supposing it a relic of Cartier's fleet.

On the 6th the French floated into the St. Lawrence, and set May, 1536. sail for their downward voyage. After a while they Return voy- anchored, just out of the current, when the savages' age. canoes, which were following, came up. The poor creatures had not yet got over clamoring for Donnacona. Cartier now put the chieftain forward to tell his people that he was content, and would return in a year. Meanwhile the Frenchmen tossed into the hovering canoes some hatchets in return for beaver and wampum. The savages were satisfied enough with the exchange to forget their grievance, and Cartier tried to get away while they continued in so happy a mind. The wind, however, did not serve him, and he was obliged to linger till the 20th. When once started, he found no obstacle till he reached the gulf. Here he buffeted awhile with adverse gales, and finally found a haven at the little island of St. Pierre. At the anchorage he found many ships from France and Britain, as he says, and may have learned more than he knew before of July. the southerly outlet of the gulf, for he shortly after passed to sea by rounding Cape Race. Early in July he was once more gliding with the flood into the basin of St. Malo.

Cartier was at once ordered by the king to make a written The *Bref* account of the voyage, and it has come down to us, *Récit.* and is usually cited, as the *Bref Récit.* It has been surmised, as four years elapsed before a new expedition was sent out, that the report which Cartier now made was not, on the whole, encouraging. He had not, indeed, discovered any mines, as had been hoped; but a copper knife which he had obtained from an Indian might indicate that his futile quest was rather unfortunate than decisive. This implement was said to come from the Saguenay region. And where was Saguenay this region? Dr. Shea thinks it evident that it did region. not mean the banks of the Saguenay River, but a country beyond, to which that river opened the way. The Saguenay had not yet been explored, and there was a chance of mines being found in that direction. There might indeed be revelations in reserve along those valleys up which Cartier had looked so longingly from Mont Royale. Then the natives had also spoken to him of an inhabited country to the south, where the climate was milder. This was, perhaps, a monition of the Lake Champlain country, which led him to imagine that a water passage was yet to be discovered, running south, which might lead to Florida, — a region, it must be remembered, broader than the present designation covers, and meaning all that the Spaniards claimed in what is now the southern and even the middle United States.

As we read the *Bref Récit*, we feel that Cartier at least was rather cheerful over future prospects; but the person necessary to be impressed with hope was Francis I. This monarch was embarrassed in making any prompt decision by the wars in which he was involved. He had listened, however, to Cartier, had read his written account, had talked with Donnacona and the other kidnapped savages, and grew to be confident in the chances of better success.

To emphasize his claim to the country in a way to impress his rival potentates, Francis now determined to create a viceroyalty in the new country, and selected for his representative a Picard seigneur, Jean François de la Roche, better Roberval, known as Roberval, from his estates. He was a gen-viceroy. tleman of some consideration in his province, — a sort of petty king, if we may believe what Charlevoix gives as the sportive designation of him, often on the royal lips. It was at His commis-Fontainebleau, January 15, 1540, that the king signed sion, 1540. the commission, giving his subject and friend full vicegeral powers, while he placed at the same time at his lieu-tenant's disposal, the sum of 45,000 livres. On Feb-February. ruary 6, Roberval took the oath before Cardinal de Tournon,

and on the next day he was commanded to follow the luckless
habit of searching the jails for recruits.   There is no certainty
that through all these preliminaries the king had determined to
have Cartier as the active spirit of the expedition, and it may
rather have been an after-thought, when he found the Picardy
gentleman not pushing the enterprise to suit his royal wishes.
October, At all events, on October 17, Henry the Dauphin
1540. Car-
tier captain- signed the paper making Cartier captain-general and
general. pilot of the fleet.   It was now sure that some spirit
would be given to the undertaking.

The outfit of the fleet was more imposing than anything
France had before arranged, and accordingly it excited the suspicion of Spain.   While the rivals of the Spanish monarch
were merely hovering about the coasts of Newfoundland, Spain
was not prepared to say that her rights under the bull of demarcation had been infringed, for it had long been allowed that
the northern regions which the Cortereals had visited, as well
as the eastern limits of Brazil, were exterior to the Spanish ap-
portionment.   But here was something that looked like a rival
claim west of Pope Alexander's line of partition.   How far
the public or the emissaries of Spain had learned of what Cartier had accomplished on his second voyage does not appear, —
certain it is that some years were to pass before any publication
was made concerning the voyage, for the *Bref Récit* was still
in manuscript.   Further, if a type of all the maps issued before
1541 has come down to us, it is equally certain that there had
been no cartographical recognition of it up to this time.   The
general impression was that the Baccalaos — as Newfoundland
and the neighboring lands were usually called — was a sterile
region, out of which little could come in compensation for any
considerable outlay.   So the Spanish ambassador in Paris reported to his master that it was best to let the French king
spend his money.   The Spaniards seem at any rate to have
exaggerated the preparations which Roberval was making, for
they imagined that thirteen ships were fitting for the voyage,
while in fact Cartier had been instructed to prepare five only,
and among them we find the familiar " Grande Hermine " and
the " Emerillon."

April, 1541. It was the king's wish that the fleet should be
at sea by April 15, 1541; but when the time came

Roberval was far from ready. It was therefore decided that a part of the expedition should go ahead, and on May 23, Cartier hoisted sail on three ships. He soon ran into foul weather, during which his vessels were separated. May. They all later rendezvoused at Carpunt on the Newfoundland coast. Here they waited six weeks for Roberval, and had abundant leisure to repair damages. But the viceroy came not. Weary of the delay, Cartier again put to sea, and entering the Gulf of St. Lawrence, pushed across it August 23, 1541. At and up the great river. It was August 23 when he Stadacona. reached his old camp at Stadacona.

The expectant natives at once asked for Donnacona and his fellows, only to be told that the chieftain had died a Christian, and that the others had married and were now great lords. There is evidence that three at least of these Indians had been baptized at St. Malo in 1538, and that all, excepting one girl, had died. The bold deceit appeased the native anxiety, and Agona, who had in the interval worn Donnacona's wreath, felt quite content with a new lease of power. In fact, he was somewhat effusive in his joy, and did his best to make Cartier share in his festive delight.

For some reason Cartier felt it best to leave his old harbor of Sainte Croix and to proceed four leagues higher up the St. Lawrence to a position near the modern Cap Rouge. September, Here he began a fort which he called Charlesbourg. 1541. Charles- He was still without tidings of the viceroy, and on bourg at Cap Rouge. September 2 he dispatched two of his ships to carry word to France of what he had done and of Roberval's non-appearance. One of these messenger ships was commanded by his brother-in-law, Jalobert, the other by his nephew, Noël.

After these had started homeward, Cartier left Beaupré in charge at Charlesbourg, and proceeded up the river. He had a conference with a petty chieftain at Hochelay, a Hochelay. spot apparently near the Richelieu Rapids. He bestowed upon this savage a red cloak with bright trimmings. Passing on through the rapids to Hochelaga, he learned that its chieftain was plotting mischief, and had gone to Stadacona as if to further some evil design. So without tarrying long, Cartier returned to Charlesbourg and made preparations for the winter. Perhaps the situation of his new fort was not favorable for

intercourse with the natives, or the savages may have kept purposely aloof; at all events, he saw little of them during the winter. His men had found some supposed
diamonds and flakes of what he thought gold, — evidently deceived by a mock metal as the pioneers of Virginia later were,
— and with such promises of wealth he was ready in the spring
to abandon the fort and sail for France. Whether he encountered Roberval on the way is a question which we may presently consider, as we follow the fortunes of the viceroy.

Winter, 1541-42.

We left this royal representative preparing to follow Cartier
with the rest of the fleet. It is to be acknowledged
at the outset that the itineraries of Roberval and Cartier during the progress of this divided expedition are difficult
to reconcile one with another. Some writers have contended
that the viceroy made but a single voyage to the gulf, and then
failed to go up the river to join Cartier, but wintered somewhere on the gulf shores. Others contend that he made a brief
preliminary voyage and then returned to France, only to start
the next spring on his chief explorations. The truth can hardly
be determined beyond dispute; nor can it be satisfactorily
established whether the viceroy and his master pilot met at
all in American waters, so as to be for any period together in
these wild regions. We have distinct statements that Roberval
sailed from Honfleur, August 22, 1541, and again from La
Rochelle, April 16, 1542. Whether this was one embarkation
with a confusion of dates, as has been often believed, or two
distinct ones, is a subject of controversy. If the voyage of
1541 was a preliminary one, Roberval could hardly have gone
beyond the gulf so as to add anything to geographical knowledge. He would have returned to France by the year's end.

Roberval.

Meanwhile Jalobert and Noël, as already stated, had been
sent home by Cartier with dispatches to the king, and their
dispatches may have given new encouragement, so that Roberval was — on the supposition of two voyages — again at sea on
April 16, 1542. This time it seems certain — whether it be
the true date of a single voyage, or the date of a second one — that Roberval departed from La Rochelle.
After a stormy passage he anchored at St. John, Newfoundland, June 8, 1542. Jean Allefonsce, whose story and

At New-foundland, 1542.

charts help us to rehearse their experiences, was in one of his ships.

We have seen that Cartier, in the spring of this year, had abandoned his post at Cap Rouge and come down the river. It has been usually said that in one of the harbors near the gulf he encountered Roberval and his fleet. We may allow it to be true, and that the meeting was not altogether a grateful one to Cartier, who could have had little disposition to return up the river for a repetition of the winter's miseries. If Cartier exhibited his supposable gold and diamonds, Roberval may have been more eager to make trial of new chances in the same field. We only know — as the story goes — that after an interview of the two, one night Cartier hoisted anchor, and when the dawn broke, Roberval found himself left to his own resources and Cartier out of sight on his way to France. Such is Hakluyt's narrative of their meeting and parting, and his name carries a measure of assurance to make it true. It has been intimated that a part of Cartier's discontent was with the necessity of leading a colony which offered no better material than the scouring of the jails.

Mention has been made of Allefonsce as in Roberval's train. This seaman was at this time a man well on in years, — in fact not much short of sixty, — and of so great Allefonsce. experience in navigation that his name is a prominent one in the maritime annals of the Norman seaports. Despite some rival claims as to his nativity, the French can best boast of his fame, for he was most likely born at Saintonge, which is a village near that Cognac which gives its name to French brandy. Champlain, who lived with a generation that had not forgotten the associates of Allefonsce, called him the hardiest mariner of his time.

Roberval apparently took Allefonsce to serve him as pilot after he had sent Cartier ahead ; and it was by Roberval's orders, after reaching Newfoundland, that Allefonsce went north along the Labrador coast to find, if possible, a passage to the west. The ice proved so dense that he gave up the search. How thoroughly he then, or at any later day, sailed about the St. Lawrence gulf is not clear. The little sketch-maps which he made, and which are preserved in his manuscript

Cosmographie, now in the great Paris library, seem to indicate personal acquaintance with its waters, even so far inland as the mouth of the Saguenay. He seems to have embraced the belief that these regions were near, or possibly identical with, Cathay, and he represents the Saguenay as broadening in its upper parts into the Sea of Cathay. If these maps of Allefonsce are the result of his own observation in part at least,

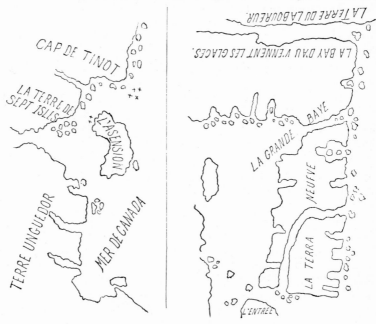

GULF OF ST. LAWRENCE.
[Two Sketches by Allefonsce.]

they may be looked upon as the earliest we have of any portion of the St. Lawrence valley made by an actual explorer.

Roberval himself ascended the St. Lawrence and reached the neighborhood of Cap Rouge by the middle of July, 1542, and began defenses where Cartier in the previous year had established his fort. The communal building — tenement, castle, or whatever it was — makes a good show in the description, with its halls, chambers, storehouses, kitchens, and cellar. The whole group of structures constituted a little intrenched camp, where the company was huddled together.

Cap Rouge, July, 1542.

Nothing but the outer danger could have brought such incongruous elements into subjection or made life endurable. The question of sustenance soon harassed them. The huge household was rough and prodigal. The stores were not of the best, and there was small chance of increasing them from the neighboring tribes, even if they could be counted on as friends. It became therefore, before long, necessary to deal out allotted rations, and it was done rigorously. In this way famine, which at one time was alarmingly near, was kept at a distance. Disease, however, could not be barred out, and scurvy began to make sad inroads upon a company weakened by many trials, and not in the past bred to wholesome ways.

As exigencies came, Roberval showed himself quite equal to his duty. He used the gibbet and lash effectively to preserve peace and insure safety to the community at Fran-çois-Roi, as the post

THE ST. LAWRENCE AND THE SAGUENAY.
[A Sketch by Allefonsce.]

François-Roi.

was now called, transformed to France-Roi by Allefonsce, and France-Prime by Hakluyt.

Fortunately Roberval, as Cartier had before him, escaped hostile attacks from the savages, and it does not appear that the French were even threatened during that perilous winter. With the coming of spring, a better feeling pervaded the company, and Roberval had the courage to think of something beside disciplining his followers. He determined to discover, if possible, what all the stories of various mines in the country were based upon. Roberval would have given much to know what the assayers had made of the sparkling fragments which Cartier had carried to France. Possibly in their treacherous interview, which in Hakluyt's narrative is made to precede Cartier's stealthy escape, that pilot may have laid before his chief the identical map which a descendant of Cartier possessed nearly fifty years later. Roberval would then have descried upon it the legend: "The Saguenay country is a rich land, abounding in precious stones."

Roberval now determined to push an expedition farther into the interior. Accordingly on June 5, 1543, — Hakluyt gives us the date, — he started with a flotilla of eight boats and seventy men. We are told that he left thirty men to guard the fort, and this total of a hundred would indicate that the winter and its diseases had claimed many victims. He expected to return to France-Roi by July 1. Whither he went it is difficult to say. Some interpret the scant account in Hakluyt as signifying an ascent of the St. Lawrence. Others make him plunge through the deep shadows of the Saguenay. It has been even stated that he established a fort on the river Mistassini, and that its remains were still traceable; but the most trustworthy explorers have never found them (*Bull. Amer. Geog. Soc.*, September, 1891).

Roberval explores, June, 1543.

At all events, he found the task of exploration, in whatever direction it lay, greater than he anticipated, and he sent back word to Royèze, who had been left in command at the fort, not to expect his return till July 20, after which, if nothing more was heard of him, Royèze was at liberty to sail for France.

The failure of Hakluyt to continue the story leaves us without a guide to the subsequent fortunes of a colony which, as the Abbé Ferland contends, could hardly have left worthy descendants, if it had established a foothold for its jail-birds. The reader needs to be apprised that in what we have gone over, the present recital is more or less forced. The dates of the several accounts are confusing. Hakluyt is more than usually uncertain, and Allefonsce is sparing of dates. Late writers, whether near or remote from the time of Cartier, have not done much to render clearer the dependence of events.

In what is to follow, the most certain element of dates comes from the somewhat surprising fondness and opportunities which Cartier, after his return to St. Malo, had for standing sponsor at baptisms, and giving evidence in court. Longrais has

CARTIER.

[The usual Portrait, but of doubtful authenticity, following the Engraving in Sulte's *Canadiens-Français*, Montreal, 1882.]

delved assiduously in the hidden sources of this kind of evidence, and there seems to have been no church or other records in St. Malo to which his scrutiny has not been applied.

In this way it is made to appear that Cartier arrived at St.

Malo before October 21, 1542. In the following spring —
say in April or May, 1543 — his name is absent from
local records, and does not reappear till autumn.
Lescarbot says that Cartier made a fourth voyage to
Canada to rescue Roberval, and there was a sufficient interval
between the spring of 1543 and October or November
of the same year for him to have done so. Lescarbot's
unsupported statement and this opportune interval are
all we have upon which to rest any such final voyage of Cartier. Concerning his remaining years at home we have a few
tangible facts.

It was probably in the interval between his second and third
voyage, and perhaps about the time he was summoned in order
to impart a little force to the dilatory performance of Roberval,

CARTIER'S MANOR.
[From Sulte's *Canadiens-Français*, vol. ii.]

that the king bestowed upon Cartier a manor, situated on the
coast a few miles out of St. Malo, which has given rise, in some
writers, to the belief that this lordship of Limoilon had made
him a noble. If such an honor could be indubitably established, it might be cited as another proof of the way in which
Cartier basked in the royal favor. It was from this abode, or
from his town house in St. Malo, that he occasionally issued in
his retirement to attend upon legal transactions, as the records
show. The most important of these citations for our purpose

is when he is summoned with Roberval (April 3, 1544) before the king, to settle the accounts of their joint expedition. The referees gave an award of nearly eighty-four livres to Cartier, which he never received, and which his heirs at a later day contended for. With this item these two men pass out of sight in the story of Canadian exploration.

April 3, 1544.

We know little of the life of Cartier subsequently, till he died at his seashore estate on September 1, 1557, probably of an epidemic then prevailing. Roberval's end is more uncertain. Perhaps he died later at sea, perhaps he was assassinated in Paris, — we have both stories given to us, — but at all events he was still living in the year of Cartier's death, and thenceforth he eludes us.

Cartier dies, September 1, 1557.

CHAPTER III.

THE results of Cartier's explorations came slowly to the knowledge of contemporary cartographers. In the year of Cartier's return from his second voyage (1536), Alonso de Chaves, the official cosmographer of Spain, made a plot of the North American coast, using, it seems probable, maps of explorations of which we have no other trace, and which gave it some trends of the coast differing from the well-known Ribero map of a few years before. Although the Spaniards were keeping close watch on the northern explorations of their rivals, it is apparent that Chaves had not heard of Cartier's movements, and this means, most likely, that the hydrographers in the service of Spain were equally ignorant of what France had been doing, and that nothing from Cartier's reports had been embodied in the Padron General, ordered in 1526, with the intention of portraying year by year the latest results of discovery. By this time Ribero, who had begun such a map, had died, and Chaves had been placed in charge of it. This map of Chaves is not preserved; but there is a map by Gutierrez (1550), known to us, which is held to be based on Chaves. This Gutierrez map gives no trace of the French voyages; nor does Oviedo, the Spanish historian, who wrote the next year (1537) with Chaves's map before him, give us any ground for discrediting the map of Gutierrez as indicating the features of that by Chaves. The next year (1538), the rising young Flemish map-maker, Gerard Mercator, made his earliest map, which shows that no tidings of the Cartier voyages had yet reached the Low Countries. He did not even recognize the great Square Gulf, which had appeared in the Ptolemy of 1511, as premonitory of the gulf which

Chaves and the Padron General.

Cartier had circumnavigated, though three years later Mercator affords a faint suspicion of it in his gores of 1541.

MERCATOR, 1538.
[Northern Hemisphere.]

We do not find any better information in the best of the contemporary cosmographers. Sebastian Münster in Germany (1540) widened a little the passage which severed Newfoundland from the main, and so did the

Maps, sixteenth century.

Italian Vopellio; but Ulpius, making the globe at Rome, in 1542, which is now owned by the New York Historical Society, seems not to have been even thus imperfectly informed. The French globe-maker, who not far from the same time made the sphere preserved at Nancy, knew only enough to make a group of islands west of the Newfoundland banks.

We turn to something more intimately connected with Cartier's own work. It might go without saying that Cartier would plot his own tracks; but we have no written evidence that he did, other than a letter of his grand-nephew fifty years later, who says that he himself had inherited one such map. We

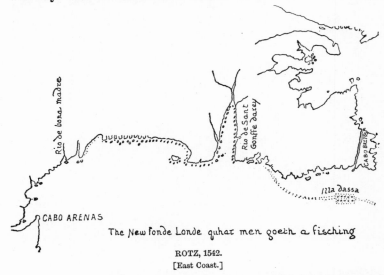

ROTZ, 1542.
[East Coast.]

must look to three or four maps, made within five years of Cartier's last voyage, and which have come down to us, to find how the lost charts of Cartier affected cartographical knowledge in certain circles in France, and placed the geography of the St. Lawrence on a basis which was not improved for sixty years.

Those who have compared the early maps find the oldest cartographical record which we have of Cartier's first voyage Rotz, 1542.   (1534) in a document by Jean Rotz, dated eight years later, and preserved in the British Museum. Harrisse thinks that back of this Rotz map there is another, known as the Harleyan mappemonde, which is deposited in the same collection ; and it is possible that a map of Jean de Clamorgan, known to have comprehended details of the earlier Cartier voyages, which has disappeared from the collection at Fontainebleau, may also have been useful to Rotz, who is held to be a Frenchman, which may also account for his acquaintance with Malouin sources. Hamy, in a recent paper (*Bulletin de Géographie historique, etc.*, 1889), makes him identical with Jean Roze of Dieppe. This *Boke of Idrography*, as Rotz calls it, contains two maps which interest us. One shows the Gulf of St. Lawrence and the opening into the river, which

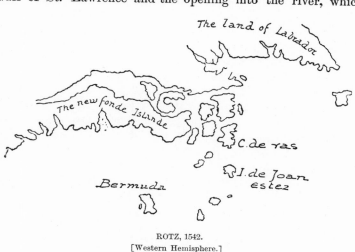

ROTZ, 1542.
[Western Hemisphere.]

indicates an acquaintance with the extent of Cartier's first explorations (1534), and may well have been made some years before the date of the manuscript which contains it. If its outline is interpreted correctly, in making Anticosti a peninsula connecting with the southern shore of the St. Lawrence River, it is a further proof that a foggy distance prevented Cartier from suspecting that he was crossing the main channel of the St. Lawrence, when he sailed from Gaspé to the Anticosti shores. The other map may be nearer the date of the manuscript, for it carries the river much farther from the gulf, and indicates a knowledge of Cartier's second voyage. So skillful a cosmographer as Santa Cruz — whose map is preserved in Stockholm, as Dahlgren has lately informed us — was certainly at this period (1542) utterly ignorant of the then recent explorations up the St. Lawrence.

Two years later (1544), there was the first sign in an en-
Cabot map, 1544.   graved map of Cartier's success, — the now famous Cabot mappemonde, — and this was a year before any narrative of his second voyage was printed. As but a single copy is known of both map and narrative, it is possible that the publications were not welcome to the government, and the editions of the two were suppressed as far as could be. The solitary map was found in Germany, and is now in the great library at Paris. The sole copy of the *Bref Récit*, published at Paris in 1545, is in the British Museum, among the books which Thomas Grenville collected.

To test this published narrative, scholars have had recourse to three manuscripts, preserved in the Paris Library, varying somewhat, and giving evidence that, before the text was printed, it had circulated in hand-written copies, all made apparently by the same penman. It was probably from the printed text that both Hakluyt and Ramusio made their versions to be published at a later day.

The suppression, if there was such, of the Cabot map is more remarkable ; for this Paris copy is the only one which has come down to us out of several editions — Harrisse says four — in which it appeared. This multiplicity of issue is inferred from the descriptions of copies varying, but it is not clear that these changes indicate anything more than tentative conditions of the plates. That the map embodies some conception of the Cartier explorations is incontestable. It gives vaguely a shape to the gulf conformable to Cartier's track, and makes evident the course of the great tributary, as far as Cartier explored it. There are many signs in this part of the map, however, that Cartier's own plot could not have been used at first hand, and the map in its confused nomenclature and antiquated geographical notions throughout indicates that the draft was made by a 'prentice hand. The profession of one of its legends — of late critically set forth from the study of them by Dr. Deane in the *Proceedings of the Massachusetts Historical Society* (February, 1891) — that Sebastian Cabot was its author is to be taken with some modification at least. The

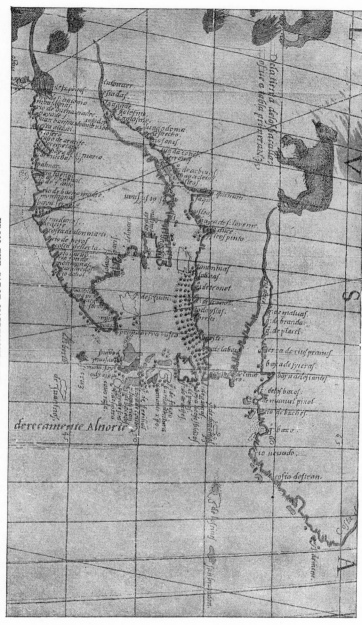

map is an indication that the results of Cartier's voyages had within a few years become in a certain sense public property. It happens that most of what we know respecting the genesis of the map is from English sources, or sources which point to England; but the map, it seems probable, was made in Flanders, and not in France, nor in Spain, the country with which Cabot's official standing connected him. It looks very much like a surreptitious publication, which, to avoid the scrutiny of the Spanish Hydrographical Office, had been made beyond their reach, while an anonymous publication of it protected

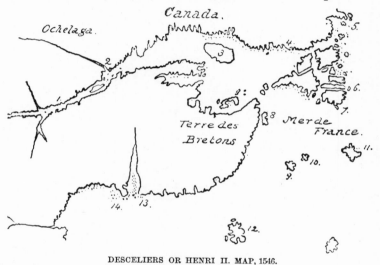

DESCELIERS OR HENRI II. MAP, 1546.

Key: 1. Ochelaga.   2. R. du Sagñay.   3. Assumption.   4. R. Cartier.   5. Bell Isle.
6. Bacalliau.   7. C. de Raz.   8. C. aux Bretons.   9. Encorporada.   10. Ye du Breton.   11. Ye de Jhan estienne.   12. Sete citades.   13. C. des isles.   14. Arcipel de estienne Gomez.

the irresponsible maker or makers from official annoyance. This may account for its rarity, and perhaps for the incompleteness of its information.   Harrisse, however, in his latest publication, *The Discovery of North America*, is inclined to recognize Cabot's direct connection with the map, and suggests that Cabot used it to enforce the claim of England to the regions which the French were now exploring, by placing the landfall of 1497 at Cape Breton.   In doing so Cabot negatived all the earlier implied and positive statements, that the landfall of John Cabot had been ten degrees farther north on the

Labrador coast. This position outside the water-shed of the St. Lawrence valley was of course less favorable to an English claim than one commanding the entrance of the valley.

Better information, mixed apparently with some knowledge derived from the Portuguese voyages, — and certainly chronicling Portuguese discoveries in other parts of the globe, — and so presenting some but not great differences, appears in another map of about the same date, known as the Nicolas Vallard map. When Dr. Kohl brought it anew to the attention of scholars, it was in the collection of Sir Thomas Phillipps in England; but there is reason to suppose that not far from the date of its making, it had been owned in Dieppe. The

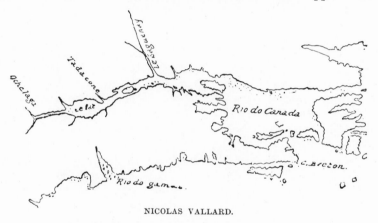

NICOLAS VALLARD.

maker of it may have profited directly from French sources, particularly in the embellishment upon it, which seems to represent events in Roberval's experiences.

There is, likewise, another map of this period which is still more intimately connected with Cartier's movements; indeed, it can hardly have been made independently of Desceliers. material which he furnished, though very likely for neighboring regions it was based on Portuguese sources. This is the one fashioned by the order of the king for the Dauphin's instruction, just before the latter succeeded his father as Henry II. A few years ago Mr. Major, of the British Museum, deciphered a legend upon it, which showed that it was the handiwork of Pierre Desceliers, a Dieppe map-maker then working at Arques.

This fact, as well as its official character, brings it close to the
prime sources ; and the map may even identify these sources
in the representations of Roberval and his men, as they are
grouped on the banks of the St. Lawrence.   I am informed by
the present owner, the Earl of Crawford and Balcarres, that
an attempt at one time to efface the legend which discloses its
authorship has obscured but has not destroyed the lettering.
The map formerly belonged to Jomard, the geographer.

There are only the sketch maps of Allefonsce which can be
traced nearer the explorers themselves than the maps
Allefonsce. already mentioned.   What this pilot of Roberval
made on the spot we know not, but he attempted, in 1545, in
a rude way to draw upon his experiences in a little treatise.
This manuscript *Cosmographie*, in which the coast-lines are
washed in at the top of its sheets, is preserved in the National
Library at Paris.   Several modern writers have used them, and
the sketches have been more than once copied.   Bibliographers
know better, however, a little chapbook, which ran through at
least four editions in the interval before new interest in Canada
was awakened by Champlain.   It was first published in 1559,
after the death of Allefonsce ; and his name, which appears in the
title, *Les Voyages avantureux du Capitaine Alfonce Sainton-
geois*, was apparently made prominent to help the sale of the
book, rather than to indicate the intimate connection of the
redoubtable pilot with it.   His manuscript *Cosmographie* had
been prepared by himself for the royal eye, while this printed
production, which was issued at Poictiers, was dressed up by
others for the common herd, without close adherence to the
manuscript.   A popular local bard sets forth pretty much all
we know of its hero in some preliminary verses.   Like all
chapbooks, the little volume has become rare ; and when a copy
was sold in Dr. Court's collection (1885), it was claimed that
only three copies had been sold in France in thirty years.

The most prolific map-maker of this period in Europe was
Baptista Agnese of Venice.   He had a deft hand,
Agnese. which made his *portolanos* merchantable.   The dex-
terity of their drawing has perhaps enhanced their value enough
to prevent careless wear of them, so that they are not infrequent in Italian libraries, and will be found in almost all the
large collections in Europe.   One certainly has found its way

to America, and is preserved in the Carter-Brown Library at
Providence. Though Agnese was making these maps for over a
quarter of a century, beginning about the time of Cartier's
activity, he never much varied from the conventional types
which successively marked the stages of geographical knowledge. He has hardly a map which can be accounted a turn-
ing-point in American geography, and his drafts simply follow
the prevailing notions.

Thus it was that for sixteen years after Cartier and Roberval had finished their work, the French public was made acquainted only with the *Bref Récit* and the scant narrative to
which the popularity of Allefonsce's name had given a forced
currency. The European scholar fared better than
the provincial Frenchman, for the third volume of
the *Raccolta* of Ramusio, which was devoted wholly to American discovery, had appeared in Venice in 1556. It is a chief
source still to be consulted for the earliest explorations of the
St. Lawrence region. It is here that we find an account of that
" Gran Capitano," identified with the Dieppese navigator, Jean
Parmentier, who visited the Baccalaos region in the early years
of that century. Here, too, we derive a scant knowledge of
Denys and Aubert, as already mentioned. But it is concerning
the first voyage of Cartier that Ramusio helps us most. Where
he got his records of that enterprise of 1534, it is not easy to
conjecture, and what he says remained for a long while the sum
of all that was known concerning it. That there were originally several manuscript texts of this narrative, varying enough
in the copying to make differences that became distinguisha-
ble, appears to be certain ; but it is not so easy to trace them
distinctively in the various printed texts which have been
published. The text in Ramusio was without doubt used by
John Florio in making the early English translation (London,
1580), which is the source of most that has appeared in that
language respecting the voyage. A Norman publisher at Rouen
printed a French text, and it is not quite certain that he used
Ramusio. It has been suspected that, in pretending to make a
translation, this editor may possibly have used an offi- Cartier nar-
cial narrative, and that his pretense was intended to ratives.
conceal a surreptitious use of a forbidden paper. When Tross
reprinted this little book (Paris, 1865), he could find only one

Ramusio.

copy, and that was in the great Paris Library; but Harrisse later discovered a copy in the Sainte Genevieve Library. The fact that the book has nearly passed out of sight might indicate, as with the *Bref Récit*, that there was either a suppression of it, or an inordinately hard use of it by readers. Two years after publishing this *Discours du Voyage* (1867), Tross surprised the critics by publishing a *Relation originale*, as if it were Cartier's own narrative of this first voyage. The arguments of Michelant, the editor, in supporting this view of its authenticity are strong, but hardly conclusive. This precious manuscript was discovered in the Paris Library in 1867, having previously escaped notice.

In the year before the appearance of the American section of Ramusio, and probably two years after that Italian editor had gathered his material, the Spanish historian, Go-Gomara. mara, showed in his *Historia General* (Saragossa, 1555), that intelligence of Cartier's exploits had reached him in some confused form. Indeed, Gomara is rarely critical in what he offers. It will be remembered that Cartier had given the name of "Sainct Laurens" to a small estuary in the gulf, and it has never been quite established when the same name gained currency as the appellation of the gulf itself, and of the great river of Canada. Nevertheless, Gomara writes in 1555, or perhaps a year earlier, that "a great river called San Lorenço, which some think an arm of the sea [*i. e.* leading to Cathay], has been sailed up for two hundred leagues, and is called by some the Strait of the Three Brothers."

We may consider that from the Rotz, Vallard, Cabot, and Desceliers maps, pretty nearly all the ground that Cartier's own maps could have disclosed is deducible by the careful student, and that a large part of our history of this obscure period is necessarily derived from such studies. Now, what was the effect of these cartographical records upon the maps of the St. Lawrence for the rest of that century?

This question brings us to consider nearly all the leading Cartogra- European cartographers of the sixteenth century, to phers, six- teenth cen- whatever maritime peoples they belong. The most tury. famous and learned of the German cosmographers, Sebastian Münster, contented himself with insularizing a region which he associated with the earlier Cortereal. Pedro Medina, the leading Spanish writer on seamanship, in his *Arte de Navegar*, and in other books, for a score of years after this, used a

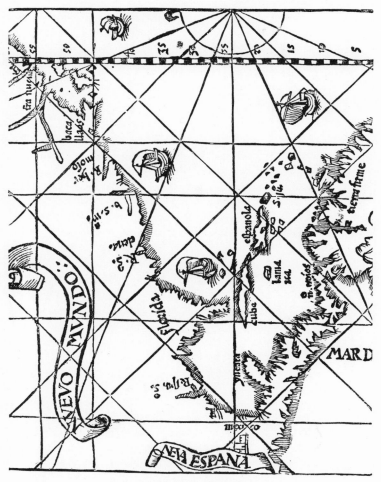

PART OF MEDINA'S MAP, 1545.

map on which there was merely a conventional gulf and river. Baptista Agnese was continuing to figure the coast about Newfoundland in absolute ignorance of the French discoveries of ten years before.

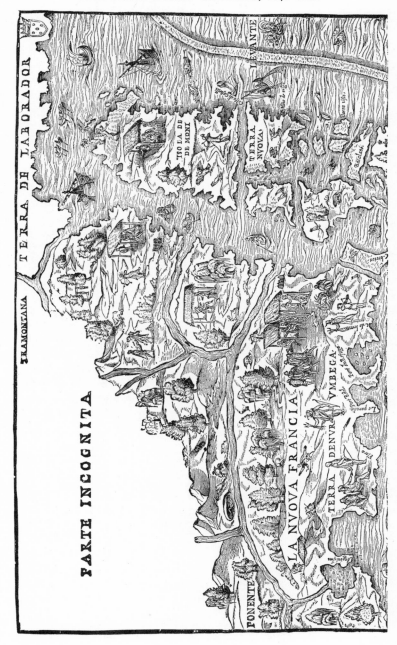

GASTALDO IN RAMUSIO (about 1550).

We are in 1546 first introduced to Giacomo Gastaldi, a Venetian map-maker of reputation throughout Italy. He gives us a map which was included in Lafreri's atlas. It looks like a distinct recognition of Cartier, in a long river which flows into a bay behind an island. This is the more remarkable because, when he was employed two years later to make the maps for the Venetian edition of Ptolemy (1548), he reverted to the old pre-Cartier notions of an archipelago and rudimentary rivers.

When Ramusio was gathering his American data at this time, he depended on an old friend, Frascastoro, to supply the illustrative maps. This gentleman, now in advanced years, was living on his estate near Verona, and in correspondence with geographical students throughout Europe. Oviedo had sent some navigator's charts to him from Spain, and Ramusio tells us that similar information had come to him from France relative to the discoveries in New France. These charts, placed by Frascastoro in Ramusio's hands, were by this editor committed to Gastaldi. The result was the general map of America which appears in the third volume of the *Raccolta.* This map is singularly inexpressive for the Baccalaos region. Something more definite is revealed in another map, more confined in its range. A study of this last map makes one feel as if the rudimentary rivers of the Ptolemy map (1548) had suggested a network of rivers, stretching inland. It has one feature in the shoals about Sable Island so peculiar and so closely resembling that feature in Rotz's map, that Gastaldi must have worked with that map before him, or he must have used the sources of that map. With this exception, there is absolutely nothing in the map showing any connection with the cartography of the Cartier-Roberval expeditions. These features stand, in fact, for earlier notions, and are made to illustrate the narrative of the "Gran Capitano."

There is a Portuguese map by Johannes Freire, which must
Freire, etc.   have been based on Cartier's second voyage, for it
leaves undeveloped the west coast of Newfoundland, which Cartier followed in 1534. Another Portuguese map, which at one time was owned by Jomard, shows acquaintance with both the first and second voyages of Cartier, as does the Portuguese atlas with French leanings, which is preserved in the Archives of the Marine at Paris, and is ascribed to Guillaume le Testu. A popular map by Bellero, used in various Antwerp publications of this period, utterly ignores the French discoveries.

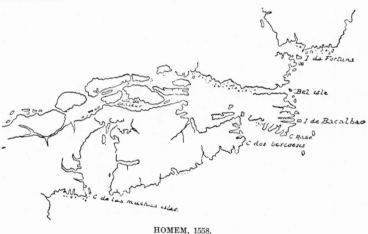

HOMEM, 1558.

The map of Homem in 1558 is an interesting one. It is in
Homem.   an atlas of this Portuguese hydrographer, preserved in
the British Museum. It is strongly indicative of independent knowledge, but whence it came is not clear. He worked in Venice, a centre of such knowledge at this time; and Homem's map is a proof of the way in which nautical intelligence failed to establish itself in the Atlantic seaports, but

rather found recognition for the benefit of later scholars in this Adriatic centre. It is in this map, for instance, that we get the earliest recognizable plotting of the Bay of Fundy. But with all his alertness, the material which Ramusio had already used respecting Cartier's first voyage seems to have escaped him, or perhaps Homem failed to understand that navigator's track where it revealed the inside coast of Newfoundland. What he found in any of the accounts of the Cartier voyages to warrant his making the north bank of the St. Lawrence an archipelago skirting the Arctic Sea is hard to say; but Homem is not the only one who developed this notion. We have seen that Allefonsce believed that the Saguenay conducted to such a sea, and there are other features of that pilot's sketches which are consonant with such a view; while a network of straits and channels pervading this Canadian region is a feature of some engraved maps at a considerably later day. Homem, living in Venice, most probably was in consultation with Ramusio, and may have had access to the store of maps which Frascastoro submitted to Gastaldi. Indeed, Ramusio intimates, in the introduction to his third volume, that this Canadian region may yet be found to be cut up into islands, and he says that the reports of Cartier had left this uncertainty in his mind. The stories which Cartier had heard of great waters lying beyond the points he had reached had doubtless something to do with these fancies of the map-makers.

When the learned Italian, Ruscelli, printed his translation of Ptolemy at Venice (1561), he added his own maps, for he was a professional cartographer. He also apparently profited by Ramusio's introduction to the collection of Frascastoro; for the map which he gave of " Tierra nueva " reverted to the same material of the pre-Cartier period which had been used by Gastaldi, showing that he either was ignorant of the claims of Cartier's discoveries, or that he rejected them. Ruscelli clung to this belief pertinaciously, and never varied his map in successive editions for a dozen years; and during this interval Agnese (1564) and Porcacchi (1572) copied him.

Ruscelli.

We have two maps in 1566 in which the Cartier voyages are recognized, but in quite different ways. The map of Nicolas des Liens of Dieppe was acquired by the great library of Paris in 1857, and the visitor there to-day can see it

Des Liens.

under glass in the geographical department. It is very pro-
nounced in the record of Cartier; for his name is displayed
along the shore of a broad sound, which is made to do duty
Zaltieri. for the St. Lawrence. The other is the map of Zaltieri, with an inscription, in which the author claims
to have received late information from the French. In this
map the St. Lawrence is merely a long, waving line, and the
river is made to flow on each side of à large island into a bay
studded with islands.

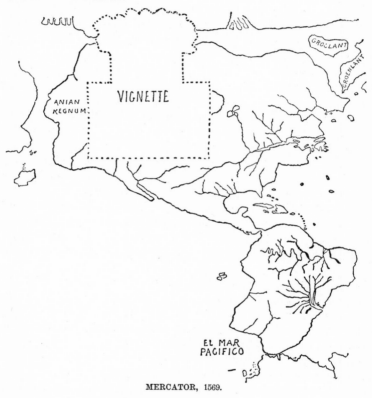

MERCATOR, 1569.

Three or four years later, we come to the crowning work of
Mercator. Gerard Mercator in his great planisphere of 1569;
Ortelius. and a year later to the atlas of the famous Flemish
geographer who did so much to revolutionize cartography, —
Abraham Ortelius. The great bay has now become, with Mer-

cator, the Gulf of St. Lawrence (*Sinus Laurentii*); but the main river is left without a name, and is carried far west beyond Hochelaga (Montreal) to a water-shed, which separates

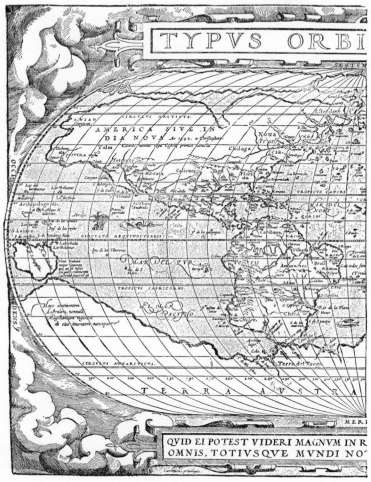

ORTELIUS, 1570.

the great interior valley of the continent from the Pacific slope. Here was what no one had before attempted in interpretation of the vague stories which Cartier had heard from the Indians. Mercator makes what is apparently the Ottawa open

a waterway, as Cartier could have fancied it, when he gazed
from the summit of Mont Royale. This passage carried the
imagination into the great country of the Saguenay, which the
Indians told of as bounding on a large body of fresh water. It
seems easy to suppose that this was an interpretation of that
route which in the next generation conducted many a Jesuit to
the Georgian Bay, and so developed the upper lakes long before the shores of Lake Erie were comprehended. Not one of
the earlier maps had divined this possible solution of Cartier's
problem ; and Mercator did it, so far as we can now see, with
nothing to aid him but a study of Cartier's narrative, or possibly of Cartier's maps or data copied from them. It was one of
those feats of prescience through comparative studies which put
that Flemish geographer at the head of his profession. By a
similar insight he was the first to map out a great interior valley
to the continent, separated from the Atlantic slope by a mountainous range that could well stand for the Alleghanies. Dr.
Kohl suggests that Mercator might have surmised this eastern
water-shed of the great continent by studying the reports of
De Soto in his passage to the Mississippi, during the very
year when Cartier and Roberval were developing the great
northern valley. There was yet no conception of the way in
which these two great valleys so nearly touched at various
points that the larger was eventually to be entered from the
lesser.

Before Mercator's death (1594), he felt satisfied that the
great mass of fresh water, to which the way by the Ottawa
pointed, connected with the Arctic seas. This he made evident
by his globe-map of 1587. Earlier, in 1570, he had conveniently hidden the uncertainty by partly covering the limits of
Interior   such water by a vignette. Hakluyt in the same year
water.   (1587) thought it best to leave undefined the connections of such a fresh-water sea. The map-makers struggled for
many years over this uncertain northern lake, which Mercator
had been the first to suggest from Cartier's data. Ortelius also
(1570, 1575, etc.) was induced to doubt the fresh character of
this sea, and made it a mere gulf of the Arctic Ocean,
stretched toward the south. In this he was followed by Popel-
linière (1582), Gallæus, (1585), Münster (1595), Linschoten
(1598), Botero (1603), and others. It is fair to observe, how-

ever, that Ortelius in one of his maps (1575) has shunned the conclusion, and Metellus (1600) was similarly cautious when he used the customary vignette to cover what was doubtful. There was at the same time no lack of believers in the fresh-water theory, as is apparent in the map of Judaeis (1593), De Bry (1596), Wytfliet (1597), and Quadus (1600), not to name others. These theorizers, while they connected it with a salt northern sea, made current for a while the name of Lake Conibas, as applied to the fresh-water basin. This body of water seemed in still later maps after Hudson's time to shift its position, and was merged in the great bay discovered by that navi-

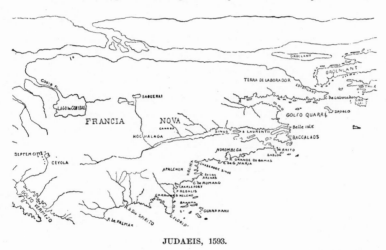

JUDAEIS, 1593.

gator. It was not till a suggestion appeared in one of the maps of the Arnheim *Ptolemy* of 1597, made more emphatic by Molineaux in 1600, that this flitting interior sea was made to be the source of the St. Lawrence, while it was at the same time supposed to have some outlet in the Arctic Ocean. The great interior lakes were then foreshadowed in the " Lacke of Tadenac, the bounds whereof are unknown," as Molineaux's legend reads.

The English seamen had become active in this geographical quest very shortly after Mercator and Ortelius had well established their theories in the public mind. Sir Humphrey Gilbert had indeed penetrated this region ; but when

English interest.

he published his map in 1576, he had helped to popularize
a belief in a multitudinous gathering of islands in what was
now called the land of Canada.   Frobisher's explorations were
farther to the north, and his map (1578) professed that in these
higher latitudes there was a way through the continent.   Hakluyt, in his *Westerne Planting*, tells us that the bruit

Hakluyt.

of Frobisher's voyage had reached Ortelius, and had
induced that geographer to come to England in 1577, " to prye
and looke into the secretes of Frobisher's Voyadge."   Hakluyt
further says that this " greate geographer " told him at this
time " that if the warres of Flaunders had not bene, they of

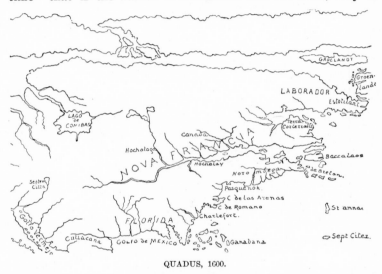

QUADUS, 1600.

the Lowe Countries had meant to have discovered those partes
of America and the northweste straite before this tyme."   Hakluyt had it much at heart to invigorate the English with a spirit
of discovery, and the treatise just quoted was written for that
purpose.   " Yf wee doe procrastinate the plantinge," he says,
" the Frenche, the Normans, the Brytons or the Duche or some
other nation will not onely prevente us of the mightie Baye of
St. Lawrence, where they have gotten the starte of us already,
thoughe wee had the same revealed to us by bookes published
and printed in Englishe before them."   It is not easy to satisfy
one's self as to what Hakluyt refers, when he implies that pre-

vious to Cartier's voyage there had been English books making reference to the St. Lawrence Gulf. Modern investigators have in fact found in English books only the scantiest
mention of American explorations before Eden printed his
translation of Münster in 1553, nearly twenty years after Cartier's first voyage. The late Dr. Charles Deane, in commenting
on Hakluyt's words, could give no satisfactory explanation of
what seems to be their plain meaning.

The year before Hakluyt wrote this sentence, he had given
up an intention of joining in Gilbert's last expedition, and had

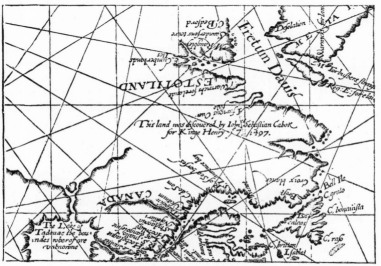

MOLINEAUX'S MAP, 1600.

gone to Paris (1583) as chaplain to Sir Edward Stafford.
While in that city we find him busy with "diligent inquiries of
such things as may yeeld any light unto our westerne discov-
erie," making to this end such investigations as he could respecting current and contemplated movements of the Spanish
and French. In this same essay on *Westerne Planting* Hakluyt
drew attention to what he understood Cartier to say of a river
that can be followed for three months "southwarde from Hochelaga." Whether this refers to some Indian story of a way
by Lake Champlain and the Hudson, or to the longer route
from the Iroquois country to the Ohio and Mississippi, may be

a question; if indeed it may not mean that the St. Lawrence
itself bent towards the south and found its rise in a warmer
clime, as the cartographers who were contemporaries of Hakluyt made it. Hakluyt further translates what Cartier makes
Donnacona and other Indians say of these distant parts, where
the people are " clad with clothes as wee [the French] are,
very honest, and many inhabited townes, and that they had
greate store of golde and redde copper; and that within the
land beyonde the said firste ryver unto Hochelaga and Saguy-
nay ys an iland envyroned rounde aboute with that and other
ryvers, and that there is a sea of freshe water founde, as they
have hearde say of those of Saguenay, there was never man
hearde of, that founde vnto the begynnynge and ende thereof."
Here is the warrant that Mercator and his followers found for
their sea of sweet water. Hakluyt adds: " In the Frenche origi-
nall, which I sawe in the Kinge's library at Paris, yt is further
put downe, that Donnacona, the Kinge of Canada, in his barke
had traueled to that contrie where cynamon and cloves are had."
Hakluyt, with the tendency of his age, could not help associat-
ing this prolonged passage with a new way to Cathay, and he
cites in support " the judgmente of Gerardus Mercator, that
excellent geographer, in a letter of his," which his son had
shown to Hakluyt, saying, " There is no doubte but there is a
streighte and shorte waye open unto the west, even to Cathaio."
Hakluyt then closes his list of reasons for believing in this ultimate passage by adding, in the words of Ramusio, that " if the
Frenchmen in this their Nova Francia woulde have discovered
upp farther into the lande towardes the west northwest partes,
they shoulde have founde the sea and have sailed to Cathaio."

Before Hakluyt published any map of his own, there were
two English maps which became prominent. In 1580,
Dr. John Dee presented to Queen Elizabeth a map
which is preserved in the British Museum. It has
nothing to distinguish it from the other maps of the time,
which show a St. Lawrence River greatly prolonged. The
second map was far more distinctive and more speculative.
Ruscelli in 1561 and Martines in 1578 had represented the
country south of the Lower St. Lawrence as an island, with a
channel on the west of it, connecting the Atlantic with the

John Dee.
M. Lok.
1580-82.

great river of Canada. This view was embodied by Master
Michael Lok in this other map, in union with other prevalent

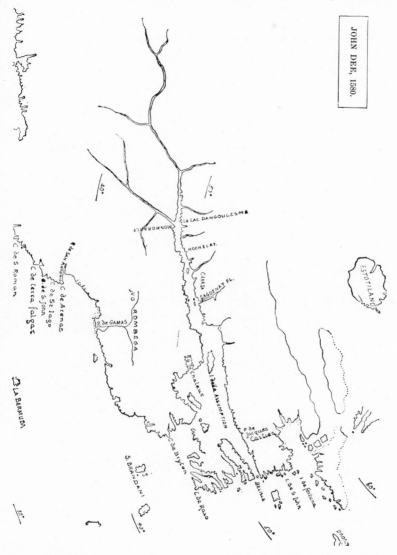

notions, already mentioned, of a neighboring archipelago between the St. Lawrence and the Arctic waters. In this way

Lok made the great river rather an ocean inlet than an affluent of the gulf. Hakluyt adopted this map in his little *Divers Voyages* (1582) to illustrate an account of the voyage of Verrazano, and curiously did so, because there is no trace of Verrazano in the map except the great western sea, which had long passed into oblivion with other cartographers, although there was a curious reminder of it in 1585, when Ralph Lane on the Carolina coast learned that the Roanoke River at its springs sometimes got the spray of the western ocean. We have already presented this Lok map to the reader [*ante*, p. 20].

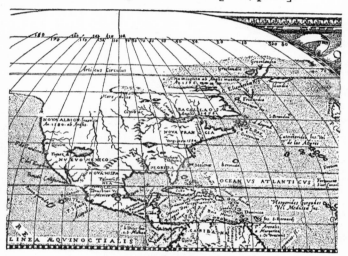

HAKLUYT-MARTYR MAP, 1587.

When Hakluyt again came before the public in an edition of the eight decades of Peter Martyr's *De Orbe Novo*, which he printed at Paris in 1587, he added a map bearing the initials "F. G." This map may be supposed to embody the conclusions which Hakluyt had reached after his years of collecting material. He had, as we have seen, already reviewed the field in his *Westerne Planting*, where he had adopted the Mercator theory of the access by the Ottawa to the great fresh-water lake of the Indian tales.

Hakluyt.

Jacques Noël, a grand-nephew of Cartier, writing from St. Malo in 1587, refers to this F. G. map of Hakluyt as putting down "the great lake" of Canada much too

Cartier's maps.

far to the north to be in accordance with one of Cartier's maps
which he professed to have. This Noël had been in the country, and reported the Indians as saying that the great lake was
ten days above the rapids (near Montreal). He had been at
the rapids, and reported them to be in 44° north latitude.

In 1590, Hakluyt was asking Ortelius, through a relative
of the Antwerp geographer then living in London, to
publish a map of the region north of Mexico and to- *Ortelius.*
wards the Arctic seas. Ortelius signified his willingness to do so
if Hakluyt would furnish the data. In the same year, the English geographer wrote to Ortelius at Antwerp, urging him, if he
made a new map, to insert " the strait of the Three Brothers in
its proper place, as there is still hope of discovering it some
day, and we may by placing it in the map remove the error of
those cosmographers who do not indicate it." It is apparent
by Hakluyt's accompanying drawing that he considered the
" Fretum trium fratrum " to be in latitude 70° north.

There was a temptation to the geographer to give a striking
character to the reports or plots of returned navigators. Mercator compliments Ortelius on his soberness in using such plots,
and complains that geographical truth is much corrupted by
map-makers, and that those of Italy are specially bad.

The maps that succeeded, down to the time when Champlain
made a new geography for the valley of the St. Lawrence,
added little to the conceptions already mastered by the chief
cartographers. The idea of the first explorers that America
was but the eastern limits of Asia, revived by Schöner and
Franciscus Monachus before 1530, may be said to have van-
ished at the same time ; for the map of Myritius of near this
date (1587, 1590) is one of the latest maps to hold to the
belief.

While all this speculative geography was forming and disap-
pearing with an obvious tendency to a true conception of the
physical realities of the problems, there was scarcely
any attempt made to help solve the question by explo- *Suspension
of explora-
tion.*
ration. There was indeed a continuance of the fishing
voyages of the Normans and Bretons to the Banks, and not
unlikely the English may have participated in the business.
Such fishermen doubtless ran into the inlets near the gulf to

dry their fish and barter trinkets with the natives for walrus tusks; but we find no record for many years of any one turning the point of Gaspé and going up the river. There was at the same time no official patronage of exploration. The politics of France were far too unquiet. Henry II. had as much as he could do to maintain his struggles with Charles V. and Philip II. St. Quentin and Gravelines carried French chivalry down to the dust. The persecution of the Protestants in the brief reign of Francis I., the machinations of Catharine de' Medici and the supremacy of the Guises, kept attention too constantly upon domestic hazards to permit the government to glance across the sea. All efforts under Charles IX. to secure internal peace were but transient. Every interval of truce between the rival religions only gave opportunities for new conspiracies. The baleful night of St. Bartholomew saw thirty thousand Huguenots plunged into agony and death. The wars of the League which followed were but a prolonged combat for Huguenot existence. Henry III., during fifteen years of blood, played fast and loose with both sides. Henry IV. fought at Arques and Ivry to preserve his crown, and abjured his faith in the end as a better policy to the same end. At last these tumultuous years yielded to the promulgation of the famous edict at Nantes (April 15, 1598), and in the rest which came later the times grew ripe for new enterprises beyond the sea.

We have seen that it was to the labors of Hakluyt and Ramusio during these sixty years that we owe a large part of the current knowledge of what were then the last official expeditions to Canada. That private enterprise did not cease to connect the French ports with the fishery and trade of the gulf and its neighboring ports is indeed certain, though Garneau speaks of this interval as that of a temporary abandonment of Canada. Gosselin and other later investigators have found entries made of numerous local outfits for voyages from Honfleur and other harbors. Such mariners never, however, so far as we know, contemplated the making of discoveries. Old fishermen are noted as having grown gray in forty years' service on the coast; and there is reason to believe that during some seasons as many as three or four hundred fishing-crafts may have dipped to their anchors hereabouts, and half of them French. Some of them added the pursuit of trade, and chased the walrus. Breton babies grew to know the cunning skill which in leisure hours was bestowed by these mariners on the ivory trifles which amused their households. Norman maidens were decked with the fur which their brothers had secured from the Esquimaux. Parkman found, in a letter of Menendez to Philip of Spain, that from as far south as the Potomac, Indian canoes crawled northward along the coast, till they found Frenchmen in the Newfoundland waters to buy their peltries. Bréard has of late, in his *Marine Normande*, thrown considerable light upon these fishing and trading voyagers, but there is no evidence of a customary passing into the great river.

Once, indeed, it seemed as if the French monarch, who had occasionally sent an armed vessel to protect his subjects in this region against the English, Spanish, and Portuguese, awoke to the opportunities that were passing ; and in 1577 he commissioned Troilus du Mesgonez, Marquis de la Roche, to lead a colony to Canada, and the project commanded the confidence of the merchants of Rouen, Caen, and Lisieux. Captain J. Carleill, writing in 1583, in his *Entended Voyage to America*, tells us that the French were trying to overcome the distrust of the Indians, which the kidnapping exploits of Cartier had implanted. Whether any such fear of the native animosity stood in the way of La Roche's enterprise or not is not evident; but certain it is that he did not sail, and the king remained without a representative on the St. Lawrence. This sovereign gave, however, in 1588, in requital of claims made by the heirs of Cartier for his unrewarded services, a charter to two of that navigator's nephews, Etienne Charton and Jacques Noël, in which he assigned to them for twelve years the right to trade for furs and to work mines, with the privilege of a commercial company. The grant was made partly to enable the heirs to carry out Cartier's injunctions to his descendants not to abandon the country of Canada.

Such reserved privileges were a blow to the merchants of St. Malo, and they drew the attention of the Breton parliament to the monopoly in such a way that the king found it prudent to rescind the charter, except so far as to allow mining at Cap de Conjugon. No one knows where that cape was, or that any mining was done there. So a second royal project came to naught.

La Roche, 1577.

It would have been better if the first expedition that really got off had never started.   A few years later, La Roche, who had had much tribulation since his last luckless effort, was commissioned (January 12, 1590) to lead once more a colony to the St. Lawrence.   By this act that king revived the powers which Francis I. had conferred on Roberval. Chartering two vessels and, in default of better colonists, filling them with convicts, La Roche sailed west and made Sable Island.   Such portion of his company as he did not need while exploring for a site, he landed on this desert spot, not without raising the suspicion that he did not dare to land them on the mainland, for fear of their deserting him.   While searching for a place to settle, heavy gales blew his exploring ships out to sea, and back to France.   Those whom he had abandoned at Sable Island were not rescued till 1603, when twelve had died.

1590.

This is the last scene of that interval which we have been considering; but in the near future other spirits were to animate New France, in the persons of Pontgravé, Champlain, and their associates, and a new period of exploration was to begin.

CHAPTER IV.

ABORTIVE ATTEMPTS AT COLONIZATION.

1600–1607.

It was in the person of François Gravé — who is usually called Pontgravé or Dupont Gravé, for he was Sieur du Pont — that France at last undertook the coloni- ^{Pontgravé.} zation of Canada. Pontgravé was a trading mariner of St. Malo. He had already, during his voyaging, ascended the St. Lawrence as far as Three Rivers. Being now desirous to back a petition which he had rendered for the privilege of trading for furs in Canada, he sought the patronage of a rich Honfleur merchant, Pierre Chauvin, seigneur of Tontuit. This person was a man of consideration and good connec- ^{Chauvin.} tions. He was a Calvinist, and had lived in Dieppe at one time. It was even averred that Henry IV. had rewarded him with a patent of nobility for his loyalty. His standing in the king's eyes was not, it would seem, an uncertain element in the chances of royal support when he allied himself with Pontgravé to promote them. But Pontgravé was not without a merit of his own, for he was no stranger in the new country, and he was not unfitted to be the agent of the monarch in strengthening the French claim in that region, to which the royal will was by no means averse. Looking for further capital to put their purpose beyond financial embarrassment, the two partners found a willing contributor in Pierre du ^{Sieur de Monts.} Guast, Sieur de Monts. It was given out that five hundred men would be carried to Tadoussac, and that a fort would be built at that point. This was a footing which might much conduce to the establishment of a government, and the royal concession readily followed.

The plan was no sooner developed than it created a jealousy similar to that which followed the combination of Noël and

Chaton, ten years or more earlier. The citizens of St. Malo promptly represented that such a monopoly would abridge the rights which they claimed to have acquired through protecting the royal interests in Canada for many years. These Malouin merchants appealed to the Breton parliament, and through it to the throne, but with no effect. Accordingly Pontgravé and his associates went on without interruption in preparing for the voyage. Four vessels were made ready, and in the largest one, the "Don de Dieu," of four hundred tons, the three leaders embarked. The five hundred men which were promised dwindled to a single hundred, and Chauvin seems to have been responsible for this, as he was for all matters which could be made to demand less expenditure and more profit.

The expedition made its landfall and passed up to Tadoussac without disaster. Here the scene from the little vessels riding in the roadstead was not a very attractive one to anybody bent on making a settlement. Over the stretch of waters there was nothing but a dim, foggy distance, for the potent river covers in its breadth at this point a score of miles, as it moves on to the gulf. Silvery porpoises mingling with the white crests of the vexed waves were all that met the eye which tried eagerly to find something to rest upon throughout the monotonous waste. A rocky point stretching to the southwest formed a bay, where trading-vessels could find an anchorage. From far up the Saguenay, in the deep shadows of its lofty crags, the savage canoeists could come down to barter their burdens of fur. The adjacent shores had no aspect to allure the agriculturist, and Pontgravé, recalling the grassy meadows and swelling upland about Three Rivers, would much rather have gone thither. Chauvin, however, only looked to the chances of trade, and he felt that at the junction of these two great rivers there was the better chance of an exchange for peltries. Accordingly, here it was determined to stay, and the people were set on shore. It was not long before a storehouse was constructed just by the brink of the harbor. Champlain found the building standing eight years later, and delineated it upon his map of Tadoussac.

Pontgravé at Tadoussac, 1600.

Once at work, Chauvin stuck steadily to his commerce for furs, and soon filled his ships. This done, he left sixteen men to encounter the rigors of the winter, with such protection as a crazy hut could afford. Even the pitying attentions of the neighboring Indians did not prevent most of this forlorn little company dying before the coming of spring.

On the return of Chauvin and the other leaders to France, they made some show of their trafficking gains; but there was little assurance to be given of a permanent colonization, or of results from discovery. Had the ravages of death among those who had been left behind been suspected, the satisfaction in the results would have been still less.

Chauvin in France.

TADOUSSAC (after Champlain).

This is Champlain's plan in his edition of 1613. KEY: *A*, Round Mountain. *B*, harbor. *C*, fresh-water brook. *D*, camp of natives coming to traffic. *E*, peninsula. *F*, Point of All Devils. *G*, Saguenay River. *H*, Point aux Alouettes. *I*, very rough mountains covered with firs and beeches. *L*, the mill Bode. *M*, roadstead. *N*, pond. *O*, brook. *P*, grassland.

Precisely what there was to prevent Chauvin himself the next year (1601) from going to the St. Lawrence does not appear; but he is known to have dispatched thither one of his ships with similar commercial success. In April, 1602, he himself made a voyage in command of two barks, and having had four months' trading at Tadoussac, he returned to Honfleur in October, to find the merchants of St. Malo still using every device to deprive him of the continuance of his privileges. Chauvin contrived to

1601.

1602.

maintain his influence with the king, and succeeded (December 28, 1602) in having his concessions reaffirmed. But the matter did not rest there, and pending a still further decision, all French vessels were forbidden to proceed beyond Gaspé.

1603.   When March (1603) came, the king had reached a determination to send to Canada Captain Coulombier of St. Malo, either separately or in conjunction with Pontgravé and the Sieur Prévert, in a single vessel, for trade and discovery, but only for one season. By this time Chauvin had

Amyar de   died, and Amyar de Chastes, succeeding to the priv-
Chastes.   ileges, entered into a partnership for prosecuting Canadian enterprise with sundry merchants of Rouen and St. Malo.

It was a good deal to Henry IV. that De Chastes was strong in the faith to which the king had been converted ; and it was a good deal more to the king that this governor of Dieppe had been one of the first to give him allegiance. These were two very good reasons why De Chastes had little difficulty in getting the new patent to establish himself in Canada.

At this point the most commanding figure in the early his-
Samuel de   tory of Canada comes upon the scene, — Samuel de
Champlain.   Champlain. Those who have searched the archives of Brouage, seeking to find a date for his birth, have for good reason always turned to about the year 1570; but they have always looked in vain. If the hero, in later years, was reticent about his birth, we do not find him more helpful in other particulars of his childhood. The authority is perhaps hardly irrevocable which makes him the son of a fisherman ; but it seems clear his father was a mariner, very likely a master mariner, and the family was respectable enough to secure honorable mention in contemporary documents. The Abbé Faillon is not without a suspicion that the forename Samuel, uncommon among Catholics and usual with Protestants, may indicate that Champlain was born in a Huguenot household. It is certain that Brouage, the place of his birth, was quite within the circle

Perhaps   of the Protestant influence that surrounded La Ro-
Protestant   chelle. The suspicion is not a welcome one to his
by birth.   Catholic biographers, and they point to his father's name, Antoine, and his mother's, Marguerite, as being conspicu-

ously of Catholic savor. The latest Canadian historian, Kingsford, does not admit even a doubt that Champlain was born a
Protestant.

The salt-works of Brouage, long the source of its prosperity,
naturally attracted buyers who were interested in the fisheries
of the new world. This mercantile concourse kept pictures
of that daring industry on those distant shores fresh in the

CHAMPLAIN.
[After Moncarnet in the Laval *Champlain.*]

minds of its people. Amid such influences the infant Champlain grew into youth and glided on into maturity.

There was occasion in the preceding chapter to picture the
martial and political turmoil of France in these latter years of
the sixteenth century. It was shown to have withdrawn attention from those fields of discovery to which Cartier had led the
way. It was among these scenes that Champlain passed his
early manhood, seasoning his formative years in the restraints
and activities of the camp, when not at home. At other times

he was accustomed to look out with a longing eye upon the
Bay of Biscay, suggestive of so much that was daring and
dangerous in seamanship.

Speaking of life at sea, Champlain later said : " I was addicted to it in my early years, and through my whole life I have
met its perils, on the ocean and on the coasts of New France,
with the hope of seeing the lily of France able to protect there
the holy Catholic religion." Whatever the religion which
rocked his cradle, Champlain as an historical character indubitably stands as the champion of the Roman Church.

The peace of Vervins in 1598 had brought all France into
peaceful subjection to Henry of Navarre, and Champlain, in his
Early   capacity as quartermaster in the army, had been in the
career.   last movements which suppressed the opposition in
Brittany. A year later (1599), he went to Spain in charge of
a French ship, carrying home some of the Spanish allies of the
League. While in the peninsula he had been placed, as an experienced seaman, in command of one of the vessels forming a
fleet which the Spanish government dispatched to their West
Indian possessions. He was absent on this service for more
than two years. It does not concern our present purposes to
follow him in his strange experiences in these southern waters.
In the West They are all set forth in a manuscript written by
Indies.   his own hand, and embellished with passable colored
drawings, which of late years has been added to the unexam-
pled Americana in the Carter-Brown Library at Providence,
Rhode Island. Once, thirty years ago, when this manuscript
was owned in Dieppe, the Hakluyt Society published a translation of it, and twenty years ago the Laval University, in their
sumptuous edition of Champlain's writings, printed for the first
time the original text and gave fac-similes of the drawings.
There is one passage in this little narrative which may detain
us for a moment, since it prefigures Champlain's conceptions of
that great northern passage to Cathay, to the finding of which
he devoted his later years. He is describing his experience at
the Isthmus of Darien. He says : " One may judge that if the
four leagues of land which there are from Panama to the little
river which rises in the mountains and descends to Porto
Bello were cut through, one might pass from the South Sea
to the ocean on the other side, and thus shorten the route by

more than fifteen hundred leagues ; and from Panama to the Straits of Magellan would be an island, and from Panama to the New-found-lands would be another island, so that the whole of America would be in two islands."

It has been suggested that Champlain, after his return to France from this southern voyage, had made some report of it to the king, in a way to attract the royal attention. At all events, since De Chastes was much about the court after he had got his patent from the king, it is not improbable that in its precincts a sturdy mariner of Champlain's joins experience would have easily made himself conspicu- De Chastes. ous to a patentee in search of a hardy coadjutor. That Champlain had attracted the attention of the king would seem to be certain from the fact that when De Chastes invited him to join the enterprise, Champlain deferred accepting till the royal assent was given. This, when given, was accompanied by an injunction which made Champlain responsible for a report of the completed explorations. Champlain himself later says, in dedicating one of his narratives to Henry IV., that he was commissioned by that king to make the most exact researches and explorations in his power.

There was much in Champlain to fit him to become a pioneer in such work. His person was rugged. His strength was equal to almost any physical task. His constitution did not succumb to exposure either of cold or heat. His senses were keen and sharpened by experience. His spirit knew not what it was to falter, when facing danger. Perhaps we must add — even if we do not go to the extent of the Abbé Faillon — that he enjoyed a hunt too much to be over-scrupulous whether the game was a squirrel or an Iroquois.

Two vessels having been made ready at Honfleur, they sailed on March 15, 1603, in command of Pontgravé, who was accompanied by Champlain in the " Bonne Renommée," while the Sieur Prévert had charge of the lesser craft, the " Françoise." The latter was to stop at Gaspé, while Pontgravé went on to Tadoussac. The little fleet had a tedious passage of forty days. After landing, they found themselves at once mingling in the filthy revelries of a camp

of Indians, who were celebrating a victory over the Iroquois.
Reeking scalps were conspicuous in the scene, and they were
At Tadoussac. the first reminders of savage warfare which Champlain
had seen, — a warfare that a few years later he was
to turn upon himself, and which was to become a heritage for
his successors.

But these horrors did not long divert him from a purpose
which he was so strenuously to pursue for thirty years. On
Goes up the Saguenay, June, 1603. June 11, he started to explore the Saguenay. It is
not clear what knowledge of this forbidding stream
had been handed down to him from earlier adventurers.
Cartier had passed it by, and it is not quite sure how far its appearance in one of Allefonsce's rude charts indicates a personal
knowledge of it. It does not seem certain that the traders who
had perhaps been up and down the main river of late years had
ever tempted the gloomy depths of the Saguenay. If they did,
they have left no record of it. Champlain went up the stream,
perhaps thirty or forty miles, but not far enough to determine
of his own knowledge its geographical relations.

The Indians contrived to let him know that the Saguenay
flowed out of a large lake, — the modern St. John, — and that
there was an affluent water-system above it. It would take a
canoe ten days, the Indians said, to make the trip back to
Tadoussac from these upper waters. There were tribes about
the lake who had told these informants that beyond the divide,
still farther to the north, lay a great salt sea. Champlain
grasped the idea of a gulf stretching south from the Arctic
Ocean, and divined the bay that Hudson was yet to make evident, and many years later he was cruelly deceived in an attempt
to find it by another route.

In a week's time Champlain was back at Tadoussac, and on
Goes up the St. Lawrence. June 18, accompanied by Pontgravé, he started up the
St. Lawrence in a small bark, taking with him a
boat for use in shallow waters. On the 23d, he observed the cataract which drops in feathery confusion from its
upper level, and gave it the name of Montmorency, which is
so familiar to the modern tourist. He saw the lofty promontory of Quebec, and supposed, as he went on, that he was passing beyond the goal of Cartier's explorations. At Three
Rivers he remarked, as Pontgravé had, how fit a place it was

for a settlement. On the 29th, he was skimming the variegated surface of a broadened expanse of the river, and as it was St. Peter's day, he applied that enduring name to the lake. Here he was for a while arrested at the mouth of a tributary on the south side, where he found an encamp- *Sorel River.* ment of Algonquins, gathering for an incursion up the stream, into the country of their enemies, the Iroquois. In attempting to ascend this river, the rapids of Chambly checked his progress. He learned from the Indians that the river flowed from a large lake, and that there was a smaller sheet still beyond. From these southern heads of the water a portage led to another river, — the Hudson, — by which the voyager would be carried south towards what Champlain supposed must be the coast of Florida, taking that name, as it was then understood, as covering a region stretching far north of the modern peninsula, until it reached the territory claimed by the French. Five years later, Champlain was to make this more apparent, with the mysteries of the distant mountains, which he saw bounding the distance on either hand, unsolved.

Reaching once more the main river, these venturesome French still breasted the current and made a way among the devious channels to the island where Montreal now stands, and looked upon its sentinel mountain. They were *At Montreal.* stopped at the Sault St. Louis, — the Lachine Rapids, — and Champlain tried in vain to get round them by a portage. Finding that he was at the end of his course, he endeavored to deduce from the bewildering statements of the savages some notion of what lay above that long plunge of waters. He got in this way a tolerably clear conception of at least a portion of the waters, which some years later he was to follow. His dusky informants took him in imagination up a large affluent of the St. Lawrence, coming from the west, and they told him that it threaded the country of the Algonquins, as later, under the name of the Ottawa, he found it to do. Following up the St. Lawrence and passing rapids and expansions of the stream, he was told he could reach a large body of water, fed through a channel, blocked by a cataract, which flowed *Hears of western waters.* out of a salubrious lake. A river flowed into this lake at its farther end, through which the boatman stemming the current could push his skiff eventually into an immense sea of salt water. This last particular the Indians were frank enough to acknowledge was derived from the reports of remoter tribes, since they themselves had never seen this ominous sea.

This hydrography is not difficult to follow. The fancy of Champlain was led in the description along the waters of Ontario, which he was yet to know by experience; up the Niagara, whose falls he never saw, and whose magnitude he failed to comprehend to the last; along Lake Erie, of which also he remained through life in much ignorance; thence by the Detroit River to Lake Huron, which he learned later to know in that portion of it called the Georgian Bay. His subsequent experience (1615) certainly showed him that it was not salt; but in his present uncertainty he could but think, as every Canadian explorer in those days thought, that the great western Sea of Cathay lay almost within his ken. He never quite divested himself of his hope to see it.

Champlain had at this time, as above intimated, derived from the accounts of the Indians a very inadequate notion of the torrent which plunges at Niagara. He speaks of it as having a volume not large enough for the main outflow of a lake, and was therefore forced to argue that the waters of Lake Erie flowed for the most part in another direction, perhaps to the south. The description presented to him by the Indians, as recorded in his *Sauvages*, is far from clear; but it seems to indicate that Lake Huron delivered the great body of its water through some other channel than Lake Erie, and that it found its way thereby into the St. Lawrence. There is an early map, made indeed at a somewhat later day, which interprets this belief by making the Ottawa this alternative channel. The geologist will observe that its configuration is curiously like what is now known to have been the water-shed of the region after the melting of the great glacier. Champlain was himself to discover that this course of the Ottawa was far from being uninterrupted.

With such vague glimpses of the unknown west, Champlain and his party returned to Tadoussac, not without hoping that the salt water reported to them could one day be reached on the way to China.

It is one of the striking features in the accounts which we have of these early days of exploration that the frequenting of a coast for traffic or fishing counts so little in contributing geographical knowledge.   It can hardly be possible that no more was observed by such mercantile adventurers than was put on record; but there must have been a scant degree of serviceable value in what they did, or the official explorers would not have

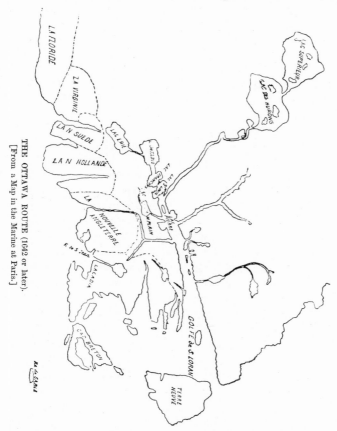

THE OTTAWA ROUTE (1642 or later).
[From a Map in the Marine at Paris.]

sought so often to cover the same fields.   The shores of the Lower St. Lawrence and the margins of the gulf had been for nearly a century at least the haunts of Normans, Bretons, and Biscayans, but Champlain felt that his record for the king would not be what it ought to be unless his official eye could survey those shores. We accordingly find him, shortly after his return to Tadoussac, making ready to follow the sin-

uosities of these lower river banks towards the gulf. It is
not our purpose now to give his experience in this
work in detail. He has set them down in his *Sauvages.*

Lower St.
Lawrence
explored.

Returning to the mouth of the Saguenay, Champlain found
the ships laden with the furs gathered in his absence, and the
expedition was ready for the homeward voyage. They had embarked several natives, and the weary voyagers daily
beguiled themselves with Indian grammar and vocabulary. On the 2d of September (1603), the stag-
gering vessels were thumping their prows against head seas off
Cape Race, and on the 20th they ran into the basin of Havre
de Grace. Here it was soon learned that, a few
months before, their chief patron, Amyar de Chastes,
had died, and the colonization scheme on which they
had returned to make report was left without a sponsor.

Return voy-
age, Septem-
ber, 1603.

Amyar de
Chastes
dies.

Pending a new movement, Champlain was busy in preparing
a map of the region, as best he could, from observation and the
Indian testimony, and in putting his notes in shape
for a report to the king. Just what the map which he
made was, we are not informed, for it was not published with his report. There could have been little in earlier
cartography to help him beyond the description of Cartier. It
is indeed possible that he might have known the maps of that
navigator and of Allefonsce. Current published maps gave
nothing but varying impressions of Cartier's results, as has
been shown in the previous chapter. The world just at this
time was getting the same vague sort of treatment of this cartographical theme in such publications as the combination *Mercator Atlas* of 1602, or in such special chance issues
as the *Relaciones* of Botero, only just published at
Valladolid. There was much in all this that would
hardly comport with Champlain's newer knowledge. But if
the map fails us, we have the text of Champlain's report, published with the royal sanction as *Des Sauvages*, late
in 1604. It was the first time he had given the
world the chance to measure his powers of observation. The
narrative was devoted to the country, its geography and physical condition, its products, its natives, and its promises. One
must determine from the way in which the book has disap-

Champlain
makes a
map.

Contem-
porary
maps.

*Des Sau-
vages,* 1604.

peared, that either the avidity of commercial speculation or the thumbing of the lovers of the marvelous, or both, has almost deprived posterity of the record, for when the Abbé Laverdière sought to reprint it twenty years ago, he had to have the copy in the great Paris Library — the only one then known to him — transcribed for the printer. Its rarity is not so great as the abbé imagined, for there are copies in more than one American library, and a comparison of the copies in Harvard College Library and the Carter-Brown Library show that it was set up twice in the same year, indicating unusual currency.

The voyage of 1603 had brought Champlain and Pontgravé into cordial relations, which were never relaxed. The greater age of that Malouin navigator gave to the friendly feelings of Champlain a tinge of filial obedi- ence. They were one in the belief that the great river of Can- ada was a channel that must be followed if a New France was to arise. Tadoussac as a goal was not to their mind. Its for- bidding sterility gave no promise for colonization, and Cham- plain's heart was set on dreams of colonization that he was never permitted to realize to their full extent.

Columbus, at the south, had accounted for the low grade of peoples which he found by supposing that he was on the out- skirts of the East, among coast tribes less susceptible to the lures of civilization than interior peoples. He argued that if he would find the wealth and luxury which Europeans dreamed of, he must get at the inland races. We know that the Geno- ese on his last voyage was bending all his energies to seek a passage through the barriers which he had found. A hundred years later, Champlain reasoned in the same strain at the north. He felt that it was a divergence from the true field of discov- ery, when it was apparent that the next expedition was to pro- mote an examination of the Atlantic coast.

When Chauvin had overruled Pontgravé's preference, and had forced the expedition of 1603 to remain at Tadoussac, he had subjected the company to a test of that region's climate which compelled the successor of De Chastes to make trial of a more salubrious climate.

It is not necessary to follow with much detail this next west- ern venture of the French, but there are some of its move- ments along the coast of Nova Scotia and New England which have some bearing on the views which Champlain grew to have of the intermediate region, bordering on the great valley of the north.

Henry IV. picked out the Sieur de Monts for a successor of De Chastes. As this new lieutenant was a Protestant, born in Champlain's own province of Saintonge, the king had a struggle to secure the coöperation of parliament.

Sieur de Monts, 1603.

The stubborn monarch carried his point, and signed De Monts's commission at Fontainebleau, November 8, 1603, creating him lieutenant-general of Canada. The new leader was directed to preserve in that country the religious rights of both Calvinist and Catholic. He was to exercise jurisdiction over both banks of the river of Canada and as far south as the fortieth degree of latitude. Within this range he was to have unchecked license to trade for furs, and to that end, in April, 1604, he proclaimed his privileges throughout all the seaports of France.

While the result of the royal struggle with parliament was doubtful, De Monts was in Rouen, organizing a commercial company among its citizens, which was to include also those of Rochelle and Saint-Jean-de-Luz. The papers of this association were signed, February 10, 1604.

Commercial company, February 10, 1604.

De Monts was joined in Rouen by Pontgravé, and at Havre de Grace the two found four vessels already laden for the voyage. Pontgravé stowed away as best he could six score of artisans in the little ship of one hundred and twenty tons, which he himself commanded. De Monts took charge of a second ship, and with him were the Sieur de Poutrincourt, whose name is associated with Acadian exploration, and Champlain, who was thus diverted for a while from the great river of Canada. The little fleet left port early in April, 1604.

De Monts and Champlain sail, 1604.

While on this expedition, Champlain passed along the Maine coast, and gathered from the Indian descriptions that there was a waterway along the line of the river of Norumbega (Penobscot), which was a practical route for canoes — if not for larger craft — between the Atlantic and the St. Lawrence. He understood, according to the popular notion of the physical possibility, that the divergent streams which afforded the passage took their rise in a large lake midway

Norumbega River.

between the ocean and the great river, and flowed north and south. He rehearsed such views in his edition of 1613, while in the same book he indicates that to make the passage northward by the line of the Kennebec requires a portage of two leagues, to reach the Chaudière. It was by this route, it will be remembered, that Amherst in 1759 endeavored to communicate with Wolfe, and Benedict Arnold in the autumn of 1775 proceeded to attack Quebec.

Champlain, following the coast, reached a little later what is now known as Boston harbor. Here he perceived a flow of water from the west. Whether it was the tide which glides by the present Point Allerton, or the current which sweeps around the northerly end of the Boston peninsula, matters little. He gave to this river the family name of De Monts, and accordingly on his and on other French maps the stream bears the name of Rivière du Guast, — a name which did not entirely disappear from the Dutch and other contemporary maps till after Boston was founded in 1630.

"This river extends," says Champlain, "toward the land of the Iroquois, a nation which is the constant foe of the Montagnais, who live on the St. Lawrence." One judges from this that the river of which the Indians had told him at the Chambly rapids, and which he thought ran towards Florida, — in fact a premonition of the Hudson, — was now identified in his thought with what we in this day know as the Charles, a meandering coast stream, which empties into Boston harbor.

For over three years, Champlain was in various parts of this Atlantic coast, and it was he who took the first steps towards an intelligible cartography of the shore line of Nova Scotia and New England. The St. Lawrence was not meanwhile wholly neglected. Pontgravé, who was scouring it in 1606 to arrest intruders, seized a vessel which De Monts and others had sent there for trade, — an action which compelled a resort to a legal settlement in France. But a greater shock was in store for De Monts. His commission had been revoked some time before, and when Champlain heard of it, the news was accompanied by a recall of the expedition, and in October, 1607, all were back in St. Malo.

There is no evidence that the French were aware at the time of the Virginia movement, which had followed the peace which

Boston harbor.

The expedition returns, October, 1607.

had been made between England and Spain in 1605. While Champlain had been searching the inlets of the New England coast, Captain John Smith was exploring the waters of the Chesapeake to find a passage to the western sea, as Captain Newport did a little later, and for near a century there were those among the English who were not prepared to believe that Virginia was other than an island, which might afford a way along its seaboard to this occidental goal. The year before Champlain left the more northern waters, the English king had granted (1606) to the London and Plymouth companies a stretch of territory along the coast from 34° in the south to 45° in the north, which was sure before long to raise a question of jurisdiction between these rival nations, and actually did bring them in conflict at Mt. Desert the same season in which Champlain left the coast.

CHAPTER V.

COLONIZATION ESTABLISHED AT QUEBEC.

1608–1613.

THE year 1608 opened with a transient change of fortune for De Monts. He had listened to Champlain's recital of his three years' experience with a renewed zest for exploration, and he was prepared to abandon the coast for the St. Lawrence. Under the same narrative, and by reason of persuasions that profit and glory could yet be found, the king so far relented that on January 7 he signed a patent allowing De Monts a renewal of his fur-trade monopoly for a single year. He coupled a condition with it, very likely at the instigation of Champlain, that an attempt should be again made to penetrate farther into the interior of the continent. The salt western sea of Champlain's first report had not been forgotten, and there were hopes, if it could be reached, of its affording the coveted way to India. De Monts was not without hopes of an extension of his trading privilege at the end of the year. De Monts's patent renewed, January 7, 1608.

Buoyed by this anticipation, and animated by the enthusiasm which projects of hazard often contribute, De Monts fitted out two ships. To Pontgravé was assigned the command of the trading part of the expedition, with orders to return at the expiration of the season. To Champlain, who was now created lieutenant-governor, was given the task of holding the country permanently, and developing its geography. This meant that an opportunity should be taken to put to the test what he had already explained to the king in his *Sauvages*, namely, " the practicability of finding a way to China, avoiding at the same time the cold of the north and the heat of the south," and he believed this route lay through the St. Lawrence. Champlain to seek a way to China.

On the 5th of April, 1608, Pontgravé sailed from Honfleur in the "Levrier," and a week later Champlain embarked,

The expedition sails, April, 1608.

it is supposed, in the "Don de Dieu," then under the command of Henri Couillard, an old associate of Pontgravé and Chauvin. On June 3, Champlain reached Tadoussac,

June, at Tadoussac.

and was at once called upon to settle a dispute which had already been begun between Pontgravé and a Basque fisherman. A little blood had been drawn, and as it would not do to risk the main enterprise by delays, the governor-general composed the quarrel temporarily, and left the ultimate decision to the authorities at home. This contest arranged, Champlain set to work building a small shallop of about fourteen tons, and it was not long before he was on his

Quebec founded, 1608.

way up the St. Lawrence. The bold headland of Quebec had attracted his attention in 1603, and he now determined to lay the foundations of a town beneath its cliffs, and very soon the level strand along the river presented a busy scene.

Champlain had not completed the laying out of his garden, when he was startled at a disclosure from one of his men. A mechanic among his followers, thinking to gain the sympathy of the Basques at Tadoussac and some consequent advantage, plotted with some accomplices to murder Champlain and offer the new settlement as a lure to the rivals down the river.

Plot to kill Champlain.

Such a secret, requiring passive complicity in many others, being hard to keep, was opportunely betrayed. Champlain, while his knowledge of the plot was not suspected, enticed the ringleaders on board a bark lying in the stream, where they were easily overpowered. The body of the principal plotter soon dangled from a tree, and three of the other chief conspirators were put in irons.

Champlain now explored the little tributary of the St. Lawrence, which causes the promontory of Quebec to jut out like a cape. On this stream he came upon traces of the fort which Cartier had built, and in his journal he enters into an argument to prove the identification, which at that time was at variance with the common opinion that the St. Croix River of Cartier was higher up the St. Lawrence.

Pontgravé having completed the lading of his ships, Champlain placed under that commander's charge the three accomplices of the recent plot, who were destined to expiate their crime in the galleys. On September 18, Pontgravé sailed for France. The little colony was left to pre- September 18, 1608. pare for winter and its hard experiences.

There was a long and harrowing wait till spring opened and the ice-floes began to jostle in the river. All in nature was more blooming than the spirits of the imprisoned col- onists, when on June 15, 1609, Champlain learned June, 1609. that a week before, Pontgravé had returned to Tadoussac. Two days later, the governor started down the river to confer with this bringer of succor. It was a sad story which Champlain had to tell his friend. Only eight of the twenty-eight whom Pontgravé had left behind a year ago were living, and half of these were broken down. The winter's horrors were too sick- ening to dwell upon, for, to increase the miseries of the French, the famished savages had hung about the settlement all the interval.

With the store of provisions which Pontgravé had brought, and with fresh men to take up the toil, the little com- munity began to improve in the summer air. Stories Pontgravé brings suc- had reached the governor, during the winter, of the cor. extent and beauty of that lake which lay towards the country of the Iroquois, and something in the nature of a pact was ap- parently made with the Montagnais, who inhabited the country about Quebec. It was agreed that if these warriors would con- duct Champlain on an exploration in that direction, he would fight in their defense if any of their enemies were encountered.

On June 18, 1609, Champlain ascended the St. Lawrence with a party of French and savages, and found two Champlain or three hundred Hurons and Algonquins encamped led against the Iroquois, not far from the river that led to this southern lake. June, 1609. These Indians were preparing to proceed with the Montagnais on a war-path towards the Iroquois. It was a bodeful meeting. The Indian chief, at a council which was held, gave Champlain to understand that he must needs cement the alliance which their friendly intercourse in 1603, and his recent promises to the Montagnais, had foreshadowed. He did not hesitate to do so by agreeing to join in their enterprise.

There is nothing in Champlain's career which has exposed him to so much censure as this prompt desertion of the part of

a mediator and pacificator among the peoples with whom he had
deliberately cast his lot. Such censors are the Abbés Faillon
and Ferland. His defenders point to the necessity of his making a promise to those whom he needed for allies, and allege
that none but a dastard could have shunned abiding by it.
By thus ingratiating himself with his savage neighbors, he
could make sure of their protection, and so advance his purpose
of western discovery, and make it easier for the Recollect and
Jesuit to venture among distant villages. Thus much he indeed
gained ; but he rendered the western path unceasingly hazardous, in acquiring the enmity of the ablest and most redoubtable
warriors of the Indian race. For over a century, the Iroquois
found no pastime equal to rendering life in Canada miserable.
They kept in perpetual anxiety every settler along the great
valley who dared to occupy a farmstead away from the palisaded
settlements. The shrieks of murdered children, the moans of
tortured parents, and devastation of households, mark the
course of French-Canadian history as long as the Iroquois maintained an aggressive confederacy. Thus it was that in making
enemies of these affiliated tribes, Champlain exposed the long
valley of the St. Lawrence to constant inroads on its southern
flanks, and no preparation for many years that the French
could make was able to check these disasters. Champlain could
hardly indeed have anticipated the century and more of border
warfare which was to follow upon the strengthening of these
savage southern hordes by an alliance with the Dutch and
English.

We need not dwell on the actual conflict of 1609, which
opened this interminable warfare. Champlain and his savage
allies sped up the river and along the lake, and at a point
Fight at   identified as the modern Ticonderoga they met in the
Ticonderoga. night a war party of the Iroquois. Waiting till day-
light, they began the battle. Champlain describes the fight, and
shows how the apparition of the Frenchmen, with their arquebuses, leveling their enemies with unseen bolts amid deadly
noises, struck terror into the ranks of the adversary and secured
an easy victory for the invaders. Colden's later narrative may
in a certain sense be supposed to present the traditional account
of the Iroquois. It confirms the powerful agency which the sudden display of the Christians' marvelous weapons had in deciding
the issue of the fight.

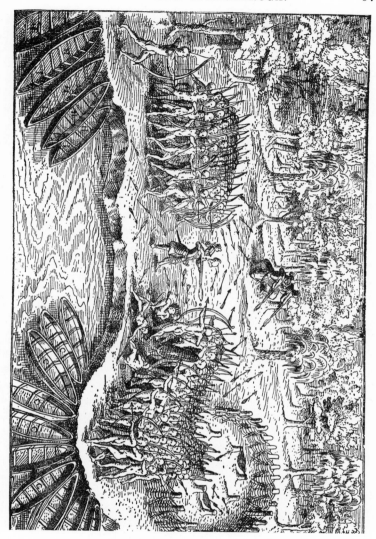

CHAMPLAIN'S FIGHT NEAR TICONDEROGA.

[From Champlain, ed. of 1613.] KEY: *A* (wanting), the fort. *B*, enemy. *C*, oak bark canoes of the enemy, holding ten, fifteen, or eighteen men each. *D*, two chiefs who were killed. *E*, an enemy wounded by Champlain's musket. *F* (wanting), Champlain. *G* (wanting), two musketeers. *H*, canoes of the allies, Montagnais, Ochastaiguins, and Algonquins, who are above. *I* (also on the), birch-bark canoes of the allies. *K* (wanting), woods.

The combat took place on July 30, 1609, on the shore where each party had landed from their canoes, and the curious reader may see how the governor depicts himself in armor and plumed helmet, firing his arquebus, if he will look at the drawing that Champlain set before his countrymen in the narrative printed for their edification. To his royal master this expedition had given a title to a fair lake and its water-shed; but while its commander was leading it, he little suspected how, not many weeks from the same time, Henry Hudson, in a search for a western passage, ascended from the ocean, by the river which now bears his name, to the country of the Mohawks, establishing claims which for fifty years the Dutch held against both French and English. Thus was prepared the way for that later league of the Iroquois and the Dutch, by which the savages acquired the European weapon. Champlain's successors were to discover to their cost what this league and that with the later English meant, when the lake to which we still apply its discoverer's name was often alive with the bustle of war.

July 30, 1609.

Dutch and Iroquois.

Returned to Quebec, Champlain prepared to depart for France, leaving Pierre Chauvin in charge; and on October 13, 1609, he landed at Honfleur. Though De Monts's privileges had expired, the governor found him by no means discouraged, and quite ready for another venture.

Champlain in France, October, 1609.

The public had no occasion to forget these recent experiences. The lively Lescarbot, a lawyer of Paris and a society wit, had, a few years before, joined the colonists of Acadia. He had not been unobservant of Champlain's career in the new world, and was now prepared to give his *La Nouvelle France* to the reading public. In it he aimed to recount what the French had so far done in securing a foothold for the king in these northern regions. The publication did not escape the notice of Hakluyt in London. This English chronicler was anxious to make it clear that his countrymen were quite ready to launch their barges beyond the divide at the head of the James River, and lead the way to Asia. He also would show that they possessed in Virginia a region of far greater attractiveness for the emigrant. His way to make this evident was to familiarize the English public with what the

Lescarbot and Hakluyt.

French had suffered in the north ; and with this end in view a portion of Lescarbot's book was translated and published in London.

Lescarbot did not leave his readers uncertain of those upon whom credit should be bestowed for what the French had already done. "Let us say," he admits, "that France owes these discoveries to the Sieur de Monts, at whose expense they have been made ; and she is likewise indebted to the courage of Champlain in exposing his life in these explorations, and in bearing some part of the charge. Champlain promises never to cease his efforts until he has found either a western sea or a northern sea, opening the route to China, which so many have thus far sought in vain." As to the western sea, Lescarbot adds : " I believe it beyond the remoter parts of that very great lake, which we hear of." He further expressed the ever-constant opinion of a school of contemporary geographers, that the great river of Canada issued from a lake which also poured its waters by another channel to the South Sea. He recalled how in Europe and Africa such a diverging flow was not unknown, instancing the lake at the source of the Nile, as such an example.

With such prestige as Champlain had acquired, increased possibly by Lescarbot's account of him, it was not surprising that he was again selected to take recruits to the colony. Pontgravé went with him, and their two vessels, after some misfortunes in working off the coast, — for the spring was a boisterous one, — finally reached Tadoussac on April 26, 1610. Champlain had laid out plans for new explorations, for the secrets of the Saguenay and the Ottawa were still undivulged. He found, however, the Indians too intent on their yearly invasion of the Iroquois country to be diverted from it, and without their aid exploration was not to be thought of. He joined their camp near the mouth of the Richelieu River, and led them to an attack on an Iroquois barricade, which had been hastily constructed, not far up the river. The attack was so successful that not a hostile savage escaped.

It was after this June onset, and while he was encamped with his allies on an island in Lake St. Peter, that he and they made

[marginal note: Voyage of 1610.]

[marginal note: Attacks the Iroquois.]

a mutual exchange of hostages, in giving and taking a young man on each side. Champlain received the savage Savignon,

Hostages exchanged.

whom he later took to France, and he gave them a young Frenchman, — there is reason to believe he is the same who later became known as Étienne Brulé. Both of these hostages, after a mutual restitution was made the next year, became of manifest value to Champlain in his later intercourse with the savages, for this interchange of interpreters enabled him to reach better conclusions as to the great lakes of the west, and as to the passages towards Florida on the south. When Champlain parted with his savage friends, two other Frenchmen voluntarily accompanied them, and one of them, Nicolas de Vignau, who went off with the Algonquins, we shall encounter again.

A few weeks later, a ship brought news of the assassination of Henry IV. The death of the king was a calamity

Champlain returns to France, Aug.-Sept. 1610.

to the colony. Having invested the Sieur du Parc with the command, and leaving sixteen men to hold the post, Champlain, with some feelings of uncertainty as to the effect in France of a change in the monarch, sailed from Tadoussac on August 13, and reached Honfleur on September 27.

It was now, while in France, that Champlain agreed with Nicolas Boullé upon a dower of 4500 livres, to be paid

Champlain receives dower for an intended marriage.

by Boullé to him, in anticipation of Champlain's marriage with Boullé's daughter, then a child. It was ten years later that he married her. Meanwhile, the dower was such an addition to his pecuniary resources that he now manifested increased devotion to the commercial side of

Voyage of 1611.

the colony, for it had not before interested him much. His next voyage to the St. Lawrence, in 1611, was almost wholly in the interests of the fur trade. He went up the river to the rapids, and selected a position for a trading-post near the site of the later Montreal. He met here his Indian allies, and the hostages on both sides were mutually restored. He listened to new stories of distant western lakes, and got reports from other savages who had followed up the trail towards Florida.

His barter for furs made him more familiar with the traders.

He found their pursuits a competition which diminished their own profits, and hampered his efforts for discovery. Referring to these traders, he says: "All they want is that the explorers should face danger in discovering new peoples and new lands for their trade, while they may find profit where the others found hardship." It was evident that the trade in peltries, if to be worth pursuing, must be put on a different basis. On his return to France in September, 1611, he undertook the organizing of the Canadian experiment on a better commercial basis, and with this task he was occupied for the greater part of the following year.

A trading company formed, 1611–12.

The whole trading interests of the Norman towns during the early years of the fur trade in Canada were much complicated by rivalries and jealousies. The study of the subject involves pretty closely the consideration of such books as the *Glanes* and *Nouvelles Glanes historiques Normandes* of E. H. Gosselin.

Champlain's plans at this time provoked opposition from the merchants of St. Malo and Rouen. He had undertaken in a measure to diminish the advantages of individual enterprise by compelling all who joined in the new undertaking to share in proportion to their contribution of capital. But aspects other than commercial were daily emphasized in public. The *Mercure François* had been established, and began its work in rendering popular the labors of the priests. In the introduction, which prepared the way, its editor had gone over the results of the expeditions of De Monts, Pontgravé, and Champlain (1604–1608), rendering them better known. A new edition of Lescarbot, and still another issue of the same book, before Champlain was ready for sea, testified to the growing interest. But the newer knowledge had little effect on prevailing views of the geography of the region, and the contemporary edition of Wytfliet's atlas showed no improvement upon the notions which had been developed out of the narratives of Cartier.

Current interest in exploration.

The distractions which had followed upon the death of the king had begun to subside. Champlain found that a renewal of political quiet conduced to draw more attention to his plans, despite the opposition that their first promulgation had raised. One feature that he insisted upon was to give dignity to the

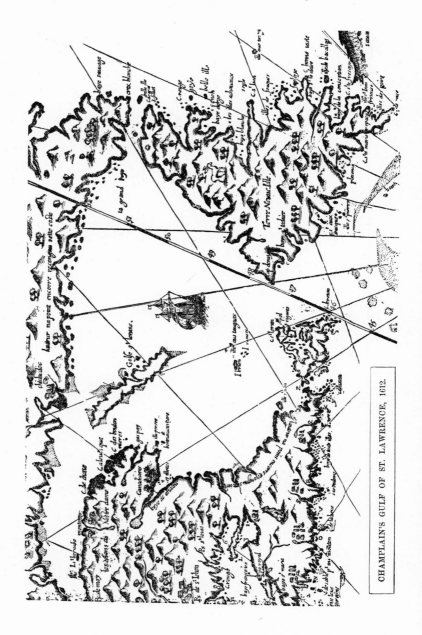

CHAMPLAIN'S GULF OF ST. LAWRENCE, 1612.

enterprise by putting it under a viceroy of enlarged powers, and on October 8 the Count de Soissons was appointed to that position. He commissioned Champlain as his deputy, a few days later. With a newly awakened zeal Soissons set about the task of familiarizing himself with the project. Champlain had hardly begun to show and explain his maps when the viceroy suddenly died.

Count de Soissons viceroy, 1612.

Dies.

The Prince de Condé was soon selected to succeed as viceroy, and more authority was assigned to him than had been before given to any royal representative in the Canadian region. There was little in respect to civil, military, and religious administration that his instructions did not permit him to undertake. His letters-patent were signed at Paris, November 13, 1612, and they were registered at Rouen, a few months later. Under these instructions the viceroy was commanded to prevent the selling of European weapons to the natives, and he was expected to do his utmost to find and open a way to China. He was enjoined also to discover the mineral resources of the country.

Prince de Condé succeeds.

November 13, 1612.

As a compensation for the considerable outlay which he might be called upon to make in furthering the equipment and business of the new expedition, the prince was to be allowed a twelve years' lease of the trade and mines of the country, with ample powers to manage it by deputy and to prevent intruders. A new commission was issued to Champlain on November 22.

Of the maps which Champlain showed to the viceroy, two were prepared to accompany the account of his experiences in the new world since 1604; and a third was perhaps one owned by Harrisse, dated in 1607, showing the coasts and harbors of New France, which has not yet been engraved. Of the maps published in it, one, dated 1612, is larger than the other, but shows a lesser extent of territory, and Champlain explains that it was " constructed according to compasses of France, which vary to the northeast." Its interior geography makes clear what conceptions respecting the great western waters Champlain had derived from the stories with which the Indians had regaled him. We find in this map Lake Champlain and the river stretching west from Boston harbor brought into close conjunction, as he had supposed them when on the New England coast. Lake Ontario is in nearly its exact

Champlain's maps.

position.   The small lakes south of it in New York State are coalesced into a single expanse of water, which he calls the Lake of the Iroquois.   Farther west a little stream flows into

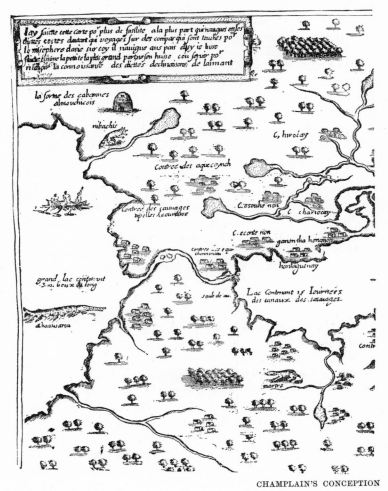

CHAMPLAIN'S CONCEPTION

the lake, conveying the waters of a natural reservoir not far off. Its position would make it stand for the inadequate conception, which Champlain had and never dispelled, of the Niagara River and Lake Erie.   At its extreme western end, Ontario

receives by a connecting channel, broken by a fall, the waters
of Lake Huron, — and farther west the map does not go. His
suspicions of the course of the Ottawa were far from correct;

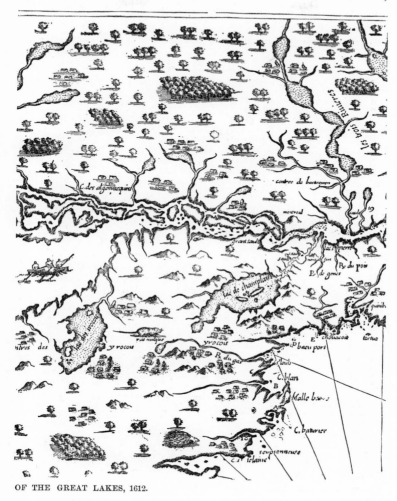

OF THE GREAT LAKES, 1612.

he made it little more than an archipelago which fringed
Ontario.

The other of the two maps he calls " a geographical map
of New France in its true meridian," and there is reason to be-

lieve that, dated a year later (1613) than the larger map, it was made even after the book which was to contain it was nearly ready to leave the press. The changes in it from the other map are marked. Lake Ontario has disappeared, and a network of rivers distinct from the course of the Ottawa appears in its place, — a conception which beguiled Blaeu and other cartog-

CHAMPLAIN'S MAP,

raphers at a later day. Another distinguishing feature is a great salt sea brought out at the north in something like its true proportions. In this delineation he profited by the report of Hudson's explorations, which had laid open the straits named after that navigator, with the great bay beyond, where Hudson had wintered. That navigator's mutinous crew, having set their commander adrift in the great bay, had brought back to Europe one of the charts which he had made. This had just appeared

when Champlain was revising this map, in an account of
Hudson's voyage which was published at Amsterdam   Hudson's
(1612), under the editing of Hermann Gerritsz, — a   map.
book usually cited by the title of the Latin edition, the *Detectio
Freti Hudsoni.* Its chart gave an approximately true delineation of the great northern bay, which forced an easy conjecture

DATED IN 1613.

that it would reveal a westerly connection with the Pacific.
Champlain must have felt that it confirmed his conception of
that great North American island which he had dreamed of at
Panama. It was a conception much in advance of the views
which Hondius, the most popular geographer of his day, was
inculcating in the different editions of the *Mercator Atlas.* We
know that such professional cartographers as Johannes Oliva
of Marseilles were still clinging to the old notions of Sebastian
Münster.

There was one aspect of the Hudson map which Champlain eagerly seized upon, and he was inspired by it with a new hope

The north- that he might yet reach this northern water, either by

ern sea. the Saguenay, by the rivers that debouched at Three

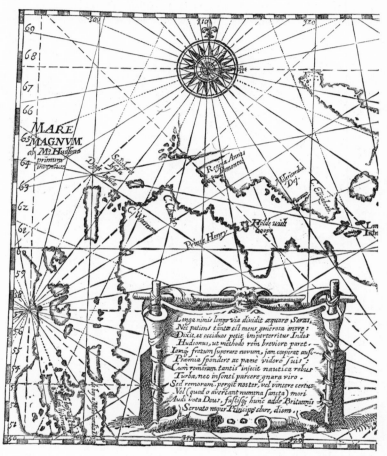

HUDSON'S EXPLORATIONS.

Rivers, or by the Ottawa. We find him possessed by such a hope in the dedicatory letter to the Prince of Condé, which he prefixed to his new book. In this he speaks of his desire to follow more persistently a search for this northern sea, which he expected to find at a point not much beyond those which he had already reached. His mind was accordingly prepared to receive any statement which confirmed this expectation.

It was just at this time that Champlain's credulity in this respect was put to a test. It will be remembered that a year

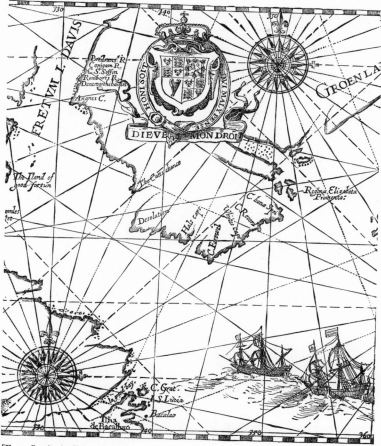

[From Gerritsz's *Tabula Nautica*.]

or two before, he had allowed a young man, named Nicolas de Vignau, to winter among the Algonquins, where he was expected to pick up what he could of their tongue and their geographical secrets. This youth now appeared in Paris. He had returned from the wilderness to Quebec, and

Nicolas de Vignau.

taken passage in one of the ships coming home after the summer trading.   Whether he started from Quebec with the purpose of ingratiating himself with the home authorities by making up a story to flatter the prevailing geographical hopes, or
whether he was induced to his deceit by finding Champlain
ready for anything which confirmed his hopes, may not be
clear.   At any rate, he told his tale.   It was that leaving his
Algonquin hosts, he had made his way up the Ottawa to a lake
which by another outlet led him to the shores of a salt sea,

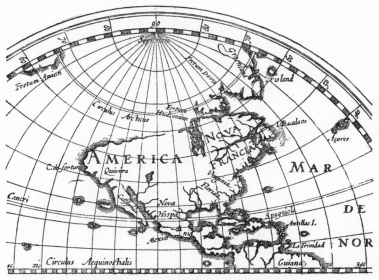

HUDSON'S BAY AND THE ST. LAWRENCE.
[As delineated in 1613 in the *Delectio Freti Hudsoni* (Amsterdam).]

where he had seen the wreck of an English ship.   This story
and the narrative of the Hudson voyage obviously confirmed
each other.   The effect was natural.   Champlain and the gentlemen of the court interested in his enterprise readily took
Vignau's story to mean the discovery of a way to these northern
waters, and a consequent path to China.   No time was to be
lost.   So in the early spring (March) of 1613, Champlain, accompanied by Vignau, was once more at sea.
Arrived at Quebec (May 8), he lost little time in
preparations, and, still accompanied by Vignau and a few
others, he was speedily on his way up the Ottawa.

Champlain
returns to
Quebec,
March, 1613.

On the little flotilla went. They paddled or poled their canoes by day, and camped on the banks at night. Explores the The broken current often compelled them to bear their Ottawa.

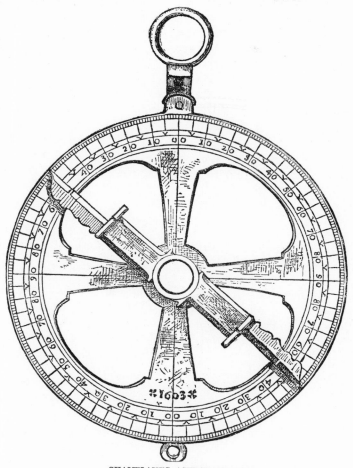

CHAMPLAIN'S ASTROLABE, 1603.
[After Cut in O. H. Marshall's *Historical Writings.*]

burdens by the portages, which the Indians had long used. Champlain noted all along in his pocket-book the latitude of his camps, and his figures are found to agree pretty well with the topographical features which he describes. Suddenly, at a

certain portage near Muskrat Lake, his entries of altitudes become more inaccurate.   Five and twenty years ago, a farmer
working in the field at this point turned up a brass astrolabe
bearing the date of 1603, and of Paris make.   These errors
of his altitudes and the line of his progress render it almost
certain that this relic was Champlain's, and that his loss of it
had left him without the means of accurate determination of
his latitude.

Champlain stopped at a village to procure an audience with
its chief.   He describes the festivals which were made in his
honor.   It was in this village that Vignau had spent his winter,
and the youth was now among his old companions.   When
Champlain asked for an escort to take him the rest of Vignau's
last year's journey to the salt sea, the fellow's rascally

Vignau's
deceit.

deceit was exposed, for the savages knew that he had
never left them on any such journey, during his sojourn among
them.   The youth could but confess his mendacity, and throw
himself on his leader's mercy.

There was nothing left for Champlain but to lead his party
soberly back to the St. Lawrence, under escort of a crowd of
canoes going down for the annual trade.

During this visit to Canada, Champlain spent but little more
than two months.   He had failed in his search at the north, but
he had at last got an intelligent notion of the course of the
Ottawa, and was able to correct his tentative maps.   When he
reached the great river, he found seven ships trading at Montreal.   The scene gave him a new conception of the growth
which the fur trade was making.

Going to Tadoussac, he embarked there on July 8, and on
the 26th of the next month, his ship floated with the
tide into the basin of St. Malo.

Back in
France, Au-
gust, 1613.

France had now transferred her chief interests to
the vast northern valley.   She saw there the best chance of
progress to the west, and the allurements of the trade in peltries
were rapidly growing upon her commercial sense.   Her settlements along the Maine coast easily lost their hold.   The Dutch
indeed did not now reach them, but Adrian Block,
in the little "Onrust," sailing from Manhattan, had
pushed around Cape Cod, and established the northern claims
of that people at Nahant.   It is to Block and the Dutch that

1613.

we now begin to look for developments in the hydrography of Massachusetts Bay. The English were more enterprising, and a party from Virginia in an armed vessel, under Samuel Argall, hovering about Mount Desert, found a convenient moment to take a settlement of the Jesuits unawares. [1613.] They fell upon it, and carried off some of the French to Jamestown, and made a like raid the next year.

SHIP OF 1613.

[From the *Delectio Freti Hudsoni*, Amsterdam, 1613.]

Champlain had been licensed on January 9, 1613, to print the book which contained his maps. The narrative, beside enabling us to follow his adventures, gives us one of the earliest descriptions of the animals and plants of our northern coasts. Men of science, however, to-day find his accounts far less satisfactory than those of the Englishmen, Hariot and White, on the Virginia coast twenty years before.

CHAPTER VI.

WAR, TRADE, AND MISSIONS. THE FALL OF QUEBEC.

1614–1629.

CHAMPLAIN now remained in France for the better part of two years. He was chiefly employed in strengthening the commercial plans of the colony, and in arranging for the introduction of priests. The fur company saw little profit in assuming the expenses of the proposed missions, and Champlain's efforts to get money for their support were necessarily turned in other directions.

The sending of Catholic missionaries was not grateful to a company in which Protestant interests were still paramount, and in which there must naturally be other grounds of dislike of such associations. The priests saw the best chance of converting the natives in making them first sedentary. The trading instinct knew that this meant a diminution of fur hunters.

So for some years there was a struggle at court. On the one side, the priests and their friends aimed to secure royal recognition of the spiritual needs of the Indians. On the other, the trading associates claimed a longer lease of their mercenary project, on the plea that they were working the country on the best terms for France and her prosperity. While the traders maintained their advantage, Champlain had nothing to do but to get along with his plans as best he could without their assistance.

Missions and the fur trade.

Champlain succeeded on his own account in making some arrangement with a few priests of the Recollect order, and it was agreed that Dennis Jamay, Jean d'Olbeau, and Joseph Le Caron should accompany him to Quebec. A lay brother, Pacifique du Plessis, accompanied the priests. Champlain and his new supporters sailed, in a vessel commanded by his old friend, Pontgravé, on April 24, 1615.

Recollects.

Champlain sails, April, 1615.

The Recollect stood for the strictest discipline that the Franciscan could endure. His loose and coarse gray vestment was girt at the waist with a cord, and his pointed hood, if not protecting his crown, hung behind. His feet were uncovered except by a wooden sole ; and he passed among men, seeming holy and patient, and he clung to poverty and humility.

It was May when the ship reached Quebec. A chapel was at once built, and on June 15 the priests celebrated their first mass. It was the first since the colonization May at Quebec. of the country, though there is some reason to believe that the early explorers may have listened to the holy words at Brest in 1534, and possibly on the rock of Quebec two years later.

It was now arranged that Jamay should remain at the settlement. D'Olbeau was soon on his way to sojourn among the Montagnais, and Le Caron started to set up his altar in the Huron villages. Sagard, in speaking of these Canadian tribes, classes the Hurons as the nobility, and the Montagnais as the rabble of the woods. To the Algonquins, who were called the burghers of the forest, no priest was yet assigned.

Champlain, in dealing with the Indian problem of his day, found himself confronted by an ethnological anomaly. Indian distribution. This part of the continent was in the main occupied by tribes of the Algonquin stock; but in the midst of this expansion of a common blood there was a sort of linguistic island, bounded on all sides by foreign races. Within this island the core was held by the Iroquois, a confederacy which represented the ideal of savage existence. Iroquois. They occupied the region immediately south of the Upper St. Lawrence and Lake Ontario. Skirting their somewhat irregular domain on all sides but the north and east lay the congeners of the Iroquois, known as the Hurons, the Tobacco nation, the Neuters, the Eries, and the Andastes, — this range of people making a sweep from the northwest at Georgian Bay to the headwaters of the Susquehanna on the south. Thus these cousins of the Iroquois pressed in upon the country of the confederates on all sides. They had found their positions by no means comfortable, for their brethren at the core, the Iroquois people, were cruelly hostile to all of them, forcing them not only to band together, but also to form alliances with the remoter Algonquins. The only exception was with the

Neuters, who suffered both the Hurons and Iroquois to raid across their territory along the Niagara, but compelled them to be amicable if they met in their villages. We have seen that Champlain had already provoked the hostility of the Iroquois, and the further alliance which he was now seeking with the Hurons through priestly service was sure to serve as a new pretext for the confederates' fierce persecutions of the latter tribe.

Champlain was quite ready to meet this hostility, and was prompt even to anticipate it. Accordingly, he planned with the St. Lawrence Indians an invasion of the Iroquois country. The route by Lake Champlain in-volved too long a march through the enemy's country, for the stronghold of the confederates, which they intended to attack, lay south of the easterly end of Lake Ontario. Moreover, the French leader expected that, by a circuitous route through the country of his allies, he could increase his force as he proceeded. The path marked out, however, lengthened the march to not much short of a thousand miles. He started on this recruiting service accompanied by Brulé, the interpreter, a French servant, and several savages. On July 9, with such com-panions, and in two canoes, he began the ascent of the Ottawa. His passage of it with Vignau had already familiar-ized him with some of its harassing obstacles, and it was because of that bootless expedition to the delusive northern sea that the tribes through whose territory he now passed recognized one whom they had already known, and would now readily serve. From the valley of the Ottawa he crossed the divide and reached Lake Nipissing, whence he continued by its outflowing stream to the Georgian Bay. Geologists have recently pointed out that a subsidence of about a hundred feet near Lake Nipissing would turn the water of the Great Lakes for the most part into the Ottawa, and make a practicable route for navigation 270 miles shorter than by Lake Erie and Ontario; indeed, the evidence seems to be that this was the channel to the sea in the geological period, and it has been in historic times the easiest route to the upper lakes known to the Indians, followed by Champlain, and adopted by the engineers of the Canadian Pacific Railway.

Champlain next crept by the lake shore along the extreme

Campaign against the Iroquois, 1615.

July. On the Ottawa.

southern part of this arm of Lake Huron, to the neighborhood of the Huron villages. Here that leader found Le Caron at his missionary work, and eight Frenchmen from the Recollects' company joined in the march. Word now reached this gathering host that a body of Andastes, living about the headwaters of the Susquehanna, were, to the number of five hundred, anxious to take part in this attack upon their common enemy. The Andastes villages lay beyond the Iroquois country to the south, and they could approach the confederates' fort from the side opposite to the Huron attack. It was accordingly necessary that communication should be opened with these proposed allies, in order that their attack should be well-timed. Brulé volunteered to reach them. He succeeded in passing the hostile villages of the Iroquois, possibly by the route indicated by the dotted line in Champlain's map of 1632, but was not able to get the reinforcement to the attack in season, as we shall see.

Moving on from the Huron country, the savage force, accompanied by Champlain and his compatriots, turned towards the southeast, and finally struck the course of the Trent, which easily conducted them to the borders of Lake Ontario. They reached its shores in the neighborhood of the modern Kingston. Here they embarked in their canoes, and crossing the lake by skirting a line of intervening islands, the native flotilla made a variegated show on the mirroring water. There is not an agreement among investigators upon the exact route which was taken, but somewhere on the shore which stretches south of Sackett's Harbor, the party landed, and concealed their canoes in a neighboring thicket. There was before them a march inland and almost due south. The local antiquaries have endeavored by examining the ground, and by following Champlain's details of his march, to determine the precise site of the fortified town of the Onondagas, which they sought. Mr. O. H. Marshall and others turn the route after crossing the outlet of Lake Oneida to the southwest, towards a position on Onondaga Lake. General John S. Clark, who has secured a more general acceptance for his views, shapes the invaders' course rather to the southeast, and brings them to a point on a small pond, where he finds remains on the ground which serve, as he thinks, to identify the spot. These traces conform in the main to a plan of the fortress, which Champlain depicts in one of the plates accompanying his narrative. The later writers, like

Shea, Slafter, and Parkman, follow General Clark's lead with scarcely any hesitation. The Indian stronghold was hexagonal in form, with four rows of lofty palisades, interlaced with withes. These walls supported a gallery for warriors, which ran around the top. From the side next the pond, water was introduced and conducted to gutters, which could be discharged upon fires, if built against the outer palisades.

CHAMPLAIN'S ROUTE, 1615.

It was before this fortress that Champlain and his allies appeared on October 10, 1615. The attack on the part of the savages was a wild hurry-scurry of boisterous movement, and some time passed before

October 10, 1615. The fort attacked.

Champlain could temper their frenzied zeal. He caused a tower to be built, and put some of his marksmen in it, to be pushed up to overtop the palisades. This worked very well; but all his precautions to regulate the attempts to fire the timbers of the outer defenses failed, through the misdirected precipitancy of his Indians. Some of the besiegers were wounded, and Champlain himself had to draw hostile arrows from his own knee and ankle.

When the assailants found they had made no impression on the defenses, they shrank as Indians always do at a repulse, and the disabled Champlain was unequal to the task of holding them to the attack. The whole mass of shrieking savages accordingly fell back under cover of the woods. They were ready, however, to renew the onset, if Brulé and his five hundred Andastes should come to their assistance. Brulé was three days away among the villages of that people, who had not yet finished their revelries at the prospect of punishing the Iroquois. Brulé proved powerless to move them on.

THE ONONDAGA FORT.
[After Champlain's Sketch.]

Five days of inaction or of paltry skirmishing followed, and the Andastes not appearing, a retreat was begun. If the shattered horde had waited two or three days longer, the succor would have come. The wounded Champlain, unable to bear his weight, was placed in a basket slung from men's shoulders, and in this mode he was borne away from a disheartening failure. It was his last expedition, and a sad contrast to his heedless onset at Ticonderoga six years before. That foolish precipitancy was avenged. His straggling force reached the lake without serious interruption from its pursuers.

Champlain retreats.

The fugitives found their canoes untouched, and embarked; and were soon on the northern shore of Ontario.

The Hurons seem to have had a purpose in keeping Champlain with them through the winter; or at least he was not able to find any guide to accompany him to the settlements. The savages tarried for a while on the border of the lake, to kill a winter's supply of deer. The rest gave Champlain's wounds time to heal. When the frosts of December ensued, and the ground was frozen, the trails became easier to traverse, and the Hurons with their guest departed for their towns.

Dec., 1615. The Hurons return home.

THE HURON COUNTRY.
[From *Creuxius*.]

It was thus that Champlain spent the winter of 1615–16 in the Huron country, in the neighborhood of Lake Simcoe. The passing months gave him opportunities to visit the adjacent and allied tribes, where he found much matter for his note-books. He records that the Indians could give him no knowledge of what lay beyond the *Mer Douce* (Lake Huron), except that prisoners taken from the more distant tribes had said that still farther on towards the setting sun there was a people who had light-colored hair and looked like the French.

Champlain hears of a distant people.

When the spring came, Champlain took advantage of a party

of Indians going eastward to accompany them. On reaching Montreal, he found Pontgravé just arrived from France, and got the latest news. On July 11, he was again in Quebec, after an absence of nearly a year. In the few succeeding days, he made plans for enlarging and repairing the buildings of the post, and on July 20 was on his way to Tadoussac. Embarking there on August 3, he arrived at Honfleur on September 10.

July, 1616.
Again in
Quebec.

Sept. In
France.

Champlain was again in the colony in 1617, but he has left no record of what he did. Pacifique du Plessis founded a mission at Three Rivers which served to give stability to a trading-post which had been maintained there for some years; and the settlement soon became and long remained a chief centre for the hardy voyageurs of the country. This class did little, however, to introduce family life, and it was hoped that, when Louis Hébert and his household arrived at Quebec, not far from the same time, a beginning was made in the more permanent elements of colonial life; but Hébert remained for a long time the only conspicuous example of a farmer in the valley. He was an apothecary by training, but he had exhibited while domiciled in Acadia a liking for the soil and its labors. He stands in the Canadian genealogies to-day as the progenitor of numerous representatives who rejoice in their descent from the man who first practically grasped the essential truth of colonial policy, and worked the soil like one bound to it.

1617. In
Canada.

Louis
Hébert.

It was during Champlain's sojourn in the valley in 1618 that his old interpreter, Etienne Brulé, returned to the settlement. The governor had last seen him when he was dispatched from the Huron company to bring the Andastes to the attack on the Iroquois fort, three years before. Brulé had now the opportunity to disclose the cause of his failure, and to explain his later wanderings. It appeared that when Brulé finally brought the Andastes to the neighborhood of the Iroquois stronghold, it was only to learn that the Hurons had departed, and there was no alternative left but a like retreat on their part. Brulé remained the following winter with his savage friends, but later, it would appear, he passed down the Susquehanna to Chesapeake Bay, and by this adventure he had established the direction of its course. If Sa-

1618.
Brulé's
wanderings.

gard's account is to be trusted, Brulé had in some manner also made his way westward, so as to find the shores of Lake Superior. He averred that it took nine days to reach the western extremity of some such water. The stories which he told of a region of copper mines point to this lake, and Sagard says that Brulé showed to him an ingot of that metal which was found there. In making his return journey, the wanderer fell among the Iroquois. He was wont to point to his wounds to show that he had undergone tortures at their hands. His own story betrays an abundance of tact in ingratiating himself with savages wherever he went. His spirit and facile habit served to convert the Iroquois enmity into a liking for him, and they made it easy for him to reach the Huron country, whence he could join the summer flotilla, descending the Ottawa.

One of the most conspicuous of the pioneers to follow up these discoveries of Brulé — whatever they may have been — was a young Norman, Jean Nicolet, who arrived just at this time in the valley, and was sent by Champlain among the Algonquins to inure himself to hardship and to learn their language. We shall encounter him again.

Jean Nicolet.

Early the next spring, Champlain, once more in Paris, procured (May 18, 1619) a license to print a new volume of his experiences. It was to cover the interval since his incursion into the Iroquois country in 1615. The book was better calculated, perhaps, than either of those preceding it to awaken the curious reader. It covered a larger field of exploration, and gave better glimpses of the country and what it could produce. It mingled the excitements of war with the horrors of torture. It afforded greater details of life among the natives. The drawings, whose production had beguiled weary hours during his confinement in the Huron villages, had passed the hand of the engraver, and helped to give a lively interest to the book. Its publication was successful enough, if we may judge by its passing to a second edition the following year.

1619.
Champlain prints a new narrative.

In the autumn of 1619, the Recollects began to make preparations for building on the St. Charles, opposite Quebec, and on June 3, 1620, six months before the Pilgrims began their meeting-house on the Burial Hill at Plymouth, these priests laid the corner-stone of the

1620. The Recollects build a church at Quebec.

earliest church erected in French America. It was palisaded like a stronghold, and there proved to be need of it. The English Separatists at Plymouth constructed their gathering-place with battlements for their small guns, and there was no need of it. For fifty years and more they lived in peace with their savage neighbors.

The Indians surrounding the settlement on the St. Lawrence were in a fair way to attain the Christian mode of warfare. If we may believe Champlain, two vessels from Rochelle, trading in the river this very season, began the practice of selling arms and ammunition to the natives. Matters had been growing more and more trying for Champlain. His colonizing purpose and the trading aims of the merchants were greatly at variance, and grew more so. Such practices as this of supplying weapons to the savages could but prove dangerous to a community which was left to pass the winters in small numbers, after the fur-ships had departed in the autumn and the traders had plunged into the wilderness. This danger was presented to the council of state, and an injunction was served on the traders to prevent the selling of arms.

Arms sold to the Indians.

In 1620, the vice-royal office was transferred to the Duke of Montmorency, who at once recommissioned Champlain, with ampler powers to enforce measures of safety. Champlain, leaving France in May, 1621, found the colony on his arrival in a sadly disorganized state. He saw that such a promise of stability as would come from greater permanence of living would do much to encourage the drooping spirits. He endeavored, therefore, to arrange for a more systematic cultivation of the soil; but he naturally encountered the opposition of the trading interest.

1621. Champlain at Quebec.

The purely mercantile character of the French occupation of the St. Lawrence did not escape the notice of their English rivals. Sir William Alexander, in a tract which he published in 1624 to induce a more active immigration to his province of New Scotland (Nova Scotia) on the part of his countrymen, accounts for the want of stability in the French colony, in that they were " only desirous to know the nature and quality of the soil and did never seek to have [its products] in such quantity as was requisite for their

Character of the French occupation.

maintenance, affecting more by making a needless ostentation that the world should know they had been there, more in love with glory than with virtue. . . . Being always subject to divisions among themselves, it was impossible that they could subsist, which proceeded sometimes from emulation or envy, and at other times from the laziness of the disposition of some, who, loathing labor, could be commanded by none."

This thwarting of the aims of true colonization by the trading associates induced Montmorency to dissolve the old company and create a new one. He again placed Champlain in charge, with renewed powers of administration, while the control of the business interests was committed to the Huguenots, Guillaume de Caen and his nephew Emeric. The older company proved too strong to be suppressed, and a rivalry between the two followed, only to result in the end in a consolidation under a single organization.

Montmorency and Champlain.

Amid all these intestine disputes, Champlain could but observe signs of larger rivalries. With Calvert at Ferryland, in Newfoundland, and that island become a base for operations, the English were not likely to remain as inactive as they had been. Champlain must have heard, moreover, how busy his neighbors on the New England coast had become. Dermer had just before this been exploring south from Monhegan; and perhaps it was at Boston harbor that he fancied he had stumbled on a western passage " which may hereafter be both honorable and profitable to His Majesty." When this same commander was at Manhattan, he had similar hopes from stories of inland watercourses which came to his ears. Not far from the same time, Purchas in England was learning that the Indians about the Chesapeake were reporting upon ships seen at the northwest, supposed by those who heard the tales to have come from Japan. And so along a northern and southern parallel there was a race for the China Seas.

Champlain's English and other neighbors.

Nor was it the English alone who gave him uneasiness. The ships for Quebec ran the gauntlet of the Basques, Flemings, and Spaniards in the St. Lawrence Gulf, and Champlain's supply-vessels were even occasionally brought under the guns of the little Basque stronghold at the Island of St. John. Once, indeed, a hardy intruder had dared to run his ship up to Tadoussac. If Champlain had chanced to see the Dutch map of Jacobsz, just

now (1621) made public, he would have read with some solici-
tude the legend of " Nouvelle Bisquaye " about the mouth of
the Saguenay. We can understand, then, why it was that
Champlain thought of the insecurity of Quebec, and planned a
larger fortress on the summit of Cape Diamond.

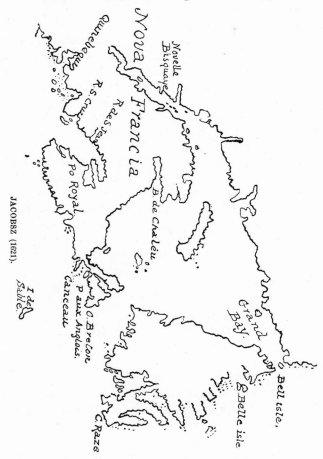

But there were other more immediate dangers for the little
colony, which hardly ever numbered in these years above a few
score souls. During the summer of 1622, thirty Iroquois
canoes were observed to pass Three Rivers, proceeding
towards Quebec. Their subsequent attack on the

1622. Iro-
quois on
the St. Law-
rence.

Recollect convent on the St. Charles is not mentioned either by Champlain or Sagard, which has thrown some doubt on the recital given in Le Clercq. Champlain indeed was absent at the time, and the Recollect father who tells us how the savages were repulsed says that he got his information from Madam Couillard, who was within the palisades all the while. This possible danger passed, it was not long before two Iroquois envoys came to Quebec and began negotiations, which in the spring of 1624 ended in a large concourse of Hurons, Algonquins, Montagnais, and Iroquois coming to Three Rivers to light their council fires and confirm a pact. If the peace had come earlier, Champlain might have profited by the quiet, and had the opportunity to confirm the stories of Brulé; but he had followed his last trail, and the mysteries of the west were left for others to solve.

1624. Treaty with the Indians.

The governor soon welcomed (1623) two more Recollects to the colony, one of whom was Gabriel Sagard, upon whose printed account of Canada we must in some measure depend, as our story goes on. With the satisfaction of being able to carry home good news of the quiet which had settled along the borders of his government, and prepared to tell the king the story of a four years' devotion to his interests, Champlain left Quebec on August 15, 1624. His wife was with him, for he had married Hélène Boullé, on his last visit to France, and she had passed these four years of novel experiences amid associations for which her early life had little fitted her. He landed at Dieppe, October 1, 1624.

Sagard.

August 15, 1624. Champlain leaves Quebec, with his wife.

During the two years which Champlain now passed in France, there were some important movements touching the future of Canada. In the first place, the Duke of Montmorency sold his viceroyalty to the Duke of Ventadour, and February 15, 1625, Champlain was created the new viceroy's representative. It is claimed that his new commission affords the earliest official record of a purpose to find a way to China. Kingsford, in his recent *History of Canada*, suggests that the language was inserted by Jesuit influence; yet in a petition in 1621 the Recollects reminded the king that " by a continuation of former explorations a passage to go to China could be opened."

1625. Again commissioned.

By 1624, when Sir William Alexander published his *Encouragement to Colonies*, the theoretical geography of Champlain respecting the western waters had become known in England. Alexander, referring to it, says that at the western end of a range of lakes, the French "did find salt water," and that great ships seen there had made Champlain believe " that a passage might be there to the Bay of California, or to some part of the South Sea, opening a near way to China." It was at this very time that the Spanish geographers were beginning to detach California from the mainland, and to open channels inland from the Pacific, so that speculative geographers found little difficulty in connecting the French reports of western waters approached by the St. Lawrence valley with these supposed developments along the Pacific coast.

At this time, moreover, Alexander was interested in a political movement somewhat ominous for New France. In 1621 (September 10), the English king had granted to him all that territory between the St. Lawrence and the sea, which lies east of the St. Croix River. " To be holden of us, from our kingdom of Scotland as a part thereof," ran this kingly purpose to carve a province of about 54,000 square miles out of disputed territory. Alexander was thus expected to colonize, and under the name of New Scotland or Nova Scotia to hold, and govern as lieutenant-general, a region that had already been included in the French king's grants to De Monts in 1603. The English patentee had not been able to start settlements when in 1624 he issued the tract to which we have already referred, as a means of propagating a colonizing spirit. As a further inducement to the same end, and to give dignity and some financial standing to his project, Alexander prevailed upon King James, and afterwards upon King Charles, to create an order of tributary Knights-Baronets, who should pay each a thousand marks into the treasury of the colony, and receive in return a grant of land to support their dignity, and these baronies were to include some at Anticosti, directly in the approach to Canada. The rank was further tokened in an " orange tawny silk ribbon with a pendent escutcheon," which they were privileged to wear. Sir William speaks of this grant to him as " the first national

Champlain's theoretical geography.

Sir William Alexander's grant.

patent that ever was clearly bounded within America, by particular limits upon the earth." The patent had certainly a distinctive limitation which told the French just what they

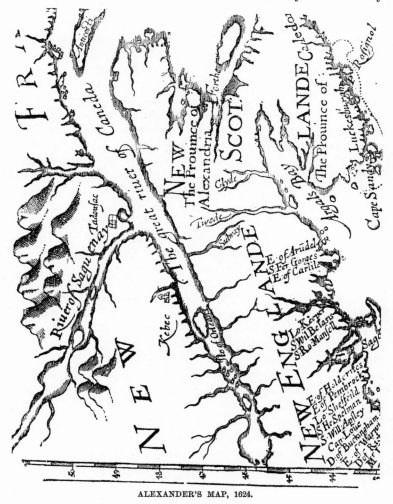

ALEXANDER'S MAP, 1624.

had to encounter, and made the bounds of Acadia a bone of contention between the rival powers for many generations.

Unfortunately, Alexander's scheme was embarrassed by the very dignity which he secured for it.   His plan of manorial rights in New Scotland was an attempt to plant mediævalism in the new world. They shut out the manly endeavor of self-respecting, though lowly owners of the soil, and the absence of such attributes in the settlers made them in the end the sport of political exigencies.

Ventadour, the new viceroy of Canada, was under the influence of the Jesuits. Champlain had always favored the Recollects. The members of this last order had prospered under the eye of the governor, and in 1624 some recruits from Gaspé had joined the little body. They had already created five missions, — Tadoussac, Quebec, Three Rivers, with others among the Nipissings and Hurons. They had, as we have noted, raised the first stone structure in the colony, the church of Notre Dame des Anges. We have seen how there is some reason to believe that in 1622 this palisaded edifice had successfully resisted an Iroquois attack. Success had emboldened the fathers, and they had petitioned the king to exclude the Calvinists from the colony; but Louis XIII. was not prepared for such a step. It came a few years later, when the strong spirit of Richelieu willed it.

If the Recollects were in this matter denied the aid of the crown, there were willing abettors in their schemes, which they could engage, and so they invited the Jesuits to make common cause with them. On June 19, 1625, the Jesuits, Charles Lalemant, Jean de Brébeuf, Enemond Massé, François Charton, Gilbert Burel, and a sixth of unknown name, appeared in Quebec. Being denied hospitality by the civic authorities, they were at once received under the roof of the Recollect monastery, and began to look about to establish a house of their own. The spot they selected was beyond the St. Charles, at the confluence of the Lairet, where Champlain believed Cartier to have wintered, and where after ninety years there were still some traces of the earlier occupancy. It was the 1st of September, 1625, when the Jesuits with due ceremony took possession of the ground, and on April 6, 1626, they found themselves in their new abode. Two days later, the Père Brébeuf, who had been among the Indians during the winter, studying their manners and tongue, and preparing for larger experiences, rejoined his companions. The Jesuits began their labors amid dissensions, which their

Ventadour viceroy.

Recollect missions, 1624.

1625. Jesuits arrive.

1626. Build an establishment.

coming had created. The return of Champlain to Quebec in 1626 did much to smooth asperities. A letter which the Père Charles Lalemant sent to Paris, and which appeared in the *Mercure François*, did not tell a comforting story.

Champlain had arrived on July 5, 1626, accompanied by his brother-in-law, Eustache Boullé. He found the colony only just recovering from the distresses of the winter. A famine had threatened the settlement, and the struggling settlers had been forced to send to Gaspé for succor. The persistency of their leaders had alone made the company desist from a purpose to abandon the place.

Champlain arrives, July.

That eighteen years of occupancy had so little served to give stability to New France was a fact forcibly pressed upon the spirit which was now animating France. Cardinal Richelieu had with an evil eye marked out his policy, and Canada was to receive the impress of feudalism. The institutions of the European past were to be evolved amid the American forests, and just at a time when there was already planned among the neighboring English, in the compact of the " Mayflower," a departure from the old-world principles of entail and primogeniture in the elevation of equal rights. The English sympathy with the Huguenots and the pretensions of the English king to territory along the St. Lawrence, as well as the mongrel combination which was now carrying on the trade of Canada, were not signs to be received passively by a man like Richelieu. The old trading companies were swept off the board, and a new company, which was commonly called the Hundred Associates, was promptly formed. The cardinal gave it his approval on April 29, 1627, in camp before Rochelle, the last of the Huguenot strongholds. On the 6th of May, 1628, the Council of State ratified the charter, and thenceforth no Calvinist was to be allowed to enter New France.

Richelieu's policy.

Hundred Associates, 1627.

These principles were hazardous in the struggle with the Dutch and English for the conquest of the continent. The Dutch West India Company was planting along the Hudson a sturdy colony of Walloons, in sympathy with the Huguenots, which Richelieu would expel. Their spirit was to live, while the manorial rights of the Van Rensselaers and the rest, compelling the people to scatter dangerously, sowed the evils that

made the country fall easily in due time into English hands, by
which a free tenure of the soil was added to the advantages possessed by these other rivals of the French.

The royal articles of 1627, creating the powers of Richelieu's
company, — which we may read in the *Mercure François*, —
gave it jurisdiction over a territory extending from Florida —
wherever that may end, for in defining bounds there was no attempt to decide it — to the arctic circle; and east and west from
Newfoundland to the great fresh lake, omitting, for a wonder, to
extend it to any salt water. Charlevoix and most of the writers following him make the grant to include Florida, but the
articles seem to be plain that the extension of the territory was
from Florida, which the Spaniards at that time actu-   Florida.
ally possessed. The conditions of this southern country had not indeed changed since the time when Champlain
wrote of it in the journal of his West Indian voyage, as " one
of the best lands that can be desired; very fertile if it were
cultivated; but the king of Spain does not care for it, because
there are no mines of gold or silver." What was of more moment to the French of the north, there were no furs there.

The principal Associates of the Company of a Hundred were
Parisians, and Richelieu was its constituted head.   The new
There was at least a quarter of the number to be   company.
found in Normandy, and three hundred thousand livres had
been contributed to carry the project on. The company promised to reinforce the feeble colony by a strong contingent of
artisans and laborers, to be sent at once, with all necessary tools
and supplies. Within fifteen years they purposed to send over
four thousand other colonists, whose support for three years was
to be guaranteed by the Associates. In the spring of 1628
their first expedition sailed, consisting of four armed vessels
convoying eighteen transports. They carried thirty-five cannon to increase the defenses of Quebec. This fleet, under the
command of Claude de Roquemont, fell into the hands of the
exasperated Huguenots and their allies, or, as Parkman expresses it, Roquemont succumbed to " Huguenots fighting
under English colors."

Roquemont had sailed in April, but an English fleet had got
the start of him, for under the pretext of relieving the Huguenots at Rochelle, the English government had declared war

against France. So the occasion was seized to dispatch an ar-
England and France at war, 1628. mament against Quebec. The instigator of the move-
ment seems to have been a French Calvinist, Michel,
but the men who gave the enterprise character were
Sir William Alexander and a Derbyshire gentleman, Gervase
Kirke. Alexander naturally looked upon the lordly territorial
claims of Richelieu as aimed in part at his own colony of New
Scotland. Kirke, who had lived awhile in Dieppe and had
Kirke's fleet. married a French woman, knew what a task was before him. The king supplied letters of marque, and
Kirke's eldest son, David, was made admiral of the fleet, with
two other sons in subordinate commands. This fleet was far
enough ahead of Roquemont to be able to land a Scotch colony
in the territory of Sir William Alexander, and to sweep the St.
Lawrence of all the French afloat, before Roquemont was expected. After this it lay in wait for its prey at Tadoussac.

On July 9, two little towers of the fort in Quebec fell down,
and in the anxious state of the garrison the sign seemed ominous. On the same day some half-famished men were scanning
the distant reach of the river to catch sight of Roquemont with
his expected succor. While their hopes were proving vain, two
refugees from Cape Tourmente emerged from the woods beyond
the St. Charles, and brought word that some Indians had come
to that post from below, who reported large ships at Tadoussac.
Shortly after, a canoe came bringing the wounded commander
of the French post at Cape Tourmente. He said that he had
escaped a party which had been set ashore from some strange
ships to assail that fort. The next day, some Basque fishermen
pulled in under the cliff at Quebec, and delivered a message
from the English admiral, which they had undertaken to deliver
Quebec sum- moned to surrender. to Champlain. It was a courteous demand from
Kirke for the surrender of Quebec. Champlain had
neither provisions nor powder adequate to a defense,
but he answered as if he had, and the messengers rowed back
with a reply as courteous as Kirke's summons, and quite as
confident. This show of firmness had its effect, and Champlain
was given a respite, not, however, free from suspense.

Meanwhile Roquemont with his fleet had advanced up the
river almost to Tadoussac, and had dispatched ahead a boat to

warn Champlain of his coming. This messenger, approaching Tadoussac, saw the English ships glide out of the Saguenay and turn down the St. Lawrence. He found cover for his boat on the bank, and Kirke's ships passed without discovering him. They were scarcely out of sight, when reverberations of cannon told him that Kirke and Roquemont had grappled in a fight. Speeding on to Quebec, the dismayed messenger carried the news to Champlain. The governor remained in a trying state of uncertainty till some Indians brought him word that the fight had ended in disaster to the French fleet.

Kirke indeed had captured such of the ships as he did not sink, and, finding both glory and booty in the victory, he gave up Quebec, and sailed for England with the prizes.

Kirke takes the French fleet.

The winter of 1628–29 was a weary and disheartening one for Champlain. There was little to eat, and by spring this little became nothing. The only hope of sustaining life was in digging roots and gathering acorns. When even these failed, the colonists clung to a hope of seizing, if they could, one of the palisaded granaries of the Iroquois. Here they could perhaps defend themselves till relief came. Most of the sufferers stood fast by their settlement; a few sought asylums among the Indians.

1628–29. Quebec.

Meanwhile Champlain was without any tidings of the effect in Europe of Kirke's enterprise. It had indeed excited a new cupidity among the English trading adventurers. In February, 1629, a royal patent was made out for Sir William Alexander, to constitute him the "sole trader" of the St. Lawrence valley, to authorize him to settle a plantation anywhere along the river from below Tadoussac to Quebec, to confiscate the property of interlopers, and to seize French or Spanish ships, and drive off the French that might be found on the banks.

One morning in July, 1629, an Indian saw some masts above the trees on the island of Orleans. Other savages came in and reported that they had seen English ships moving up the channel. Champlain could doubt no longer that the enemy had returned. Before long, the hostile vessels glided into the basin, and looked like cockboats as the governor with a little squad of pallid and ragged adherents looked down upon them from the ramparts of the feeble fort.

1629, July. Quebec surrendered.

They saw a boat with a white flag row to the strand. The officer bore a new demand for surrender. Champlain asked for a fortnight to consider it; but an immediate compliance was insisted on. Kirke was not unreasonable in his terms. He offered honorable privileges, and engaged to transport all who desired it to Europe. There was no alternative, and the demand was met. The next day, the red flag of England floated from Cape Diamond. The English admiral had sent his brothers to arrange for the capitulation, while he remained at Tadoussac. Under these commanders, the troops which had come in the ships were landed, and quartered in casemate and barrack. Provisions were at once put ashore, and the storehouses were filled with unwonted supplies. Thirteen of the French colonists, looking perhaps on the change as a deliverance, as Charlevoix intimates, were induced to live under the English rule. Of these there were seven who were of importance to the victors, because of their woodcraft and experience with the Indians.

Those who preferred to leave embarked with Champlain on one of the English ships, and on July 24 started for Tadoussac. Champlain This vessel ran ahead of her consorts, and while thus embarks. unsupported she met a French ship under Emeric de Caen. This vessel had slipped by Tadoussac unnoticed. The hostile crafts cleared for action, and it seemed for a while that De Caen would avenge the fall of Quebec; but British pluck prevailed, and the Frenchman struck his colors. The prize was taken to Tadoussac, where on August 19 the terms of the surrender were ratified by the English admiral.

It seemed now to one in Quebec as if the English domination of North America was likely to be assured, and not to be left, as was the case, to the uncertainties of a hundred and thirty years yet to come. Lord Baltimore at Avalon, in Newfoundland, had indeed seen a sorry time with his colony in the face of the French, to say nothing of English enemies, and he had just carried his people to the Chesapeake. Here he found that the chartered rights of the Virginia company, with all the extensions to a supposable western ocean, had been surrendered to the crown, and under a royal governor, the most ancient of the English settlements was to gather new vigor, a part of which he was to feel. In the region which lay towards the French, and had been called North Virginia, but which, since Captain John Smith had described the country, was more commonly known as New England, there was an ominous movement. In March, 1629, while Champlain and his stricken followers were dragging their emaciated bodies into the sun on the rock at Quebec, Charles the First was confirming the Massachusetts charter, as granted by the company at Plymouth in Devon, which since 1620 had claimed to 48° north latitude. In the interpretation which the colonists gave to the new charter, it carried its northern limits above the source of the Merrimac, well within a region which the French had claimed. The charter gave also to the grant an indefinite extension to the western sea, whose shores both French and English were anxious to reach. Smith had complained that with all his praises of the New England soil, it had hardly lured the emigrant like the more fertile south. But the year in which Quebec was lost to the French was the same in which Puritanism claimed New England. The party which Endicott brought to Salem in 1629, with instruction to buy the land of the natives, were the precursors of a race unequaled as colonists. They differed from the French in the north in many respects, but in none more potently than in bringing to these American wilds the life of families. The long struggle they sustained along the New England frontiers with the horrors of savage war showed how stubbornly they could cling to their ideal.

A few days before the English fleet which bore Champlain was descried from the Hoe at Plymouth, the council for New England, sitting in that town, made a grant to Gorges and Mason, which assured the control of the country on " the Iroquois lakes " to their associates of the Laconia company. This, with all its mistaken geography, would have meant to the English in Quebec, had they known it, a close contiguity to their conquered post. But all visions of a compacted English territory were soon dispelled.

CHAPTER VII.

QUEBEC RESTORED. EXPLORATIONS OF NICOLET. DEATH
OF CHAMPLAIN.

1630–1635.

ON the return of the English fleet to Plymouth, November 20,
Nov. 20,   1629, it was discovered that before Quebec had capitu-
1629.   lated, a treaty of peace between England and France
had been signed on April 23. On November 29, Champlain
was in London, endeavoring with the aid of the French ambassador to arrange for the restitution of the untimely conquest;
but there were complications to be removed. On the preceding 2d of February, the English king, in anticipation of the
Alexander's conquest of Canada, had granted, as we have seen, to
charter.   Sir William Alexander, a charter of " the county and
lordship of Canada in America." This document spoke of the
" expected revealing and discovery of a way or passage to those
seas which lie upon America on the west, commonly called the
South Sea, from which the head or source of that great river or
gulf of Canada, or some river flowing into it, is deemed to be not
far distant." The charter granted jurisdiction over the islands
in and over fifty leagues of territory on each side of this river,
" up to the source thereof, wheresoever it be, or to the lake
whence it flows, which is thought to be towards the Gulf of
California, called by some the Vermilion Sea." This also included all the lands adjacent to the passage from the source of
the river to the Gulf of California, — " whether they be found a
part of the continent or main land or an island (as it is thought
they are) which is commonly called by the name of California,
— which are not really and actually possessed by others, our
subjects, or the subjects of any other Christian prince or constituted orders in alliance and friendship with us."

But all this was a short-lived or rather premature colonial

grandeur. Not many weeks later, it was agreed, in ignorance of what was happening on the St. Lawrence, that all conquest made by either English or French after April 24, 1629, should be restored to the condition existing before such cap- Canada to be ture. It was because of this agreement that Cham- restored. plain was now making his protestations in London.

Alexander and the Kirkes, with all who had ventured their money on the success of the Quebec expedition, were not in good humor when they saw that the lordship of Canada, and all the royal protestations which had encouraged them, were likely to vanish in thin air. These disappointed gentlemen had influence enough to protract the negotiations for the restitution, and when Champlain at last came to Paris, by the end of December, the issue was not reached, nor did the negotiations move rapidly during the following year (1630). Alexander and his friends lost no occasion to urge that the 1630. French had always been intruders within the limits of New Scotland. The English king, never willing to acknowledge the French rights to Canada, was making up his mind to such a qualified restitution as would not prejudice the English claim to the country.

King Charles had married, in 1625, a sister of Louis XIII., and only a part of the dower agreed upon had as yet been paid to him. It was a good time now to demand 1631. The queen's the rest. On June 12, 1631, he informed his ambas- dower. sador in Paris that if the French court did not pay this deficit there would be no restitution of Port Royal and Quebec. Here was substantial ground for diplomacy, and we can read the correspondence in the report of the Canadian archivist for 1874. The outcome was the treaty of St. Germain-en-Laye, on March 29, 1632. The agreement embodied in this 1632, March. St. Germain-treaty was very likely hastened by the fact that De en-Laye. Razilly, a leading member of the Hundred Associates, was known to be fitting out a fleet, which might be intended to wrest from the English by force the object of the lingering negotiations.

The treaty which Charles thus concluded was easily advanced by his pressing need of money, and the promise of the remaining dower. The king's letter, preserved in the Harleyan collection, and only printed by Mr. Brymner of the Canadian

archives, in 1889, has made this manifest. The terms for
restitution of the French posts in Canada bore hard on those
faithful subjects who had used his letters of marque to add to
his dominions, and who saw their conquests given up for his
royal necessities. Accordingly, the satisfied monarch was quite
willing to send ten thousand pounds sterling to Alexander as a
sop, while he ordered the evacuation by Alexander's son of the
region in the vicinity of Port Royal, where Charles La Tour
had earlier been installed as a representative of French interests. Charles was at the same time not inclined to throw too
much doubt on the numerous charters which under his royal
signature had covered all the region in dispute, and with char-
acteristic duplicity professed to his subjects that he intended to
carry on the plantation of New Scotland by the creation of more
baronets. Further than this, the rights of the Council of Plymouth, established in 1620, going as high as 48° north latitude,
and the patents given to De Monts in 1603, still remained to
keep alive a conflict of jurisdiction. The dispute was not finally
settled till Wolfe perished on the Plains of Abraham.

Charles was nevertheless quite ready to fulfill the new obligations of the treaty, and so the restitution of Quebec soon followed. As the De Caens had suffered from the inability of the
French government to protect them while at Quebec,
Emeric de Caen was sent out to receive the surrender.
At the same time he was allowed a year's privilege of
trade, to recoup himself in his barter for furs. In July, 1632,
the French reached Quebec. They found the English occupants had passed the period of their possession not without
tribulations. During the first winter, forty of the ninety men
who held the place had died. Those who ruled them had no
vigor to prevent illegal trading on the river, and the Basques
had plied their traffic with small hindrance. During the second
summer, they had received some recruits, and there were about
seventy English in the town when De Caen, on July 13,
received its surrender. The French accounts say that
the English commander sailed down the river with his
ships heavily laden with furs. Some of the hatchets which
Kirke had used in the barter for skins were recognized two years
later by Henry Fleet among the tribes of the Potomac.

Richelieu had in mind to control, as his wont was in most

Emeric de
Caen sent
to Quebec,
1632.

July.
Quebec sur-
rendered.

things, the religious missions in Canada. He tried first to induce the Capuchins to take charge of them, but for some reason that order found its way to Acadia instead. Missions.
The Recollects had appealed to Rome to have a bishop in Canada, which was not a way to ingratiate their order with Richelieu, and in a spirit both of defiance and defense that minister sent the Jesuits instead. This exclusion of the Recollects has sometimes been said to have been the result of Jesuit intrigue. At all events, on April 18, 1632, two Jesuit fathers, Le Jeune and De Noüe, sailed from Havre for 1632. Jesuits arrive.
Quebec. Some weeks later, at Tadoussac, Le Jeune saw for the first time, as they came on board the ship, some of the uncouth and filthy creatures whose interests, as he understood them, were to fill so large a part of his devoted life. A heedless cruelty was at once mated in his mind with their squalor, for he labored in vain to induce them a few days later to spare some Iroquois prisoners from the horrors of the stake. The Jesuits perhaps realized how fit an introductory experience all this was to the work they had come to do. Shortly afterwards, we find the two priests restoring the dilapidated mission house on the bank of the St. Charles. The policy of the Jesuits was reasonable, and it was not savage. " The power of the priest established," says Parkman, "that of the temporal ruler was secure. . . . Spanish civilization crushed the Indian, English civilization scorned and neglected him; French civilization embraced and cherished him."

On August 28, 1632, Le Jeune wrote to the provincial of his order in France detailing his experiences. It was the earliest of that series of wonderful letters, known *Jesuit Relations.*
as the *Jesuit Relations.* These reports for forty years and more supplied the most that was known of life in the Canadian wilds to the great mass of French readers. Charlevoix speaks of the avidity with which they were read, and Parkman praises the good faith of their authors, — a Protestant recognition of good intent that their contemporary rivals in other ecclesiastical orders did not accord. There are few allusions to these narratives in the writers of their day, though Creuxius used them in writing his account of Canada in 1664, as Chaulmer had done in his *Nouveau Monde* in 1659.

Although the final edition of Champlain's narratives bears the

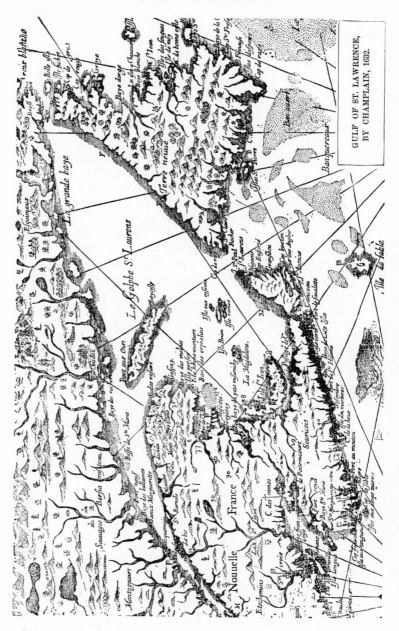

GULF OF ST. LAWRENCE,
BY CHAMPLAIN, 1632.

date of 1632, there are some reasons to think that it was really issued the following year (1633), after Champlain had returned to Quebec. This book, in which several Paris publishers seem to have been conjointly interested, contains in the first part a condensation of his previous publications, and in the second a continuation of his experiences from 1620 to 1631. The last year's doings were apparently not written by Champlain himself. Indeed, it is manifest to more careful critics that the volume, including its map, failed to receive Champlain's personal supervision, and was prepared for the press by another hand. Some have been

Champlain's final edition, 1632-33.

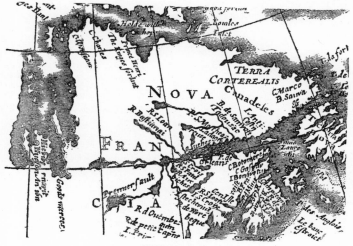

HONDIUS, 1635.

led to believe that a Jesuit father — possibly one who had been in Canada — edited the book in the interests of his own order, and issued it, notwithstanding the date on the title, after Champlain had departed from France in March, 1633. These critics rely upon a difference in style in what they claim are Jesuit interpolations, and they point to inaccuracies and obscurities which could not have come from one so well informed as Champlain. The obscuration of the Recollects, which the book shows, is something, too, in such judgments, that could not have originated with Champlain. This edition, says the modern historian, Kingsford, "was an engine to influence opinion, so that Canada, restored to France, should be given over en-

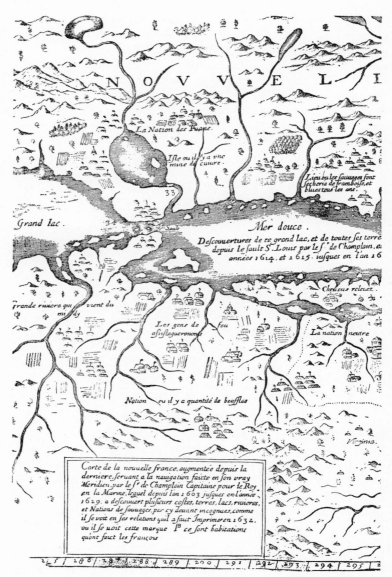

THE GREAT LAKES,

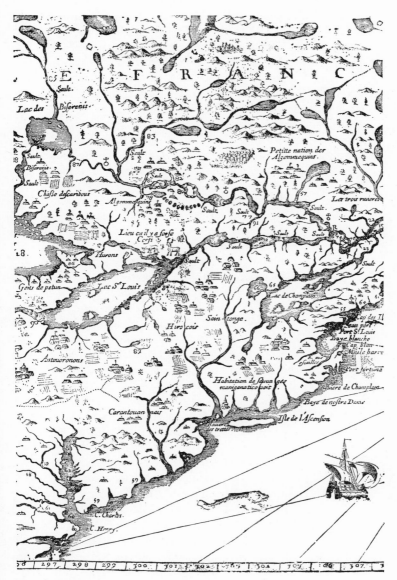

BY CHAMPLAIN, 1632.

tirely to the Jesuits." In most copies a certain passage which is thought to reflect on Richelieu, the Jesuits' patron, is canceled.

In the large map there is perhaps some, but less reason to suspect an alien hand. We get from it the first cartographical intimation of a great lake beyond the *Mer Douce.* In an explanatory legend Champlain says that the Saut du Gaston, commemorating a brother of Louis XIII., was near two leagues in width, — it represents the present Sault Ste. Marie, — with its waters coming from a very large lake beyond; and in the map we find its western extension cut off by the margin of the Champlain's sheet, — a convenient limitation to the vague know-
1632 map. ledge which was then current. It will be observed that we get in the stream which enters Lake Ontario at the west end the first fairly accurate location of the Niagara cata-
Niagara. racts. Champlain never comprehended the magnitude of these falls any more than Cartier did when he seems to have heard of them, a hundred years before. Sanson, when he published his map in 1656, represented the conception of Champlain; but we get no particular description of the cataract till we find one, drawn from hearsay, however, as we shall see in Galinée's journal, when this priest accompanied La Salle along Lake Ontario in 1669. This stream, which shows the falls near its outlet in Ontario, comes from Lake Huron through a region which with better knowledge is made the basin of Lake Erie. Very curiously, there seems to be the beginning of the Straits of Mackinaw, with its island, nearly in the proper place, while the inlet which stands for Green Bay, amid the country of the Puants, is thrown over to the northern side of Huron.

Champlain, on returning to his Canadian government, had borne with him a new commission, representing all the prestige with which Richelieu and his Hundred Associates could clothe their representative. He sailed from Dieppe on
1633. Cham-
plain in   March 23, 1633, and on the 23d of May the morn-
Canada.   ing gun at the fort on Cape Diamond boomed a welcome to the restored governor. The salvos stirred many an echo, but none in nature was more responsive than that in the heart of Le Jeune, when his attention was first arrested by the sound as he was stirring with the early duties of the day at

the Notre Dame des Anges. He knew that it meant a friend
had come to take command in place of a Huguenot. Perhaps he
did not know that in the train of the returned governor came

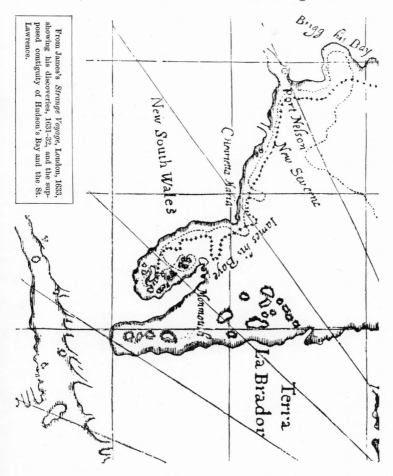

From James's *Strange Voyage*, London, 1633, showing his discoveries, 1631-32, and the supposed contiguity of Hudson's Bay and the St. Lawrence.

men of his own order; but it was not long before he found the
Jesuit missions strengthened in the coming of Brébeuf,   _{Jesuits.}
Massé, Daniel, and Davost.

But it was in his civil rule that Champlain had most to fear.
The English, thinking to improve their trade in the gulf, manifested a purpose to advance to Tadoussac and begin a compe-

tition with the French for the native trade. In May, 1633,
representatives of the Canadian tribes assembled at
Quebec to sit with Champlain round the council fire.
The French governor urged his allies to repel the
advances of the English. An Indian from Three Rivers, Capi-
tanal, impressed the listening Jesuits with oratorical powers
that they had not associated with the native tongue. Champlain in reply was allured into picturing that good time when
the French and the Indians should be one, giving and taking
in marriage. If such a consummation were possible, Champlain
was aware that much must be done to hedge the little colony
about, so that such feelings of mutual trust might grow. A
post must be established somewhere below on the river to
prevent the English coming up and the Indians going down.
A fort must be built at Three Rivers, strong enough to check
the raids of the Iroquois; and a light troop of three hundred
French soldiers needed to be kept ready for quick movement
along the river. Champlain's letter of August 15, 1633,
urging these measures upon Richelieu, produced little
effect. The self-reliant governor soon became convinced that he had not much more to hope from the new company than he had experienced from the old. A year later, he
renewed the representations, but with no better result.

It is not probable that Champlain was aware of the movements which the English were making from the Atlantic side,
or he would have been even more solicitous of succor from
France. The Indians had impressed on the minds of the English, as they had done upon the French, the same faith in a
great interior basin of water. Captain Thomas Young, in
1633, sailing up the Delaware, where the Swedes were conduct-
ing a lucrative fur trade, speaks of that "Mediterranean Sea,
which the Indian relateth to be four days' journey beyond the
mountain." Young had resolved to find it. He expected first
to reach a smaller lake, connected with the larger by a strait.
The rapids of the Delaware checked his progress. He now
desisted for the season, with the expectation of building a vessel above the falls during the following year. He supposed
that, setting out from such new point, he would still have a voyage of a hundred and fifty or two hundred leagues to overcome.
He apparently harbored the same notion as prevailed in Can-

Marginal notes:

1633, May. Indian council.

Richelieu apathetic.

ada, that this intermediate lake would, when reached, disclose
passages both to the North and to the South Sea, and Supposed in-
in this event the conflict of rivalry could not be far terior basin.
off. Two years later, an English edition of the great *Mercator-
Hondius Atlas* shows this great interior water lying west of
Ontario.

In June, 1634, a fleet arrived at Quebec, and in it came
Father Buteux and two other priests. The whole 1634. Jesu-
population of Canada at this time was scarcely more its arrive.
than sixty souls, and of this number only two households could
be said to have fastened themselves on the soil. In fact, all
results of consequence in the colony's life could be traced to
the summer traffic in furs, and development stopped with that.
The neighboring English and Dutch were pursuing the
same trade. Half the people in Albany lived by it. The skins
came from New England as well as from the Iroquois and beyond, and large shipments were made to Holland from Manhattan. But there was this difference, that these people were
generally becoming a product of the soil, and were rapidly increasing, particularly along the New England coast. There
were at this time near four thousand English settled about
Massachusetts Bay, and the great immigration was begun which
before 1640 was to bring something like twelve thousand colonists to the country. The people founded a college, French and
and began to build ships, and were trading in the re- English col-
moter inlets, and bringing wheat from Virginia. The onization.
little colony of New Plymouth were supporting a trading-
post on the Kennebec, close up to the divide which separated
them from the French, and were maintaining it against French
privateers, not always successfully. All this meant with such
a people permanence and colonial growth. Though there was
some wildness in contemporary opinions among the English as
to the westward geography which they were slowly developing,
there was not in official circles the same confident expectation
of reaching by western exploration the great China Sea, which
prevailed in Paris and Quebec. When, in 1635, the Plymouth
Company of Devon surrendered its charter, which had carried
their claim to 48° north latitude, they distinctly averred that
the " sea to sea " limits of its terms were the equivalent of about

three thousand miles. The colonies of Maryland and Virginia,
backed by the Alleghanies, were more prone to imagine a
western sea not very remote beyond the darkened ridges of
those mountains.

Life on the St. Lawrence, with almost a generation of colonization behind it, was quite another thing, and Champlain was
not a man to be blinded to its essential failure. With something of chagrin, but with a determination to make one more

1634. Three   stride in the western march, he sent off in July, 1634,
Rivers.   an expedition prepared to start a new settlement at
Three Rivers, which in all these years since Pontgravé had dis-
cerned its advantages had been left untried. He directed a
fort to be built on the very site where the Iroquois had in the
past destroyed a stronghold of the Algonquins, and one step
more was taken on the way to Cathay. This step meant that
the church should once more send still farther west its precursors of civilization, and, after much persuasion, the Hurons,
who had come down on one of their trafficking visits, were at

Jesuits go   length prevailed upon to take back with them some of
west.   the Jesuit priests. The savages much preferred men
with packs and arquebuses to those in cassock and hood. The
French, in bidding Brébeuf and his companions good-by, grati-
fied the savage humor by a discharge of cannon. Brébeuf was
not without some military fervor himself, and we soon hear of
him, teaching the Hurons to build their palisades in a square
with flanking towers at the angles, as better fitted than their
round inclosures to give the French arquebus its best effect in
helping repel an attack.

Late in July, Champlain went to Three Rivers to observe the
progress of the fort. It was his last journey so far west, and

August.   on August 3 he was back in Quebec. Shortly afterwards he gave a God-speed to Le Jeune, who went to
assume charge of the new post, taking Father Buteux with

September.   him. They arrived at Three Rivers on September
8, and three months later found themselves in the
midst of an epidemic, which put their courage to a severe test.
While it was raging, Le Jeune began with his own hand a register of baptisms and deaths, which now remains the sole doc-

Early rec-   ument transmitted to us of these old Canadian days.
ords.   The early records of Quebec were destroyed a few

years later, when the Chapel of Notre Dame de Recouvrance, which Champlain had erected to commemorate the recovery of the town from the English, was burned in 1640.

The establishment of the first seigneury at Beauport marked a new stage in the progress of the French scheme of colonization. A seigneurial tenure to tract after tract was given in the following years to any enterprising person who would undertake to plant settlers on the land, and accept in return a certain proportion of the grist, furs, and fish which the occupant could secure by labor. *Seigneury at Beauport.*

It was on July 22 that Champlain held his last council at Quebec, inviting the Hurons, who had come down the river with their customary constancy, to participate. The burden of the governor's address to them was that if they would only worship the Frenchman's God, they would flourish under his benignant protection and have no difficulty in overcoming the Iroquois. He told them that they only needed to embrace the white man's faith, if they would have the white man take their daughters in marriage. There was room, he said, in Quebec for a goodly number of their young children, if they would only commit them to the custody of the kind French, who would give them shelter and food in their holy houses, and be like grandparents to their tender wards. *1635. Champlain's last council.*

It was probably late in July, 1635, that Champlain learned of the return of Nicolet from the mission on which he had dispatched him the previous year. It will be remembered that in 1618, not long after this young Norman had arrived in the valley, Champlain had sent him among the Indians to prepare him for future service as an interpreter. Nicolet may have made an occasional visit to the settlements in all these intervening years, but there is no definite evidence of it. It seems likely that his was not a familiar face when he appeared at Three Rivers in the summer of 1633, in the train of the Algonquin traders, come thither for their summer traffic. By the next June (1634) he was ready for new labors. These many years among the Algonquins and Nipissings, suffering their perils, had quickened his senses for the hardiest tasks of the forest. *Nicolet.*

The Canadian writer, Benjamin Sulte, has shown it to be reasonably certain that Champlain had started Nicolet at this time in the train of Brébeuf and Daniel, who left Three Rivers for their missions on July 1, 1634. Nicolet's intention was to go far enough west to learn something more definite than had yet been acquired from the Indian stories, as Sagard tells us, of those distant western people, who had neither hair nor beards, and who journeyed in great canoes. It was the common tale that these stories had passed eastward from a distant nation who lived by water that was not fresh, and who had migrated to their present homes from the shores of a great sea. Such were the geographical and ethnological riddles that Nicolet was now expected to unravel. Parkman suggests that the brocaded gown which he is known to have taken with him was in reference to this hairless people who, in the prevalent opinion, must have been thought a race of the Asiatic Orient.

Nicolet's course lay up the Ottawa, and by Lake Nipissing to Georgian Bay, and thence to the Huron villages. Here he renewed old friendships, and secured the services of seven of the tribe for guides. Launching their canoes at the head of Georgian Bay, the party skirted the eastern and northern shores of Lake Huron, and found at last their progress checked Sault Ste. Marie. at Sault Ste. Marie. Nicolet was the first European who had reached this point, and, encamping on the southern bank of the passage and in the present State of Michigan, he opened the first communication which white men had with the ancestors of the modern Ojibways. There is no clear evidence that he pushed by land beyond the rapids, so as to get a satisfactory view of the great lake beyond. Its existence, conjectured by Champlain, was yet to be proved by others.

From the Sault, Nicolet and his companions retraced their way, and, following the shore of what is now called the northern Straits of Mackinaw. peninsula of Michigan, they came to the Straits of Mackinaw, — that dominant position in the geography of North America, reached in just a century from the time when Cartier tried the great northern portal of the interior at the Straits of Belle Isle. Nicolet could hardly have suspected the commanding stand at which he had at last arrived. With all his surmises, he even did not know the great channel which led to it from the landfall of Cartier, for the existence of Lake

Erie was but faintly conceived; and the route by the Ottawa, with all its obstruction, was the only passage which he knew. To the south of him lay the great lake whose position Champlain had so recently misconceived in placing it to the north; and at the head of Lake Michigan and the extremity of Green Bay — shortly to be tested by Nicolet himself — lay the inviting portages which were in due time to conduct the French into that great valley which the English had not dared to enter over the Appalachians, nor the Spaniards to invade from the Gulf of Mexico. There was no dream yet of the great affluents of the Mississippi, which by the Missouri were to conduct the explorer to the Columbia and the Pacific, and by the Arkansas were to open a way along the Colorado to the Gulf of California. All this was shadowy in men's minds, and the speculative geographer of the time had not yet made it clear whether the canoe which was carried over the southern portages would float to the Atlantic, the Mexican Gulf, or the South Sea.

Nor could our adventurous explorer have divined what lay in the farther west, — that channel of the Sault, where the rapids had baulked him, leading to the long stretch of Lake Superior, which the Jesuits, who were now at Three Rivers, were yet to unfold; the devious passage to the Lake of the Woods and Lake Winnipeg, and the Indian trail which would have led him equally to Hudson's Bay or along the Mackenzie River to the Arctic Ocean; and the turn off at Lake Athabasca, which would have conducted him to the northern tributaries of the Columbia.

These were the possibilities to be made clear in coming years, — the route to China was to dissolve to this.

From the Straits of Mackinaw Nicolet passed on to Green Bay, and proceeded to its southern extremity. Here he encountered the tribe whom we know as the Winnebagoes. Winnebagoes. His damask robe and his pistols, belching fire as he stalked to meet the savages, made them look upon him as a strange spirit. The explorer soon found that his familiarity with the Algonquin and Huron tongues availed him little, for the Winnebagoes were the first of the Dacotah stock that the white man had seen. The messages of good-will and peace which Nicolet brought to them were not rejected; and mutual professions were enforced by speech and feast.

Leaving his new-found friends behind him, Nicolet pushed up the Fox River, threaded its tortuous ways, passed its frequent lakes, and reached the villages of the Mascoutins, — a Mascoutins. tribe whose name had been familiar, by report, twenty years before, for they had a fame for daring courage which had extended far to the east. He was now among a folk of the Algonquin stock, and was better able to understand the stories which they told him of other water away towards the south, three days off. It was to be reached by ascending the Fox still higher, and then by crossing a short portage, whence he could "Great descend to the "great water." This designation, in water." the misconception of its import, long nurtured a belief in some expansive sea. The story which Nicolet heard in reality prefigured the channel of the Wisconsin, flowing into the great central stream of the Mississippi valley, destined to remain a mystery for forty years yet to come.

For some reason Nicolet did not attempt to make this momentous passage of the low lands, which here constitute the ridge between the great valleys of North America, and it was left for Joliet and Marquette to establish the truth.

We follow Nicolet in these wanderings mainly from his story, as repeated by Vimont in the *Jesuit Relation*, published six years later. That we find no published record till 1640 has led writers on the subject to assume that this exploit of Nicolet Date of must have taken place in 1639 instead of 1634. It Nicolet's expedition, was Sulte who made the earlier date a certainty. 1634. He published his conclusions in 1876 in a volume of miscellanies, and reinforced his argument in the *Collections* of the Wisconsin Historical Society in 1879. Later students have hardly questioned his conclusions, but some popular writers have been ignorant of them.

We have not represented that Nicolet passed into the Wisconsin River. It is fair to say that the language as given by Vimont has sometimes been interpreted to mean that Nicolet actually did float his canoe on that tributary of the Mississippi. Instead of this, however, it seems far more certain that Nicolet Illinois and pushed directly south and reached the tribe of the Sioux. Illinois, where he saw something of the Sioux, who were in that neighborhood on an expedition from the country farther west.

On his return down Green Bay, Nicolet is known to have exchanged friendly courtesies with the Pottawattamies, scattered along the western shores of Lake Michigan. Pottawatta-mies.

It was probably in the early summer of 1635 that, having parted with his faithful Hurons in their villages, Nicolet joined the customary flotilla descending the Ottawa for the summer trade, and reached Three Rivers some time in July.

Unfortunately, we are without any knowledge of the effect which Nicolet's story may have had on Champlain, and we are left without any conception of the reason why such portentous events should have failed of any recognition which has come down to us, till Vimont recounted the story. It was left for Sagard to condense the narrative in his subsequent history. It may have been in recognition of his services that Nicolet received one of Champlain's last appointments, in being made commissary and interpreter at Three Rivers. We soon find in the contemporary records evidence of Nicolet's unmistakable activity in that region.

The last letter preserved to us which Champlain wrote makes no mention of the great exploit which we have just been recording. This missive is dated August 15, 1635, and in it he still tries to impress upon Richelieu the necessity of further succoring the colony. He speaks of the English as haunting the lower St. Lawrence, and professing to do so with their king's permission. The Dutch and the Iroquois to the south still troubled him ; but thoughts of them did not harass him long. 1635. Champlain's last letter.

About the middle of October, Champlain fell under a stroke of paralysis. For two months and a half he suffered, and at last on Christmas Day, 1635, the end came. 1635, Dec. 25. Champlain dies.

The intrepid governor lay dead in his own Quebec, the incipient city of blasted hopes. Trade had supported it, and had stunted it. A summer of activity and a winter of inaction was its story, year in and year out. In the long and hot July days the people had found enough to do, and there was enough for their amusement in the varying procession of Huron canoes which came down the St. Lawrence and emptied the living and furry burdens on the strand beneath the cliffs for the annual traffic. The merchants sold implements and trinkets to the savages, loaded their barks with peltry, and sailed away, to leave those who remained, despondent, listless, nursing their misfortunes, and too few for generous enterprises. The merchants' ships took their factors back to France, to a constituency which counted gains, and cared nothing for those who rendered profits possible.

The dream of empire which Champlain had cherished had come to this. There was a fortress with a few small guns on the cliffs of Cape Diamond. Along the foot of the precipice was a row of unsightly and unsubstantial buildings, where the scant population lived, carried on their few handicrafts, and stored their winter's provisions. It was a motley crowd which in the drear days sheltered itself here from the cold blasts that blew along the river channel. There was the military officer, who sought to give some color to the scene in showing as much of his brilliant garb as the cloak which shielded him from the wind would permit. The priest went from house to house with his looped hat. The lounging hunter preferred for the most part to tell his story within doors. Occasionally you could mark a stray savage, who had come to the settlement for food. Such characters as these, and the lazy laborers taking a season of rest after the summer's traffic, would be grouped in the narrow street beneath the precipice whenever the wintry sun gave more than its usual warmth at midday. It was hardly a scene to inspire confidence in the future. It was not the beginning of empire.

If one climbed the path leading to the top of the rugged slope, he could see a single cottage, that looked as if a settler had come to stay. There were cattle-sheds, and signs of thrift in its garden plot. If Champlain had had other colonists like the man who built this house and marked out this farmstead, he might have died with the hope that New France had been planted in this great valley on the basis of domestic life. The widow of this genuine settler, Hébert, still occupied the house at the time when Champlain died, and they point out to you now, in the upper town, the spot where this one early householder of Quebec made his little struggle to instill a proper spirit of colonization into a crowd of barterers and adventurers. From this upper level the visitor at this time might have glanced across the valley of the St. Charles to but a single other sign of permanency in the stone manor house of Robert Gifart, which had the previous year been built at Beauport.

We know that the Jesuit Lalemant did the last service, and Le Jeune spoke a eulogy when they laid the dead hero away. As time rolled on, the place of his burial was forgotten, and it is not many years since the growing fame of one who has not been inaptly called the Father of Canada prompted the antiquary to search for the sacred resting-place of the dead. Theories as regards the identity of its site have been more than once advanced and abandoned within the last thirty years. It seems, after all has been said and done, that the present better judgment allows that every trace of the mortuary chapel where he was laid to rest has been swept away. It was in what is now an open square in the upper town. If Champlain's remains were taken to another place when the chapel was destroyed, the act was done without any record which has been preserved.

CHAPTER VIII.

FROM THE DEATH OF CHAMPLAIN TO THE REORGANIZATION
OF THE GOVERNMENT.

1635–1663.

WITH the death of Champlain, Canada was left without a ruler, except for the supervision exercised by the governor of Three Rivers. Charles Huault de Montmagny had been appointed in Champlain's place as early as March, 1636. It does not seem probable that the death of Champlain, at a season when the St. Lawrence was ice-bound, could have been known in Paris so early in the year. If it was not known, the superseding of Champlain must already have been determined upon, and very likely at the instigation of the Jesuits. It was June when the new governor reached Quebec. Almost immediately Le Jeune and his brotherhood felt that they had gained a sympathizing friend. Montmagny had scarcely set foot to ground before he fell prostrate at the sight of a cross. He lost no time in standing godfather to a converted heathen. A neophyte had but just died, and Montmagny conspicuously walked in the funeral procession.

When his piety was thus manifested, the governor turned to more worldly affairs. Quebec had become a rather pitiable home for some two hundred souls, but such as it was, it made the centre of the interest which France had in the new world. The ruler who had arrived was a far less enterprising man than the one whom these two hundred Frenchmen, barring the Jesuits, were mourning. If Champlain had lived and continued in office, there would probably have been early occasion to chronicle some expedition to the west to follow out the hopes which the story of Nicolet had raised. As it was, that adventurer's story seems hardly to have met any immediate response, and

Montmagny.

Arrives, 1636.

it was not till several years had passed that it found, as we
have seen, a record in the chronicles of the priests. A triumph
of the church might have been sooner recognized.

Montmagny's purpose was rather to consolidate the colony
and render it more defensible with the scant force at his command. So he strengthened the fort, and marked out an upper
town on the adjacent plateau. This project was quite beyond
what seemed to be necessary; for there was very little of permanent interest in the town among the scant population which

Le JEUNE.
[From an old Print.]

filled the tenements along the lower strand. This population
was largely made up of the fur traders, who only came and went.
The priest was a steadier denizen, but he was likely to wander
back and forth through the wilderness. It was his career to
keep the missions in fitful, if not constant, communication with
the town. The gliding nuns were barely more than birds of
passage alighted on the way to heaven, and flitted from cabin
to hospital.

The black-robed Jesuits exercised an influence that will be
viewed differently according to the measure of sympathy which

attaches to their devotion and dominance. These qualities in Jesuits and that body have been held to be concomitants of hardi- Franciscans. hood and heroism, but an age less addicted to senti- mentalism, and a faith more imbued with spiritualism, are apt to diminish reputations once exalted. The exclusion of the Franciscans accounts for much that is lacking which might have made life more endurable under their balmier and strength- giving influences. It was only those that shunned the settle- ments and lost themselves in the woods, and became in some respects more skilled in woodcraft than their Indian compan- ions, who breathed the fresh air that supports reliant men, — or at least the enemies of the Jesuits thought so, when they con- templated those who fled from their priestly influence.

The missions which Brébeuf and his companions had insti- tuted among the Hurons in 1634 were still the outposts of the church, and for some years we have the reports respecting them annually sent to Quebec by Lemercier. It has been reck- oned that these adventurous missionaries had gathered into what they called the fold of Christ perhaps a hundred out of the sixteen thousand souls making up the Huron communities. It was not theirs to reckon the cost against so paltry a gain. The happiness of a single soul was enough.

Every attempt to preserve communications between these remote stations and the main settlement was a hazardous one. The Iroquois were a danger both seen and unseen, and their fierce ubiquity stood appallingly in the way of exploration out- side of the Huron country.

In 1637, the authorities at Quebec began to gather a few fam- 1637. St. ilies of the Montagnais in a little settlement at St. Joseph's. Joseph's (Sillery), the better to protect them from the savage Iroquois. The trembling creatures were not safe even 1640. there, and by 1640 some nuns who had been admin- istering to the sick among them were withdrawn to Quebec for safety. The confederates were everywhere on the war-path. Letters from the remoter missions were not infre- quently intercepted by them. The black-robes in Quebec, anx- ious for the safety of their brothers afar, had frequent intervals of suspense that only good luck relieved.

A report from the Huron country at this time makes men- tion of a map which the Père Ragueneau had drawn of this western country, but it has unfortunately not come down to us. It might have shown in truer position than Champlain Ragueneau's had given it, the great cataract, which Vimont was map. now calling Onguiaahra. This director of the Canadian missions also forwarded to Paris a letter of Le Jeune, written in September, 1640, in which it is said that an Englishman, coming by the Kennebec route, accompanied by a single servant and some Abenaki Indians, had reached Quebec, in the previous June, on the way to find a western sea; but that the French governor had turned him back. In the same *Relation* it is reported that a prisoner to the Fire or Tobacco nation, coming from the southwest, had represented Tales of the west and south. that a region beyond his home was so mild that corn could be planted twice a year, the last crop being gathered in December.

It was such stories as these that both created and answered the yearning of the geographical sense in its uneasy moods. Every hint of a salubrious climate and a possible western way was comforting and reassuring.

While the Jesuit *Relations* were making such stories current, they offered something much less vague in the reports, which showed that Nicolet had already reached regions which were unknown before, and that a new mission had Sault Ste. been established at the Sault Ste. Marie. Communi- Marie. cation with this distant station was evidently to be maintained by chance and at long intervals, if maintained at all.

The priests who had accomplished this exploration in 1641 were the Fathers Raymbault and Jogues. They had 1641. Raymbault and started for the mission of Ste. Marie at the foot of bault and Jogues. Georgian Bay, near the Huron villages. Leaving in June, they were in September at the rapids between Huron and Superior, where only Nicolet had preceded them. They found two thousand savages encamped there, or about ten times the number usually abiding at the Sault. Among them were the Pottawattamies, who had fled north before wandering bands of the Iroquois, and were now fraternizing with the Pottawatta-Ojibways. The priests heard from them of the great mies, Ojib-ways river and of a valorous people along its banks. This (Sioux). unknown tribe, by a clipping of their full name, we know to-day under the designation of Sioux. It was while here at

the rapids that one of the Jesuits — Father Raymbault — passed
Raymbault dies. away, and Vimont, in reporting the occurrence to his
superior in Paris, said that Raymbault hoped to reach
China across the wilderness, but God diverted his path to
heaven !

By this time the French were beginning to perceive that the
possession of the shores of Lake Erie would render the passage
from Ontario to Huron safer and easier, and without the loss
of time required for the route by the Ottawa.   But an impending Iroquois war put off the fortunate day.   With the firearms
which the confederates had obtained of the Dutch at Albany,
— the main station of that people, for New Amsterdam had at
this time little more than a score of dwellers, — they had
increased both their daring and their power of offense.   An
appalling stroke soon came.   In August (1642), twelve Huron
canoes, returning from their summer traffic with the French,
1642. Jogues taken. were waylaid by a band of Iroquois in ambush, and
Father Jogues and some adherents, again on their way
to the missions, fell into the hands of those savages.
The victors with their prisoners made a circuit through the
woods near the mouth of the Richelieu, to avoid the fort which
the French had constructed on its banks.   Their canoes were
soon dashing against the stream on the way to Lake Champlain.   South they passed, and entering the passage near where
Champlain had taught the Iroquois the value of firearms thirty-
three years before, the victorious party pushed out into the
upper tributary lake.   Father Jogues was perhaps the first of
Europeans to see the untamed glories of Lake George.

Blaeu's *Atlas* of 1635 shows how much at fault the Dutch
Lakes Champlain and George. Geographi- cal errors. were at this time as to the position of Lake Champlain ; indeed, taking the English notion as expressed
in the Laconia patent, it seems almost as if before
this experience of Jogues, and even afterwards, both
the Dutch and the English were inclined to confound the
waters on the west of Vermont with Lake Winnepesaukee in
New Hampshire.   At the same time they brought in their maps
the Lacus Irocociensis too far south.   This notion long prevailed in the Dutch maps, taking the hint doubtless from that
of Champlain in 1613, and was accepted by Ogilby and other
English cartographers for forty or fifty years after Jogues's

adventures. The map of the *Mercator-Hondius Atlas* in 1636 seems to indicate that a conception of this water tributary to Lake Champlain, now known as Lake George, had been derived from some source before that date, though the basin of the two lakes is placed after the prevailing misconception.

We have no occasion at this point to depict that sort of martyrdom, emulating the stoical endurance of the pagan, which the Jesuit historians delight to honor, in the tortures which these captive priests experienced. The scene of this suffering is of more importance to us now, as that of the first acquaintance of the French with the southern water- Southern water-shed of Ontario. We have Jogues's own account of of Ontario. it, both in what he wrote and in the personal testimony which he gave his countrymen, when, the next year (1643), he was rescued by the neighboring Dutch from his savage tormentors. He was sent by them to France, and returned once more, after an absence of two years, to other miseries. It was while at one of the Iroquois villages (June, 1643) that Jogues de- 1643. Jogues scribed the seven hundred warriors which he found among the about him, and said that they had three hundred Iroquois. Dutch arquebuses among them, and that their war parties were departing to the north to make havoc along the St. Lawrence.

Before Jogues had returned to Quebec, a brother Jesuit, Bressani, endeavoring to open communication with the Huron mission, which had been shut off for three Bressani. years, was likewise captured by one of these marauding bands of the confederates, and went through the same miserable ex- perience of torture, to be rescued in his turn by the Dutch in much the same way. In another year this Italian zealot also was facing once more the perils of a mission life.

There is a strange story to tell of the way in which a new and permanent settlement was pushed forward to an island Founding of at the mouth of the Ottawa, gaining another step in Montreal. the westward occupation. To see the piety of those who were instrumental in the founding of Montreal, one needs to be in the spirit of the movement. Without such sympathy, it is not difficult to perceive its grotesqueness sooner than its religious fervor.

Different persons in France, having no knowledge or inter-

CARTE DE
L'ISLE DE MONTREAL
ET DE SES ENVIRONS

Dresfée fur les Manuscrits du Depost des Cartes Plans
et Journaux de la Marine.

Par N⁰ Bellin Ingenieur et Hidrographe de la Marine.

1744

MONTREAL

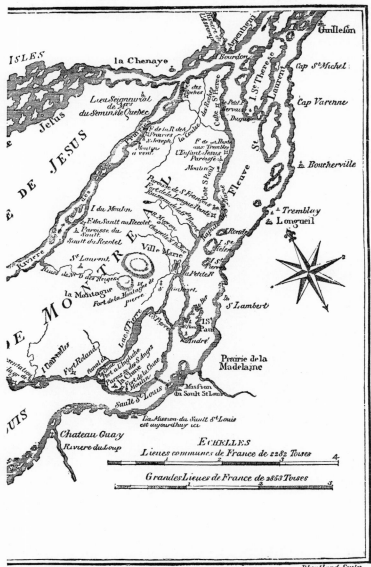

AND VICINITY.

course with each other, behold visions of a spot in the Canadian wilds where they are separately impelled to found hospitals and establish religious orders. The *Jesuit Relations* had indeed told their readers something of what this spot was, where now stands the chief commercial city of Canada; but

MAISONNEUVE.
[From Sulte's *Canadiens-Français*, vol. iii.]

the story loses something of its lesson to the faithful, if each enraptured visionary knew anything of it in so obvious a way. As it happened, two of these ecstatic men met by a miracle, embraced like old friends, and took a walk together to outline their conjoined plans. The Abbé Faillon, who tells us of it, might have walked with them, he knows so much of it all, and in this nineteenth century tells us the whole story in more than one of his books, with a pleasing and unquestioning faith. We read in his pages how Olier and Dauversière, with others who were allured by the ecstasy, got what money was needed, and secured the island by a grant from the Hundred Associates. These

JEANNE MANCE.
[From Sulte's *Canadiens-Français*, vol. iii.]

astute fur traders, however, were careful enough in their grant to guard the perpetuity of their own rights of trade from the infringements of priest, nun, and invalid. At this juncture, Paul de Chomedy, Sieur de Maisonneuve, stepped forward, sword in one hand and psalter in the other, Sieur de Maisonneuve.

as the commanding spirit who was to govern this little colony.
With equal opportuneness Mademoiselle Jeanne Mance, fit
Jeanne governess for those of her sex, appeared at Rochelle,
Mance. ready to embark with this strange embryo colony.
Where she was going she neither knew nor cared ; she was im-
pelled to do the work of the Lord, and would fain attempt it.

So with this miraculously compounded company, Maisson-
neuve and the lady were wafted to sea in one of the ships,
while Olier and the other leaders stayed behind to make other
worldly preparations. When the pioneer ship arrived at Quebec, it was too late to ascend the river beyond, and, obliged
to delay, the eager colonists did not find a ready welcome at

the hands of the
constituted author-
ities. The soli-
citude which was
expressed at the
dangers pictured
for them in so ex-
posed a situation as
Montreal was evi-
dently not so much
the result of anxi-
ety for their wel-
fare, as jealousy of
t h e i r movement.
T h i s ungracious-
ness did not wear
off during the win-
ter, and Maison-
neuve's company,
quartered at Sil-
lery, were quite
ready, when the
spring opened, to

MADAME DE LA PELTRIE.

move up to their destined plantation. In the mean while their
Madame de supreme faith had attracted the attention of Madame
la Peltrie. de la Peltrie, and she was ready to leave the Ursu-
lines at Quebec and join the new-comers.

In May, 1642, the flotilla of the enthusiasts reached the site

of Montreal. Father Vimont welcomed them to the spot with
a holy ceremonial, accepting them as a charge of the
order of Jesus. So Montreal was begun on the green
1642.
grass of the river-side, skirted about with a screen of the forest,
just as the buds were swelling.

The experiment curiously reversed ordinary ways of settlement. The town was not founded to invite the erection of
a hospital as the ills of life demanded it, but a hospital was
to be put up to invite settlers to put a town about it. It was
a piece of good luck that the Iroquois let them alone for the
interval while they were constructing their buildings and palisading their ground. The river itself proved a bitterer foe
than the savage, and at one time nearly drowned them out. It
was to celebrate their deliverance from this disaster that they
marched out to the mountain which had attracted Cartier, and
set up a cross on its summit.

Montreal, thus placed and fortified, under the zealous cap-
taincy of a man like Maisonneuve, proved an important post
for the western progress of civilization. It was suitably situated to form a base for the protection of the Ottawa route on
the one hand, and on the other hand it was well planned for
an advance of population by the main stream of the St. Lawrence.

There was little hope for the future, however, with the Hundred Associates still farming out the resources of the
country. The piety of the religious orders was
The Hundred Associates.
shocked at the company's inertness in all that might conduce to
the conversion of the heathen. Those who had the good of the
colony most at heart failed to see any purpose in the Associates
to increase the colony or improve its condition. Its spirit had
manifested no purpose but to fill its coffers.

The charter of the company had given power to establish
fiefs or seigneuries, with the obligation upon those who received
them to settle immigrants upon the soil. It was a gift which
compelled the possessors of the grants to incur outlays and per-
form duties which were variously fulfilled. Up to 1641, there
had been eight seigneuries established, and we have seen how at
Champlain's death the erection of a stone manor
house at Beauport had marked one of them. When
the abolition of the company took place in Febru-
New France and New England.

ary, 1663, there had been sixty-five such manorial grants of importance, beside some of little account. This all signified an

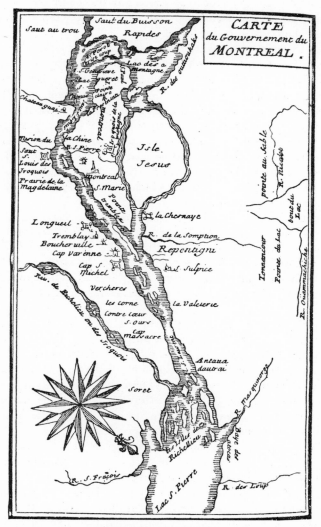

MONTREAL AND VICINITY.

old-world and disjointed way of settling the country, subversive of homogeneous activity. The result was what might have been expected, and in striking contrast to that union of sentiment among the English colonists which, at this time (1643), brought about the New England confederacy, representing in Massachusetts Bay alone something like twenty thousand souls, throwing off their bondage to the traditions of the mother land, and enacting of themselves their code of laws in a " Body of Liberties."

Canada had scant hope in the peace with the Iroquois, which was close at hand. Couture, who had been captured with Jogues, had been adopted by the Mohawks, and had used his exertions to foster among them a spirit of amity towards the French. It so happened that a number of the Iroquois had been taken by the Algonquins, and clemency had been shown to them at the instigation of the French. This incident gave persuasiveness to Couture's appeals, and the Mohawks were induced to send an embassy to Three Rivers to Mohawks propose a peace. propose a peace. With much parade the emblematic belts were hung up and counted, and the hatchet was thrown away.

But the peace proved delusive. Unfortunately, the Mohawks only had proposed and concluded it. If the Senecas and the other confederates refused to abide by it, there was some gain in holding the Mohawks alone to their agreement. Jogues, who had now come back from France, was 1646. Jogues sent to them. sent, in May, 1646, to try to hold that tribe to their pledge. In a month he was back in Quebec, but no great confidence resulted. In August, he was sent again, but he was waylaid in his path by a wandering band of Mohawks and led as a prisoner to their town, only to be struck down as he Jogues killed, 1646. entered a lodge, whither he had been invited to a feast. Brained by a hatchet which had not been thrown very far in token of amity, a soul singularly dear to Catholic hearts passes from history.

There was no longer any doubt that the Mohawks were determined for war in alliance with their brothers. The War opens. confederates at this time numbered perhaps three thousand warriors, — such is Parkman's estimate, — and this horde must have been much less in extent than the Huron and Algonquin could oppose to them in combination, to say nothing of what the French might add. The Iroquois superiority consisted rather in an indomitable fierceness concentrated by a union of energies.

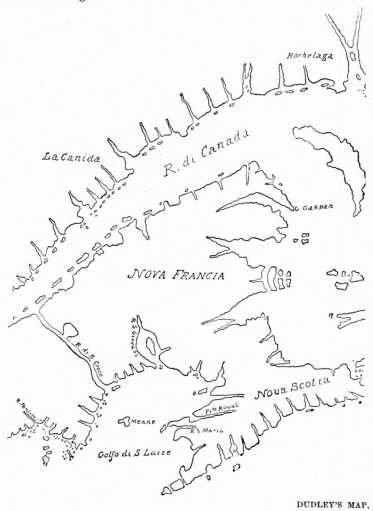

DUDLEY'S MAP,

With allies so ineffectual as the northern tribes were, the French could hardly hope for a successful issue of the war. They certainly had no force of their own to protect the country which they claimed to possess. Their whole line, from the St. Lawrence Gulf to Lake Huron, was particularly vul- The valley nerable. The church had pushed her missionaries exposed to inroads. up the Saguenay to the nations of

Sanguenai

the Porcupine and the White Fish, and if the traders of these distant tribes carried back from Tadoussac, season after season, some remnant of the priests' instructions, the new faith was far less abiding than the fear of the Iroquois, from which they did not escape even in their northernmost limits. The passing of these marauding bands was constantly break-

La Gran Bala

ing the peace along the Frenchmen's northern bounds. Canada was scarcely less endangered along its southern flank. The English were seated along the coast of Maine, and no one yet was quite certain that, among the valleys stretching from the sea towards the St. Lawrence, there might not be a feasible approach for an enemy. Robert Dudley, indeed, was showing at this time, in his maps, that there was a waterway to connect the Bay of Fundy with the St. Lawrence. Farther west, the approach to Canada by Lake Champlain was a deadly opportunity for her inveterate enemies. The French had not yet dared to confront these foes along the shores of Ontario and Erie, and the Canadian bushranger knew as little of these shores as Champlain had known fifteen years before. Lalemant had described the Niagara River in 1641 without even referring to the great cataract; but Ragueneau in his *Relation* of 1648 first mentioned it as of

I Sable

" frightful height." The French knew much more of Winnebago Lake, far more distant as

1647.

it was, and their pioneers had possibly walked from the Fox to the Wisconsin, to mingle the water of the St. Lawrence valley, dripping from their leggings, with the current that reached in its flow the tropical south.

The great western track still lay along the Ottawa, and among the friendly Hurons. While this tribe protected the route, its villages at the same time invited the Iroquois attack. It was soon to come.

In 1648, a band of the confederates, chiefly Mohawks and
Senecas, invaded the Huron country in the absence of
its warriors. They devastated one of their chief towns
and scattered its inhabitants. This was in midsum-
mer. Winter came on and gave a false security, and before it was over the enemy fell upon St. Ignace (1649) and made a more dreadful havoc.

The Hurons attacked, 1648–49,

Two of the most conspicuous of the black-robes were here

BRÉBEUF.
[His bust in silver at Quebec. His skull can be seen through the oval in front.]

among their neophytes. Gabriel Lalemant, Parisian by birth, a professor by training, had carried into the wilderness the delicacy and air of a student. Father Brébeuf, quite the reverse in appearance, a giant in frame, brawny and active, was fit to measure strength with the hardiest savage whom he taught. Both missionaries summoned an almost immeasurable courage to bear the tortures which they suffered amid the burning town.

The blow could not be parried, and one after one the fifteen Huron towns succumbed or were abandoned. The dispersal of the sufferers
was complete. The Hurons were destroyed as a people. Such as survived fled east and west, — some will yet be encountered as we follow future explorers towards the distant west; some gathered under the protection of the French in the neighborhood of Quebec; while others purchased immunity from further spoliation by migrating to the Seneca country and merging themselves in the Iroquoian confederacy.

and destroyed.

The Huron country never again knew the traces of this people, and only the modern archæologist, wandering between the latter-day villages of an alien race, finds in the forests the evidences of the former occupants.

No event in Canadian history had heretofore attracted so much attention in Europe as this foreboding dispersal of the Hurons. The *Relations* of Ragueneau, which gave the details of this disaster, were eagerly enough sought to warrant editions in French at Lille as well as at Paris, and for European scholars in general there was demand for a third edition in Latin.

The Canadians themselves had never before felt so distressingly the results which followed in the train of Champlain's infelicitous onset at Ticonderoga half a century before. Their rulers were even ready to turn to the English for help. Four years before (1647), Winthrop of Massachusetts had made advances looking to a treaty of commerce with the powers at Quebec, prompted perhaps by the presence there of La Tour of Acadia, who had had, a few years before, some pleasant relations with Boston. The English governor's death, however, had intervened to prevent any such consummation. There was now an opportunity for even a closer alliance than trade could suggest, and Father Druillettes, who was serving at a mission near the sources of the rivers in Maine, was sent (1651) down their courses to the sea, with instruction to make his way to Boston for a conference. He was well received at the Puritan capital. His ambassadorial office protected him from laws which that community had sought to level against Romanists. A Boston merchant even provided a locked chamber for Druillettes's devotions, where he could set up his altar unobserved. Eliot, the New England apostle to the Indians, quite opened his heart to the priest, and the two mutually and with apparent interchange of sympathy rehearsed their experiences in a common vocation, for Eliot had been five years preaching to the Naticks, and he had now four hundred neophytes in his fold.

1651. Druillettes sent to Boston.

He meets the Apostle Eliot.

The contrasts of this meeting of the Jesuit and the Puritan are some of the most striking in our colonial history. With kindred aims, they leaned far from each other in their representative methods. It was the kind of opposition which Doyle describes in his *Puritan Colonies.* "The French missionary

well-nigh broke with civilization; he toned down all that was
spiritual in his religion and emphasized all that was sensual, till
he had assimilated it to the wants of the savage. The better
and worse features of Puritanism forbade a triumph won on
such terms." When, just before this (1649), Parliament had
established the " Society for the Propagation of the Gospel in
New England," the new organization expected to act largely
through the federal commissioners of the colonies, for the min-
isters and magistrates were one in their life. The story of civil
and religious exertion in New France is largely one of variance.

Druillettes on his part was struck both in his intercourse at
His obser-   Boston and Plymouth — where Governor Bradford on
vations.   a Friday gave him a dinner of fish — with the thrift
of the New England character. He marked their numbers,
which in contrast with Canada seemed prodigious to him, and
saw how their population was now increasing by nature and
not by immigration. He found such a people an instructive
contrast to the thin settlements at a few points along the St.
Lawrence. " The zeal of propagandism," says Parkman, in
commenting upon this observation of the Jesuit, " and the fur
trade were the vital forces of New France. Of her feeble population, the best part was bound to perpetual chastity, while
the fur traders. and those in their service rarely brought their
wives to the wilderness. The fur trader, moreover, is always
the worst of colonists, since the increase of population, by diminishing the number of the fur-bearing animals, is adverse to his
His mission   interests." Druillettes's mission, however, failed. The
fails.   commissioners of the united New England colonies,
to whom the appeal ultimately went, considered it bad policy
to divert the Mohawk from his northern path, and to expose
their own frontiers to his ferocity.

Not only had the Huron villages been destroyed, but the Iroquois had depopulated the Indian country all along the waterway from Montreal to Georgian Bay. They had rendered
passage so unsafe between the rapids above Montreal and Ta-
Iroquois   doussac that the fur-trade stations from Three Rivers
raids.   to the Saguenay were in effect abolished. The Iroquois had pushed with more audacity than ever up the gloomy
channel of the Saguenay, and had driven the upper Montagnais

back to Hudson's Bay. Everywhere north of the St. Lawrence and Ontario, Algonquin and French alike shuddered at the name of the confederates. The missionaries had withdrawn from their outposts, and they told in the settlements of the horrible sufferings which their brothers had undergone at the Iroquois stake.

When commerce and the missionary spirit was at this low ebb, and the fugitive French from exposed positions had thronged into the settlements, an Iroquois embassy appeared with a proposition for peace. They further offered an invitation to the inactive missionaries once more to set up the cross in the villages of the confederates. This unexpected step had not been taken without some motive. The Hurons whom the Iroquois had adopted had brought among them a faith drawn from Christian teaching, which adversity had not wholly obliterated. Such sharers of this belief had in some degree accustomed the proud Iroquois to the emotions which they had never succeeded in subduing by torture, and the constancy of the missionary had become to their savage mind a virtue, worth acquiring even from a foe.

There was another more prudent impulse. The Iroquois had now turned their warring energies against the Eries and Susquehannas, so that they could no longer be the middlemen of those tribes in furnishing furs to the Dutch at Albany. They were thus cut off from the profits of such a commerce. Their only compensation lay in restoring such a trade with their northern neighbors along the St. Lawrence and beyond.

The peace gave an opportunity, heretofore denied, for a reconnaissance of the southern shores of Ontario. Father Poncet, who had been one of the first of the missionaries to answer the appeal of the Iroquois, returning (1653) in the inclement season from the Mohawk villages, passed by trail along the lake shore and then descended the river to Montreal, — the first of white men it is thought to view the Thousand Islands of the St. Lawrence. The next year (July, 1654), Father Simon Le Moyne entered for the first time the Oswego River, and passed thus into the heart of the Iroquois country. During Le Moyne's sojourn among these savages, he found a Christian's delight — as the

Peace, 1653.

1654. Le Moyne among the Iroquois.

term was understood — in urging the Iroquois to further daring against the Eries. In September, he was back in Montreal, and found his warring impulse approved, in the belief that such diplomacy would keep the confederates to their pact with the French.

Iroquois constancy was hardly of such stable quality, and the Mohawks, who had kept aloof from the final agreement, felt themselves as free as ever to fall as they could on anything human along the borders of the St. Lawrence. Faith and confidence could not long subsist under such a fast-and-loose policy.

1656. Mohawks attack the French. In 1656, the Mohawks, jealous of a movement by the Onondagas to receive a French colony, intercepted its pioneers on their way thither. They feigned regret after they had done their mischief, and then went skulking down the St. Lawrence to fall unsuspected upon the poor Hurons, who were clustered at the Island of Orleans, in fancied security. The same vagabonds plundered some outlying houses of the French, near the rock of Quebec.

During the few years of the Jesuits' missions in New York, the priests had not failed to notice the departure of Iroquois bands towards the southwest. They learned that this route took their warriors to the affluents of a stream which emptied finally into that great river of the west so often magnified in the Indian speech. It led, as they told the missionaries, to a region where other white people lived, who said prayers like the black-robes, and called their flocks to mass by a bell. Did this mean the Spaniards of that indefinite region which was called Florida, and skirted the Mexican Gulf, or that other region known to other brothers of the Society of Jesus along the Gulf of California? It was the great geographical problem of the vast interior of North America.

The Dutch dominie, Megapolensis, tells us that the Jesuit Le Moyne had, in his wandering among the missions, found a spring where oil flowed on the water. This has been supposed to refer to the modern Oil Creek, a tributary of the Alleghany River. This, if true, establishes the fact that the Jesuit had at this date passed the divide, and had reached a part of the great valley of the Mississippi.

This brief occupancy of the Iroquois field by the Jesuits

served to make it apparent that these confederates held in their country one of the most striking geographical vantage-grounds on the continent. The northern incline of their ter- *Geographical* ritory swept its waters into the broad basin of the St. *vantage of* Lawrence and the lakes. Eastward, the Mohawk could *the Iroquois.* bear their canoes to the Hudson and the Atlantic. Southward, the sources of the Delaware and Susquehanna rippled onward to the great bays that indented the coast at Pennsylvania and Virginia. To the southwest lay the channels that fed the Ohio and the vaster stream which gathered its waters from the Rocky Mountains and beyond Lake Superior, and glided on to the Mexican Gulf.

This enormous reach of diverging waterways did much to give the Iroquois their dominance as a confederation; and it was thus perceived by the French. When later the Jesuits were driven out of the country, this geographic *Understood by the* conception was well understood by Talon, the most *French.* enterprising and ambitious leader which the French in America ever knew. But the time was not come for the exploration westward along these tributaries of the Ohio.

It was mainly the priest who had thus far watched the westering paths from the Iroquois haunts. It was the trader who was to lead by the more northern routes. " Not a cape was turned," says Bancroft, in speaking of these western adventures, " nor a river entered, but a Jesuit led the way." The rhetoric is too sweeping. It was not always the Jesuit when a priest, and oftener than not, the trader rather than *Priest and* the priest. What gold was at the south among the *trader as pioneers.* Spaniards, beaver-skins were at the north among the French. The Canadian *gentilhomme* devoted himself to the venturesome pursuit for furs, and became a roving bushranger, followed by men with packs. The priest sought the trader's escort, and followed as occasion provided him a seat in the canoe. Sometimes, indeed, the man with a pack and the man in a cassock were rivals in the advance, and followed the same trail; but oftener the trader was ahead. Most of the Catholic writers are fond of claiming this pioneer work for the missionaries; but the Abbé Ferland is better informed when he allows that it was oftenest the wood-ranger who opened the track for the priest.

The dispersion of the Hurons affected both the priest and the trader. That portion of this afflicted people which had gone west sought the islands of Green Bay, but only to be The Hurons pushed farther by their pursuers. They went on till wander. they reached the Iowas of the plains. Here, in the open country, they longed for the forest, and turned north to the region of the Sioux. Provoking the enmity of that tribe, they turned again south, and found temporary respite on an island in the Mississippi, below Lake Pepin. Passed by their dispersion beyond the reach of the priest, the missionaries sought the

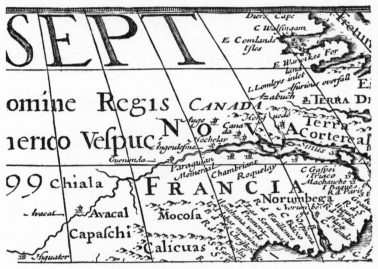

VISSCHER, 1652.

distant west to find others to convert. The old country of the Hurons stripped of its population, the trader also sought the more distant west, to open his trade with other peoples.

But before following new adventurers to the west, let us look at affairs as they were going on in the settlements. 1658. D'Argenson, governor. A new governor, the Vicomte d'Argenson, had arrived in 1658 to enter upon a difficult task. He found the Iroquois again on the alert, and he had scarce a hundred men to bear arms against them. He found the priestly orders which ruled at Montreal and Quebec by no means at peace with each

other.   There had been a struggle between the Sulpitians and
Jesuits to secure a partisan bishop, and the Jesuits had been
the most influential with the Pope.   Laval, the titular bishop
of Petræa, arrived in June, 1659, to assume the chief   Laval ar-
ecclesiastical power in Canada.   He entered upon his   rives, 1659.

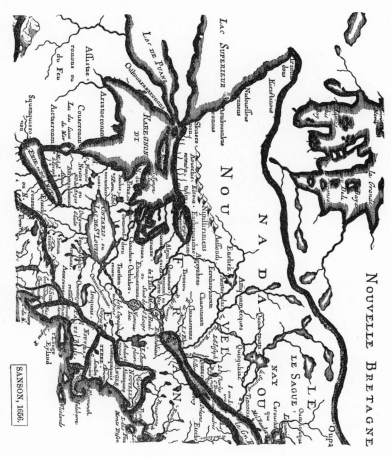

duties in a militant spirit, and the civil rule did not wait long
to feel the severity of his power.

The country which Laval would lay at his feet if he could
was hardly comprehended by Europe, except in France, and not
everywhere there.   Under the influence of the *Relations* which

the Jesuits had annually printed in Paris, the royal cartographer
had improved upon the geography as Champlain had
left it. Sanson, who had been for nearly ten years
the official geographer of France, embodied in his
American map of 1656 all the material which he could command. His configuration of the lower lakes had entirely su-
perseded the drafts of Champlain; but he had not ventured

Maps of New France, 1656, etc.

HEYLYN'S COSMOGRAPHIE, 1656–62.

upon more than a vague extension of those waters farther to
the west, leaving these parts to be improved in his later revi-
sions, ten years afterwards. The Gottfried map of
1655 showed how great an advance Sanson's better
knowledge could accomplish in 1656; but such promi-

Sanson, Gottfried, Blaeu, Creuxius.

nent cartographers among Sanson's contemporaries as the Englishman, Heylin, and Blaeu and Visscher of the Low Countries and Germany, were apparently ignorant of what even Champlain had done. Blaeu for some years continued to make a mere lace-work of rivers stand for the great basin of the St. Lawrence. When Creuxius summarized the narratives of the Jesuits and made a map to accompany his *Histoire du Canada*, he found that Sanson had in the main done the work for him. He still left Michigan and Superior incomplete. He was late enough (1660–1664) to have made something out of the stories of the Ohio, which Le Moyne had brought from the

VISSCHER, 1660 (?).

Iroquois country, but he passed them all by. He even failed to recognize the divide which those who passed to Huron by the Ottawa route had made so well known. These were small faults compared with the entire absence of every development since Champlain, which Du Val in the same year rep- Du Val. resented in his map. This contemporary cartographer shows how slowly the map-makers of Europe moved forward to a conception of this great northern valley.

The time had come to carry still farther the western verge of the map, as Sanson and Creuxius had left it.

Medard Chouart, Sieur des Grosseilliers, had come as a lad
to Canada, and his young manhood was passed in
learning woodcraft as a trader at Lake Huron.   As
early as 1645, he seems to have dreamed that a route from the
Great Lakes to Hudson Bay could be found.   By 1653, he had

Grosseilliers.

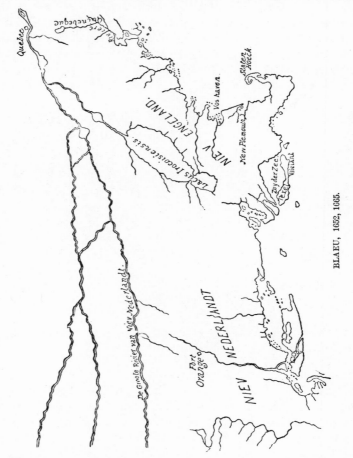

married and settled down among the voyageurs who congregated at Three Rivers.   Here, two years earlier, Pierre
d'Esprit, the Sieur Radisson, had arrived, a lad
when Grosseilliers had reached man's estate.   In one of Radisson's expeditions the Iroquois had captured him, and had

Radisson.

tried to hold him by adoption; but he eluded their watch, and escaped to the Dutch at Albany. Here he was sent down to Manhattan, and, going to Europe, he had returned to Three Rivers in 1654, to find that his sister had become the wife of Grosseilliers. This brought the two men into close relations.

At this juncture, there were fresh stories of a great river at the west flowing to the China Sea. The Mère de l'Incarnation says that the reports had come from distant _{1654.} tribes. This was, perhaps, the earliest mention of such a river obtained from the western tribes, since Nicolet had reported it, twenty years before. We read in the _{Stories of a western river.} *Relation* of 1654 that it was only nine days from the country about Green Bay to the sea which separates America from China.

We know that in August, 1654, two French traders went west and penetrated the country beyond Lake Michigan, and in August, 1656, they led back an Ojibway _{1656.} flotilla with a burden of furs, and reached Quebec. It has been a question who these daring Frenchmen were. Sulte conjectures they were the two brothers-in-law from Three Rivers. They may have been of the party of thirty Frenchmen who started for Lake Superior in 1656, accompanied by the priests Garreau and Druillettes. These last were attacked on the way by Iroquois; Garreau was killed, and the expedition failed.

There is much less certainty that at about the same time, as is claimed, some Englishmen pushed west from the headwaters of the James River in Virginia, and _{Alleged English expedition.} passed the mountains. The story is told in Coxe's *Carolana* as coming from a memorial presented to the English monarch in 1699, and the exploit is ascribed to a Colonel Abraham Wood, who had been ordered to open trade with the western Indians, which he did in several successive journeys. No satisfactory confirmation of the tale has ever been produced.

There is no question that Grosseilliers wintered on the shores of Lake Superior in 1658–59, where he had fallen in _{Lake Superior, 1658-59.} with some of the Sioux and had heard of the great river. He was again on the St. Lawrence in 1659, and was there joined by Radisson. A new expedition was _{1559. New expedition.} planned, and the two started once more with an es-

cort. They were too conspicuous a band to escape the Iroquois,
and it was soon decided that the savages could be better eluded
by a smaller following.   So with a few Indian guides the two
traders pushed on together.   The narrative of their journey

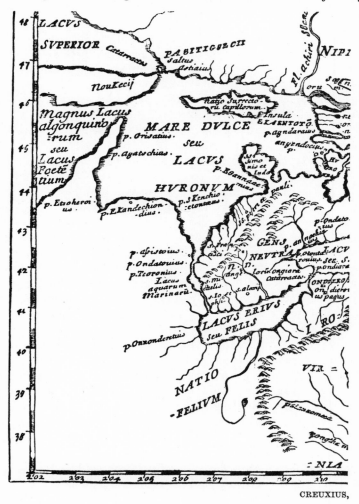

CREUXIUS,

enables us to follow them along the southern shore of Lake Superior, where the pictured rocks excited their wonder.   Radisson records that he was the first Christian who had seen them.

They went on to La Pointe, — the modern Ashland, — and here tarried awhile for their Huron guides to visit some kinsmen at the south, where we have seen those Indian wanderers had already been gathered.

DATED 1660.

Where the two Frenchmen went after this is in dispute. There are those who have held that they pushed directly south from Superior, and others have contended that they returned by the Sault Ste. Marie, and, passing the Straits of Mackinaw, went up Green Bay and took the route by the Fox and Wisconsin. Radisson himself says : " We went to the great river which divides itself in two, where the Hurons had retired. The river is called the Forked because it has two branches, one towards the west, the other towards the south, which we believe runs towards Mexico." They seem to have encountered a band of these fugitive Hurons, who represented the river which passed

At the Mis-sissippi.
the island where they lived to be as large as the St. Lawrence. If the two traders reached the true Mississippi, as some have conjectured, they saw it a dozen years before Joliet floated on its waters.

They did not push very far in this direction, as it would ap-

Lake Supe-rior.
pear, but turned north and wandered about the extreme western end of Lake Superior, and were thus the earliest to define its western limits. Here they found themselves among the Sioux, and heard their strange tongue.

Charlevoix at a later day intimates that in their first contact with the language of this Dacotah family, the French had fancied they perceived a Chinese accent. They thought also that they observed in the customs of the Sioux something like the habits of the Tartars. There was a story circulating at the time, as a part of the argument to prove the close connection of Asia and the Asiatic people with the more distant American tribes, which the French reached. It was to the effect that a Jesuit, Father Grelon, after having served at a mission on Lake Huron, had later been stationed in Chinese Tartary, where he had met a woman who had belonged to his flock in Canada. The theory was that she had been sold from tribe to tribe, and so had passed on to Asia, which could only have happened, as was contended, by the two continents approaching each other nearly, somewhere in the north, or being in fact one.

The result of this intercourse of Radisson and Grosseilliers

1660. At Three Riv-ers.
with the Indians of this remote west was that in the summer of 1660 they led a flotilla of sixty Lake Superior canoes back to Three Rivers. The crews of the summer ships awaiting their cargoes were glad of the furs. The voyageurs lingering about the post found much interest in the stories which were told of these remoter tribes, and of their strange tongue.

Grosseilliers, making a new outfit, started west once more in August (1660). He was accompanied by several Frenchmen, and gave escort to an aged Jesuit missionary, René Ménard. The party passed the winter among some Ottawas on the southern bounds of Lake Superior. These Indians did not prove very tractable converts, and the missionary determined to seek a remnant of the Hurons to the south, which he had heard of as living somewhere in what is now the State of Wisconsin. Ménard started with a single servant. The route was intricate and laborious, by sluggish streams, through tangled swamps, and it involved many portages. In crossing one of them, the aged priest lost the trail of his companions, and was never seen again. A camp kettle which he carried with him, together with his breviary and cassock, were later found in different places among the western tribes. It was never known whether he died by exposure or was killed by wandering savages. If Perrot can be correctly interpreted, Ménard and his companions had already got a sight of the great river.

1696. Grosseilliers starts west with Ménard,

who dies.

We learn from Boucher that all of the party who accompanied Grosseilliers in 1660 to the wilderness, and who were still alive, returned in the summer of 1663 to the settlements, with new conceptions of the geography of that remote region.

Grosseilliers's party returns, 1663.

It was in 1660 that the earliest census of Canada was made, and this shows a total of 3,418 souls, and an appreciable part of this number had been born on the soil. The inhabitants of New England, at the same time, numbered not far from eighty thousand. The Indian element was not included in either calculation; and in Canada, taking the valley below Lake Huron, the savages had never before borne so small a proportion to those of European origin. The statement may possibly be exaggerated that neither along the Ottawa route, nor on the shores of Lake Huron, was there an Indian to be found; but it is certain that there could be but few. "To such an extent," says Father Jocker, "the daring and resoluteness of a few thousand savages had prevailed over an enemy more than ten-fold their own numbers and not wanting in warlike qualities, but incapable of combined action

Iroquois prowess.

and destitute of able leaders." This had been accomplished by a body of Iroquois, reduced at this time to scarcely more than twelve hundred warriors, with perhaps a thousand savage associates, made by adoption their helpers and dependents. Even such a depletion of their numbers did not prevent their still investing the vicinity of Montreal, and even Quebec, with their prowlers, so that for the denizens of those posts to venture beyond support was to invite destruction. Fathers Dablon and Druillettes, ascending the Saguenay to its sources in 1660, found that beyond the Lake of St. John and along the shores of Mistassin, the Montagnais crouched in fear of the Iroquois.

CHAPTER IX.

REORGANIZED CANADA.

1663–1672.

MEANWHILE, a political change had come over Canada. Mazarin had died in 1661, and Colbert, then a man somewhat over forty, had been made comptroller of finance and minister of marine. He was a forceful character. He brought administrative clearness and pluck to bear on industrial and commercial problems. New France was soon to feel the influence of a controlling spirit in old France. Colbert, 1661.

In 1661, an old soldier, Baron Dubois d'Avaugour, had arrived at Quebec as governor. He was a brisk administrator, of unceremonious habits. He was not the man to stand in awe of Laval, and the two held adverse views as respects the propriety of selling liquor to the Indians. A struggle was the consequence. The ecclesiastic sought to coerce the governor by the terrors of excommunication, but the soldier was not alarmed. So Laval went to Paris and succeeded in getting D'Avaugour recalled. The Sieur de Mézy was appointed in his place, — a man destined in turn to become Laval's tormentor. The ecclesiastic and his civil associate reached Quebec September 15, 1663, and on the 18th the governor carried out the churchman's policy by an edict against the liquor traffic. The Jesuits had righteously triumphed. D'Avaugour governor. His contest with Laval. Sieur de Mézy governor, 1663.

D'Avaugour had in his short term of service risen to a high conception of what Canada under fitting patronage might become. Such a portal as the St. Lawrence, he said to Colbert, belonged to the grandest empire of the world. He urged the minister to send out soldiers. They could build forts, root out the Iroquois, he said, and then be turned into colonists. Though a hundred families — counting five hundred souls — were forwarded by the king, with the view of maintaining them a year, it was yet some years before the necessary military force to put the colony in security could be spared from France.

Just at this time (1663), the great change in the administrative control of the country took place. The Hundred

1663. The Hundred Associates abandon their charter. Associates abandoned their charter, and (February 24) New France was restored to the crown. In April the king created a sovereign council to administer the

COLBERT.
[From Sulte's *Canadiens-Français*, vol. iii.]

government of the new royal province. Quebec, which was made the capital, was then a town of 800 people, out of the 2500 which constituted the population of the colony.

But a more comprehensive plan was ripening, under Colbert's instigation, and on May 24, 1664, the monarch instituted the great Company of the West, to govern " for the glory of God and the honor of the French king" the vast range of lands in America, to which the king laid claim. This extent included in North America all New France from Hudson's Bay to Virginia and Florida, embracing the spaces back of the Alleghanies preëmpted in the English charters, and throughout which the new company was to receive the monopoly of trade for forty years. It was not long before the Canadians themselves saw that the country was not worth maintaining in the face of such a monopoly of its commerce. The company, to quiet the discontent, made concession of the trade of the Upper St. Lawrence; but retained that of the lower parts of the river.

1664. Company of the West.

To exercise the general control over all his American possessions, the king dispatched Alexander de Prouville, Marquis de Tracy, to be lieutenant-general over that part of America possessed by France. For the more immediate control of New France he created Daniel de Rémy, Sieur de Courcelles, governor, and made Jean Baptiste Talon intendant. This last office made an associate ruler share in some respects the governor's responsibility, and in others hold him in check.

Marquis de Tracy.

Sieur de Courcelles governor; Talon intendant.

In the early summer of 1665, Tracy, having made a circuit by the West Indies, reached the St. Lawrence, and on June 30 he landed beneath the rock of Quebec. He was now a man of sixty-two. He brought with him some of the troops which D'Avaugour had pleaded for, a few companies of the Carignan-Salières regiment, and these were joined by other companies shortly afterwards. A final quota came in September in the train of Courcelles and Talon. Beside these veterans of the Turkish and other wars, the ordinary accessions to the colony of late had been large, for at least two thousand persons had come over at the royal charge. It seemed as if a new invigoration was in store for the colony. With a force of twelve hundred veterans there was a chance that the frontiers towards the Iroquois could be defended. Within three weeks, Tracy began the erection of forts on the Richelieu, and later he fortified an island in Lake Champlain, where Fort St. Anne became the base in time of still other forward movements.

1665.

But New France was to gain more from the intendant Talon, who had Colbert for his supporter, and his abilities as an ener-

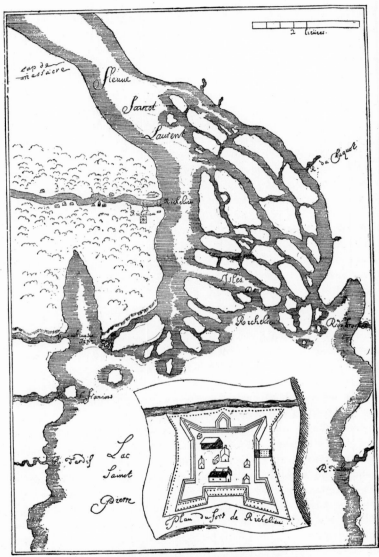

LAKE ST. PIERRE AND THE SOREL RIVER, 1666.
[After Sulte's *Canadiens-Français*, vii.]

getic reformer soon showed that he could, in some ways, overtop
the vice-regal power of the governor. In gorgeous Courcelles
state, Courcelles was supreme; he outranked the in- and Talon.
tendant as a military leader, and was vested with powers to treat
for foreign relations; but in matters of police, justice, and finance,
the intendant was clothed with a power which grew strong
under such vigilance as Talon bestowed. The administration of
Canada had never before known so alert an eye. Everywhere
the people were thrilled by the intendant's energy. No one
had had, in this wilderness, such an ambition for France, and
the French lilies must go wherever man could carry them.
Talon hoped that immigration would follow the symbol, and
he strove to promote it. He went in his purposes further than
even Colbert dared to go, and the home minister was forced
to intimate to his agent that France could not be drained
of its life-blood to furnish settlers for the St. Lawrence. The
English had just captured New Amsterdam, and Talon fancied
that French gold would tempt them to sell it. There was something to the English more alluring than French gold, and that
was an alliance with the Iroquois, and they succeeded easily to
this inheritance from the Dutch.

The vantage-ground which Nicolet had secured at the west
was never fairly appreciated till Talon became intendant of
Canada. He now entered upon the task of proving that explorer's prevision to be worth confirming. The intend- Talon and
ant showed that he had a wonderful faculty of making western
others work for him, and support themselves while discovery.
doing it, and he manifested this in nothing more than in his
prosecution of western discovery. Margry prints various extracts
from Talon's letters, showing his determination to make French
rule pervade the great interior of the continent, and we know
that the Spaniards manifested not a little jealousy at Talon's
projects. They knew that he intended to awe them at the
south, if only he could find a continental stream flowing to the
Gulf of Mexico, with a convenient strategical point near its
debouchement where he could build a fort.

Talon in due time impressed upon the king the necessity of
establishing posts towards the south by which the rivals of

France could be kept from working westward. A renegade Frenchman, one Louis de Page, was at the same time striving to make the English king occupy in force the Isle à Coudres, just below Quebec, so as to prevent succor of the upper country by a French armament, while an English force raided the lakes and secured the country lying towards the Mississippi. Talon held that somewhere in Ontario a fortified station was necessary as the base of an advance towards Florida. The governor entered into the spirit of Talon's purpose, and undertook in

1666, Jan. Courcelles invades the Mohawk country. January, 1666, an armed reconnoissance of the Mohawk country, for this tribe seemed little disposed to respect the peace which the other confederated tribes had made with the French. Courcelles's force increased as he passed Three Rivers, and he commanded not far from five hundred men when he reached Fort Thérèse, well up the Richelieu. He lacked efficient guides, however, and led his force too far to the east, so that on February 20 he found himself at Schenectady. Here he learned that the Dutch rule on the Hudson had given place to the English. This, and the time which his mistake had given to the Mohawks for preparation to receive him, as well as the inclemency of the weather, rendered it prudent for him to retrace his steps, and his baffled force turned to the north.

The Mohawks' escape from what might have been a heavy chastisement hardly conduced to incline them to peace, while the increased power which the French had shown convinced them that it was not to be so easy in the future as in the past to deliver a rapid blow on the St. Lawrence and then retreat. So not one of the uncertain offers of peace which the Mohawks made were as assuring as was expected, and Tracy resolved to deal a blow himself, before the season was over.

October. New invasion under Tracy. In October he was on his way up Lake George, with six hundred troops, as many Canadians, and a hundred Indians. No such force had been seen in Canada before. He fell upon the Mohawk villages one after another, only to find them deserted. He consequently encountered not the least resistance in his devastating march. The dispersion

1667. The Mohawks ask for peace. of the Hurons was avenged. In the spring of 1667, a Mohawk embassy came to Quebec suing for peace, and there was a respite from danger for twenty years all along the St. Lawrence valley. When Tracy returned to

France, — as he did shortly afterwards, — he could carry the comforting assurance that he had conquered a peace. It had long been a complaint of Colbert that the horrors of an Iroquois war sprang largely from the habit of the settlers in pushing their cabins too far from support, in order to meet the fur trader nearer his supply. With a peace assured, the remonstrance lost its force, and the increase of the colony for the next two years shows how the field of habitation was growing constantly wider. The census which marked 3,418 souls at the end of the Iroquois war (1666) two years later had run up to 5,870. 1666. Census.

The peace opened new prospects, and there were chances now to solve the geographical doubts in every direction.

We will look first at the one respecting the north. Twenty years before this, Ragueneau had been questioning the northern Indians hanging about the Huron missions, Explorations north and had learned that their hunters had reached the North Sea in their quest for furs, and that it lay in a straight line towards the pole more than three hundred leagues away. In October, 1660, when Grosseilliers and Radisson had followed up a northern tributary of Lake Superior to Lake by Peré, Grosseilliers, etc. Nepigon, one of their party, named Peré, had discovered beyond the divide a stream, by which it was supposed they could descend to Hudson's Bay.

At a later day, Grosseilliers had sought to test all these conjectures, and during his wanderings it has been asserted, but with no definite proof, that he had actually reached James's Bay, the southern bend of Hudson's Bay, and found that the English, seeking a passage westward farther north, had not yet been there. Returning to Quebec with Radisson, full of enthusiasm for the opening of a new trade, if he had not discovered its exact channel, Grosseilliers had proposed an expedition, by water, descending the St. Lawrence and rounding the Labrador coast. There was not only no response to his enthusiasm by the managers of the company, but he was even fined for trading in the north without a license. The rebuff was enough to make him eager to seek other masters, and he went to Boston to find Grosseilliers in Boston. them. Here he fell in with a Captain Zachary Gillam, who was quite ready to make a hasty run in his ketch to James's

Bay, and Grosseilliers went (1664–65) with him. They accomplished little more than to find the way and re-   1664–65.
turn to Boston.   Here they met Colonel Carr, one   Sails to Hudson's Bay,

HUDSON'S BAY.

of the royal commissioners to receive Manhattan from the
Dutch, and so impressed him with the chance of a new access

to the trade for peltries that Carr wrote about it to Lord Arlington. Carr undertook to secure for the two Frenchmen — for Radisson was with Grosseilliers — a passage to England, and in August, 1665, they sailed from Boston. While in London, they had the favor of an interview with Prince Rupert, and this conspicuous personage and his friends combined to give the adventurers an outfit in two ships, one of which was the "Nonsuch," Captain Gillam, with whom they had sailed to the north from Boston two years before. It was to the New England capital that the expedition, after a successful venture at the north, returned, and we find Wait Winthrop, in December (1671), writing from Boston that Zachary Gillam had come back "from the northwest passage with abundance of beaver." Thence the ships sailed for England, where it became known that the explorers had built and equipped a fort on what they called Rupert's River, thus making a lodgment in the country.

and, Aug., 1665, from Boston to England, thence to Hudson's Bay.

1671.

This was success enough to give form to that great commercial enterprise which had a long history as the Hudson Bay Company. It was soon chartered by the king, and we find the aristocratic names of Prince Rupert and others among its corporators.

Hudson Bay Company.

The future of this monopoly was hardly then divined. The secretary of the Royal Society, when he heard of a grant of vessels to Grosseilliers, wrote to Boyle just as if a northwest passage had already been discovered. There seems to have been no serious purpose in the conduct of the affairs of the company beyond the fur trade and its profits, and neither discovery nor the conversion of the Indians proved to have that share in its interests which was the pretense of its charter.

In November, 1670, word had somehow come to Talon in Quebec that two English vessels were in Hudson's Bay. The Montagnais at this time had been pressed so hard by the Iroquois that they had abandoned the lower Saguenay. So it happened that hunters of the Montagnais had probably sought security in the direction of the northern waters. From them, through the missionaries, it is probable that the news had reached Talon. The natives of this bay region had heretofore traded with the French through the

Nov., 1670. Talon hears of the English ships.

intermediate Ottawas, and Talon was anxious to dispense with such middlemen. He was quite sure, moreover, that the present movement of the English to divert that trade was under the instigation of Grosseilliers. The next year (1671), the intend-

1671. Sends Albanel up the Sague-nay. ant sent Father Albanel up the Saguenay to open the way for a French occupation by founding a mission near the bay. In the following June (1672), that priest pushed on from the upper waters of that river, and by

1672, June 28. At Hud-son's Bay. the 28th he was on the shores of the bay. The country was now taken possession of for the French king, perhaps within sight of vessels flying the English colors, for the Jesuit reported seeing them. We get some account of this undertaking in Father Dablon's *Relation* of 1671-72. Talon at the same time informed the king that he was considering a proposition to send a small bark to the bay by water; but he seems to have been no better prepared for the task then than when Grosseilliers had proposed it. It was not long before the factors of the Hudson Bay Company heard of Albanel's doings, and the officers of the company in England were memorializing the government in the matter of encroachments, and still later La Barre took his turn in complaining to the ministry in Paris of English encroachments.

Let us turn now to the explorations towards the west. The

1665. Ex-plorations west. summer of 1665 had brought down to the settlements a flotilla of canoes from Lake Superior for the annual trade. In August, they were to go back, and under an escort of about four hundred of these savages, a few Frenchmen, including Father Allouez, who was sent to take the place of the luckless Ménard, started on the long return journey. On September 2, he was at the Sault Ste. Marie, and, passing into the great lake beyond, he bestowed upon it the name of Tracy, " in

Allouez on Lake Supe-rior. acknowledgment of the obligations we are under to that man." Later in the same month, Allouez was at the bay where the modern town of Ashland stands, and on the principal island near the inlet, which the French called La Pointe, he founded the mission of the Holy Spirit, with a village of the Chippewas near by, and built a bark chapel for his altar.

There were about eight hundred warriors in the neighborhood, made up of wandering bands of the Algonquin stock, and the father lost no time in making the savages feel that the new representative of his royal master was determined to pursue their old enemy, the Iroquois, until that hated foe was either exterminated or should succumb. It was in his intercourse with these various tribes that the name of the "great water," of which the savages had so often spoken, took form in the phonetic rendering of Allouez as "Missipi," in his enumeration of the tribes which were said to *Hears of the "Missipi."* live along its banks. The priest was inclined from what he heard of that stream to suppose that it entered the Sea of Virginia, as the Chesapeake and its neighboring oceanic waters were sometimes called.

It was during some of his excursions hereabouts, in which he sought to find the great mass of native copper, often described, that Allouez fell in with parties of the Sioux *Sioux country.* (Nadouesiouek). They represented their country as lying to the west of Lake Superior, forty or fifty leagues towards the "Missipi," and as being a prairie region. The savages seemed to speak of their home as the extremity of the earth, but yet represented another people to be still farther west, while beyond the latter lay the great fetid ocean. To the north of them were other tribes, with some that eat meat raw beyond; and still farther was the North Sea, bordering a country which confined the water-shed of Hudson's Bay.

These descriptions were in due time to find their way to the public in the *Jesuit Relations*, and the geographers recognized in them a decided progress in the development of this great Western Mystery.

In 1668, Marquette had founded a mission on the southern side of the Sault Ste. Marie, the earliest in what is now the State of Michigan. Here he was soon joined *1668–69. Marquette and Dablon.* by Dablon, and in September, 1669, Marquette was sent to La Pointe to take the place of Allouez, who had other work to do.

There had been for some time among the tribes on the Fox River, near the head of Green Bay, a few young Frenchmen seeking trade, and yielding to their unbridled passions. They were of a class now beginning to be felt, which has *Coureurs de bois.* passed into history as the *Coureurs de bois,* — a lawless gang, half trader, half explorer, wholly bent on divertisement, and not discouraged by misery or peril. They lived in a certain fashion, to which the missionaries themselves were not averse, as Lemercier shows when he commends the priests of his order as being savages among savages. Charlevoix tells us that while the Indian did not become French, the Frenchman became a savage. Talon speaks of these vagabonds as living as banditti, gathering furs as they could, and bringing them to Albany or Montreal to sell, just as it proved the easiest. If the intendant could have controlled them, he would have made them marry, give up trade and the wilderness, and settle down to work. It was his attempts to do this that drove them into the woods and threw them into the English trade. Their alienation helped the English and embarrassed the French. It was left for Frontenac later to regulate what could not be suppressed.

Father Allouez tells us how he was urged by the savages themselves to go among the tribes at Green Bay and influence to soberer practices a group of these men who congregated there. It was on this mission that he left La Pointe, with the further hope of making some converts among the neighboring Indians. He returned first to the Sault, and left there for his new post òn November 3. Here he spent the winter, and founded the mission of St. Francis Xavier among the Pottawattamies. In April (1670), he ascended the Fox, and found Indians on Lake Winnebago mourning the losses they had experienced in a recent attack by the Senecas. On the Wolf River, an affluent of the Fox, he founded another mission, that of St. Mark, and for a while administered at both missions. In some of his further explorations he reached the head of the Wisconsin, and records that it led to the great river " Messisipi," six days off. The *Relation* of 1669–70 repeats this new story of the great river in speaking of it as more than a league wide, and flowing from the north to the south. It adds that the savages had never reached its mouth, and it was not certain whether it flowed into the Gulf of Florida or into that of California.

1669-70.
Allouez at
Green Bay.

Marquette, whom Allouez had left at La Pointe, was living a disappointed life. He had the remnants of the Hurons and Ottawas about him, who had settled here to

Marquette at
La Pointe.

be, as they hoped, beyond the reach of the Iroquois. Wandering bands of a multitude of tribes came to the post to trade with the French, and among them were parties of the Illinois, living at this time apparently to the west of the Mississippi. Bands of the Sioux, who came too, said to Marquette, as they had to his predecessor, that they lived on the banks of this same broad river. While the poor priest was pondering how he could make his way to this great water, and was picturing more fruitful fields for his labors, a feud was gathering between the Hurons and the ferocious Sioux, these Iroquois of the west, as Marquette called them.

This warfare for a time interfered with a cherished scheme which Marquette had formed of going south to the Illinois, and establishing a mission among that people. He had already undertaken to acquire their tongue from some wanderers of the tribe, and from these Indians he had learned that in coming to La Pointe they had passed a great river, which flowed towards the south, but none of their tribe had ever reached its mouth. According to the stories which Marquette heard from them, there was to the south of the Illinois a people who gathered corn twice a year. The Shawnees had told them, they said, that this distant people wore glass beads, and Marquette conjectured that this fact indicated contact with Europeans. It took thirty days to reach this other people, going south from the Illinois country. There were other stories which came to his ears, as of a river at the west flowing to a sea where large canoes under sail had been seen, and where the tide came and went.

Marquette, in reasoning upon such statements, reached a different conclusion from Allouez, in supposing that the mouth of this river must be, not on the Atlantic side, but on the Pacific, at the Gulf of California. "If I get the canoe," he adds, "which the Indians have promised to make me, I intend with another Frenchman, who can speak with these lower people in their own tongues, to navigate this stream and come in contact with these lower tribes, and so decide the question of the ultimate direction of this great river's flow."

Believes the great river flows to the Pacific.

The reports which at this time were coming in to the Jesuit councils at Quebec, and which were embodied in their *Relation* of 1670–71, speak of the Mississippi, as they had now learned to call the great water, as flowing south either into the Vermilion

Sea (California), or into that of Florida, "since what is known of great rivers in that direction is that they flow into one or the other of these seas." "The Indians say," the report goes on, "that for more than three hundred leagues from its mouth it is wider than the St. Lawrence at Quebec, and that it flows through a treeless prairie land, where the only fuel is turf or dried excrements. As it nears the sea, the woods again grow, and in this region the inhabitants seem like the French, have houses in the water, and cut trees with large knives." This is interpreted by the writer in the *Relation* to mean that the people have ships and hew out planks. "All along the river from the Nadouesse [Sioux] to the south there are many tribes of different customs and tongues, and they make war on each other."

The feud with the Sioux had so extended that the Huron and
Marquette follows the Hurons, 1670-71.
Ottawa fugitives, unused to victory, moved away from La Pointe to avoid a conflict, and Marquette followed them. We shall see that Dollier found him at the Sault Ste. Marie, in 1670. The next year (1671), we find him among the Hurons on the north shore of the Straits of Mackinaw, where they had stopped in their flight, and here Marquette founded the mission of St. Ignace. At the same time another
André with the Ottawas.
priest, Louis André, who had first joined Marquette at La Pointe, settled with the Ottawas in their retreat at the Great Manitoulin Island. The chastisement which had been given by Tracy to their inveterate enemies, and of which they had heard, seemed now to embolden the Ottawas to move toward their old country, west of Lake Huron.

But before this there had been an imposing ceremonial at
Nicolas Perrot, 1670.
the Sault Ste. Marie. Among the better class of the wild wanderers of the woods was one Nicolas Perrot, who had been long enough among the Indians to acquire some ascendancy over them. His countrymen had confidence in him, — another point in his favor. He was now in the full prime of physical vigor; young enough to endure and show others how to endure. He was twenty-six or thereabouts. In the summer of 1670, after he had spent a winter among the western tribes, a long line of fur-laden canoes trailed along the Ottawa route under his guidance.

Perrot came to Quebec at a time which was opportune for Talon's projects. The intendant had, before this, dispatched Joliet to the extreme west to seek for the mines of copper, said to lie thereabouts, but that pioneer had failed to discover them. Talon was now ready to send an official expedition of larger aims, with the certainty, as he thought, of establishing such relations with the tribes of that region as would serve, in some measure at least, to balk the English in their efforts to draw the Indian trade to stations on Hudson's Bay.

There might well have been in Talon's mind other plans of the English which troubled him. The scheme of the rival crown in granting charters along the Atlantic seaboard during the preceding sixty years could hardly have been unknown to the French government. The charter of Virginia formulated a claim for extension "up into the land throughout from sea to sea west and northwest," and this description stretched their claim, as later discoveries had shown, over the very country which for nearly forty years the French wood-rangers and priests had been exploring. The opinion which has been since advanced, that the annulling of the Virginia charter in 1624 by *quo warranto* was equivalent to an abandonment of this right of extension beyond the Alleghanies, was hardly in mind then, and the English Commonwealth, in 1651, certainly reaffirmed this inordinate sea-to-sea pretension. The later charters of Massachusetts and Connecticut recognized this extravagant right, though the subsequent grants to the Duke of York and Penn were in disregard of it. It has been asserted that the authorities in Virginia just at this time were giving practical expression to their alleged rights beyond the mountains in sending out expeditions to find and determine the direction of the streams of the great inland water-shed. We need not regard stories trumped up at a much later period to enforce the English claim along the Ohio, such as that which Thomas Hutchins tells of a Captain Bolt reaching the Mississippi by this route in 1670. It is to be feared that there is no weightier ground for believing that in September, 1671, just after the French had made the ceremonial at the Sault Ste. Marie, soon to be described, Governor Berkeley of Virginia sent Captain Thomas Batts, with a party of English and Indians, over the mountains

Virginia charter.

1671. Alleged English expedition over the Alleghanies.

to observe the course of these western currents. We shall revert to this story in the next chapter.

Of the sufficiently accredited and far more imposing effort at continental occupation, to which in the very same year Talon was giving direction along the Great Lakes, Simon François Daumont, Sieur St. Lusson, had been selected the leader. He had been commissioned the previous year, September 3, 1670. In October, the party started. There was a small retinue, but what was vastly more important, the indispensable Perrot was of the number. When the party reached the Manitoulin Islands, St. Lusson remained there in camp for the winter. Toward spring, Perrot, who had instructions both from Courcelles and Talon, went on to the more distant regions to prepare the Indians for the scene they were to witness. We get the story in good part from Perrot's own memoirs. This narrative served Charlevoix in his account of the events; but it was not given to the modern scholar till Father Tailhan edited it from the manuscript in Paris in 1864. It had been in good part used by La Potherie, and the English reader had known something of it before in such parts of it as Colden included in his *Five Nations*. This memoir makes reference to other writings of Perrot, involving his knowledge of savage life and history, but no other manuscript has come down to us.

1670-71. St. Lusson's expedition.

Perrot's memoirs.

It was the purpose of the authorities to have an august ceremony at the Sault Ste. Marie in the following summer, and Perrot's mission in going ahead was to arrange with the tribes neighboring to Green Bay that they should accompany him to the Sault in the spring (1671). He seems to have elicited a showy welcome among these tribes, where he was regaled with feasts and exhilarated with mock fights. By May, a large concourse of savages had assembled at the appointed place. There were not only those who had come with Perrot from Green Bay, but others had responded to the call of messengers sent west and north, and even from the east, they came, as far as from Lake Nipissing, — fourteen tribes in all, as their representatives were counted. St. Lusson had come, as was expected, and in his train was Louis Joliet, a name already become conspicuous in this western exploration, as we have seen, and he had apparently been the earliest to visit Green Bay (1668) since the time of Nicolet. It was on the 14th of June that all was ready, and we may follow the *Relation* of 1671 in describing what took place.

To the top of a hill near the Sault, St. Lusson led the motley throng, — soldier, priest, and savage, all in their holiday array. We have the signatures of those who were conspicuous in the ceremonials, attached to the instrument, recording their assumption of power for the French king over all the territory from the North to the South Sea, and extending to the ocean on the west. What such a range meant, not one of them knew. Among these signatures we read the names of four Jesuits, Claude Dablon, Gabriel Druillettes, Claude Allouez, and Louis André. Druillettes was the most interesting of this group, both from the experience which a long life had given him, and from his knowledge of the English, whom he had known a score of years before when he had been sent to Boston to gain their alliance against the Iroquois, and whose rights they were on the point of contesting in a regal act of possession. It devolved upon Dablon as the superior of the lake missions to bless a wooden cross which had been prepared. The dusky faces of the encircled savages, with glimmering eyes, wide with wonder, were turned from all sides towards this central group of Europeans. As the huge cross was lifted from one end and dropped into its cavity, the uncovered French chanted a hymn of the seventh century, —

1671, June 14. The ceremony at the Sault.

> "Vexilla Regis proderunt
> Fulget crucis mysterium," etc.

This done, a plate on which was engraved the royal arms was set on a post close by the cross, while the *Exaudiat* was sung and a priest offered a prayer for the king. St. Lusson then, lifting a sod and holding forth his sword, took formal possession of the soil in the name of His Most Christian Majesty. *Vive le Roi* was the shout of the Frenchmen in recognition of this claim of sovereignty; and the wild Indians howled in concert.

Father Dablon has preserved for us the curious speech which Allouez made to the assembled savages. Allouez was, on more than one such occasion, the preferred spokesman of his order. He was not unused to the Indian method of harangue. He told

them that the great monarch of France fought amid his warriors
until he was gory with the blood of those he had slain.   The
mighty king of the French did not resort to scalping to score
the number of his victims, because the streams of blood which
he caused to flow were a much better reckoning!   There was
much else of like grimness in the Jesuit's speech.

There was something fortuitously grand in the geographical
conception of these Frenchmen at the Sault Ste. Marie.
There was hardly a spot on the continent that opened
more striking vistas of domination along such lines of
transit as nature had provided here.   Marquette had divined it
in relation to the missionary service.   "Mackinac," he says,
" is the portal of the southern tribes, as the Sault Ste. Marie is
of those of the north and west, and many nations pass these
gates to reach the settlements of the French."

The geo-graphical position of the Sault.

Talon could but have an inadequate conception of what his
representative had done.   In making a report to the home government of what St. Lusson had accomplished, the intendant
had expressed the opinion that this officer had penetrated to a
point not more than three hundred leagues from the " extremity
of the land " at the Vermilion or South Sea, and that thence one
would have to sail fifteen hundred leagues to reach China and
Japan.

From Lake Superior as a centre, the French had reached at
this time some pretty definite conclusions as to a route to Hudson's Bay ; but of the great tracts of the Canadian northwest
with its icy sea towards the pole, and rocky barriers towards the
setting sun, there was yet nothing, even in the Indian reports,
to shape the ideas of its future.   To the south and southwest
the expectation was more definite, and it was not long before
the great water of the Mississippi was to be revealed, if it had
not already been glimpsed.

The same *Relation* (1671) which had given an account of
the ceremonials under St. Lusson contained the earliest map of a completed Lake Superior, which in
a few details as to missions was rectified in a part of
the edition of the *Relation* for the next year.   Parkman holds
that this Jesuit map has been unduly praised for accuracy in

1671. Jesuit map of Lake Superior.

comparison with other Canadian maps of that day; but it is doubtful if any better was engraved. It was certainly a surprising improvement upon what the leading cartographers of Europe at this time were letting pass for the geography of this region. The Dutch Montanus a year before (1670) had reached no conclusions from all that had come to his knowledge, except that there was some sort of a big sea thereabouts. After the Jesuit map was published, a German editor of Montanus, in 1673, reëngraved the Dutch map, and let it stand as before. Ogilby, though he based his English work on Mon- Montanus, tanus in its text, seems for the whole western region Ogilby. to have advanced scarcely beyond Champlain. This English geographer had not even heard of the Ottawa route which *Relation* after *Relation* had emphasized, and neither Michigan nor Superior, in even a rudimentary shape, appear in his map, showing how little recourse was had by the northern geographers of Europe to the records of the French missionaries. This neglect of opportunities is nowhere more apparent than in the map of his province of Maryland, which was made for Lord Baltimore in the very year of St. Lusson's pageant. This was a survey by Augustine Hérman, a Bohemian engineer, who paid for a tract of land assigned to him by the lord proprietor, by this cartographical service. The map was published in London, in 1670, and in a legend upon it we read : " These mighty high and great mountains [meaning the Appalachians] are supposed to be the very middle ridge of Northern America. And, as Indians report, from the other side, westward do the rivers take their original issuing out into the west sea."

Ogilby had made of Lake Erie a mere river, — but we need now to show how quite other notions had prevailed for a year or two, of this last of the Great Lakes to be Lake Erie. developed.

When Talon wrote to Colbert, in 1670, that he had sent resolute people to go farther west than any one had gone before, it is supposed — and indeed it may be held to be certain — that he meant to refer to St. Lusson, as he added that one such had gone to the west and northwest. He probably also had La Salle in mind when he said that another had gone south and southwest. We get upon debatable ground at this time in trying to find out precisely what this new actor on the scene did in these

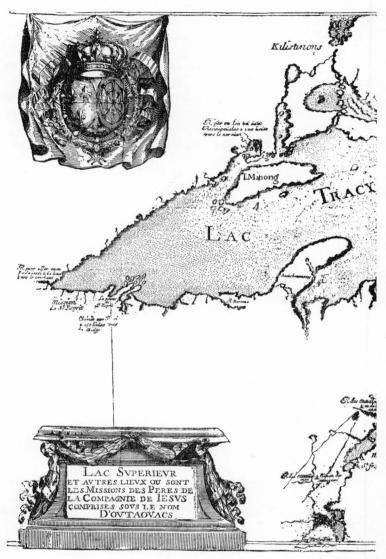

LAKE SUPERIOR.

[From the *Jesuit Relation*, 1672.]

years before Marquette and Joliet made their unquestioned visit to the Mississippi in 1673.

OGILBY, 1670.

René Robert Cavelier, of an old and rich burgher family at Rouen, is known in American history as the Sieur de la Salle, from an estate of his family near that Norman town. Early in life he was a Jesuit novice, or at least the evidence is suggestive, if not conclusive, that he was ; and it is usually said that he left the order because of his unwillingness to curb his independent spirit. A defection of this sort — grant it true — would naturally deprive him of the sympathies of that order, and that it did has been sometimes inferred from the studious absence of all reference to him and his doings in the published *Relations* of the Canadian Jesuits. The only direct statement that he had been connected with the Jesuits comes from Hennepin, — a dubious authority, — and some writers on Canadian history, like Kingsford, have failed to find any corroborative evidence. His own nature hardly fitted him for the servility of the Jesuits, for he had an ardent temperament difficult to restrain, and an ambition suited better to independency than to a religious subjection. His enthusiasm made friends for him ; but his headlong conduct sometimes lost them.

La Salle.

His relations with the Jesuits.

His character.

Having a brother in Canada of the Sulpitian fraternity, he was led to join him. He was about twenty-three when we first find him at Montreal. It will be remembered that this town had been founded by priests of the Sulpitian order, not far from the time when La Salle was born, and that order's incorporated seminary was now the feudal lord of a large landed property thereabouts. The Iroquois wars had operated to hinder settlement of their outlying lands, but now that peace had come there were eager bidders for grants of lands, and among them was the young La Salle. From this source he received a tract of territory just at the head of the rapids above Montreal, admirably fitted as a station for the fur trade, as Champlain had pointed out over thirty years before. The spot was several miles from the thinly peopled squares of the town, surrounded by forests, and fit to be converted into an outpost of the settlement, and such the Sulpitian fathers expected La Salle to make it.

At Montreal, 1667.

It was apparently near the close of 1667 that he secured his land, and during the winter he began to clear it. By the end of 1668, he had ten or twelve acres under cultivation, and had begun a palisaded village. He granted land both within and without these defenses to such as could be induced

1668.

to become his tenants, and a large common was set aside for the public use.   He began buildings for his own occupancy, evidently with the intention of leading the life of a resident seigneur, and he protected himself from over-neighborly intrusion by leaving broad unoccupied acres — more than four hundred, it is said — about his homestead, wherever this was, for there is some contro-

LA SALLE.
[From a copy of an old Engraving given by Gravier.]

versy as to its exact position in his grant.   Here he lived for a while, by no means inactively.   He went on excursions towards the north, and we are told that he became satisfied there was no practicable communication to be had that way with any western sea.   He conned the Indian tongues, and gained some proficiency in such studies.

La Salle, however, was too much fascinated with the visions

of an explorer to make a good settler, and when some Senecas, in the winter of 1668–69, visited his post, he was freshly aroused by the way in which they depicted to him the course of a great river, rising in their country and making its way to the southward for such a distance that it would take eight or nine months for a canoe to follow it to the sea. The story is comprehensible to-day by combining in one the courses of the Alleghany, the Ohio, and the Mississippi, but to La Salle's imagination it was a vision of the great waterway which had been looked for from the time of Cartier. In the turn which geographical conceptions respecting the interior of North America had been for some years taking, it seemed probable then that this outlet of the long river must be in the Gulf of California. It was a grateful thought that this would make it a ready channel to the South Sea, and give the French access to a route to China, quite as convenient as that of the Spaniards from Acapulco.

1669. Senecas at his post tell of a great waterway to the southward.

To embark on such an enterprise as to search for this river accorded quite with La Salle's temper; but as he had invested all he had in his seigneury, he was without the necessary funds for an equipment. With the hope that he could secure countenance, and perhaps more active aid, from the authorities at Quebec, he went thither. Courcelles gave him letters patent, authorizing him to make discoveries, and commended him to the kind notice of the rulers in Virginia and Florida, if he should chance to come within their jurisdictions. With these credentials La Salle returned to Montreal, and began a treaty for the sale of his estate; but before it was concluded, he entered into certain contracts with those who were to accompany him, including the Sieur de la Roussilière, who was to be the surgeon of the expedition. These contracts indicate that he was not at all sure what direction he should ultimately take, whether to the north or the south, and he evidently meant to leave himself free to profit by circumstances as they might arise, for his men bound themselves to follow him in either direction.

La Salle plans an expedition.

Meanwhile, there were other considerations to enter into his plan. Dollier de Casson, a Sulpitian priest, had passed a winter in the Nipissing country. He had a daring habit, which had been nurtured in early life as a trooper of

Dollier de Casson.

Turenne's army, and more recently under Courcelles in his inroad into the Iroquois country. During this winter in the wilderness, Dollier had seen a slave of the Indians, whose own country was afar off towards the southwest, and he had sent the savage to Montreal. Here the fellow inspired Queylus of the Sulpitian mission with a desire to reach with his missionaries this distant land, of which its native spoke so glowingly. In the autumn of 1668, that Sulpitian had established a mission station for his order at the Bay of Quinté, on the northern verge of Lake Ontario, and he was quite in the mood of adding to the Sulpitian agencies another in this distant region, some seven or eight hundred leagues away, as they understood the slave's story. Queylus represented to Dollier that the chance of guidance thither, which this man offered, was an opportunity not to be lost in the service of the church. Dollier had agreed to the proposition, when Laval opportunely came to Montreal, and gave Dollier a letter of authority (May 15, 1669), and commended him to the assistance of the Jesuits, wherever he might encounter them. Laval recommended him to work among the Ottawas of the Mississippi region, using that tribal name in a generic way, and applying it to all that people's kindred, wherever they might be found.

Just here it occurred to Courcelles to strengthen the chances of success by uniting La Salle's and the Sulpitians' parties in one enterprise, and he urged upon the Sulpitians to abandon the direct western route, which they had proposed, and to follow the more southerly direction which La Salle intended. Galinée, another Sulpitian, somewhat versed in surveying processes, had been joined with Dollier, and the two now came into Courcelles's plan. The expedition thus took on a sort of double control, which did not argue well for its success. Queylus, not having great faith in La Salle's proficiency in the native tongues, added a Dutchman to the company, who could talk in Iroquois, but who unfortunately had little knowledge of French.

On July 6, 1669, La Salle concluded the contract for the sale of his landed property, and on the same day the little flotilla floated out into the St. Lawrence and headed upstream. The party was more than half of La Salle's

[marginal notes:] Queylus. — 1669. — La Salle and the Sulpitians join, — and start, 1669, July 6.

choosing. The twenty men which constituted it, in their seven canoes, looked back to those who wished them God-speed with not all the assurance that sometimes emboldens doubtful enterprises, for there was by no means a certainty that the peace with the Iroquois was stable enough to last till their intended

LAVAL.
[From Sulte's *Canadiens-Français*, vi.]

intercourse with those Indians was passed. Two canoes of Senecas returning to their homes led the way as guides.

In following the events of the expedition, we must depend upon the journal which Galinée has left, now preserved in the great library at Paris. Of the map which accompanies it there is a copy in the library of Harvard College, from which the annexed sketch is made.

Galinée's journal and map.

The contents of this journal were first made known to American scholars by Mr. O. H. Marshall in 1874, but the full text appeared later in Margry's documentary publication.

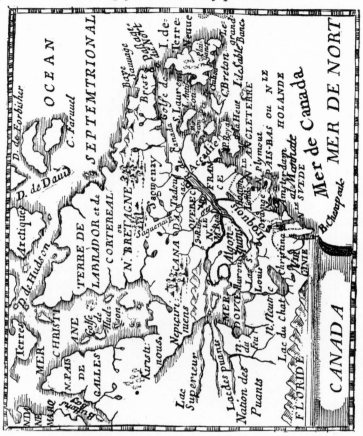

[From P. Duval's *Géographie Universelle*. This atlas of a French Geographer Royal served to keep up the notion (1658–1682) that the Ottawa and not the Niagara conducted the waters of Lake Erie to the sea.]

The object of La Salle was first to go to the Seneca villages, where he hoped to obtain guides for further progress. The canoes passed into Lake Ontario, and, following the southern shore, they reached Irondequoit Bay on August 26, 1669. On this same day, Fremin and Garnier, who were holding the Jesuit mission among the Senecas,

August 26.
At Ironde-
quoit Bay.

left their post for Onondaga to attend a general council of the Jesuits then working in the Iroquois country. It has been suspected that they got word of the landing at Irondequoit and absented themselves conveniently, in order to harass the Sulpitians by depriving them of the means of communication with the Indians. From the landing, La Salle, Galinée, and a few others made their way to the mission, only to find that the Jesuits, to whom the letter of Laval accredited them for kind offices, were gone. What Fremin and his companion had anticipated — if the theory of willful desertion is allowed — was soon apparent, for it does not appear that La Salle's acquaintance with the Iroquois tongue was of much service, and the strangers were sadly at a loss in trying to communicate their desire to secure guides. The savages could do nothing but feast the newcomers. They after their own fashion added to the entertainment by putting to the torture a prisoner whom it was supposed they had captured on the bank of the very river of which La Salle was dreaming. What intelligent intercourse the French had seems to have been brought about by the aid of a servant of Fremin, whom that missionary had left behind, and through him La Salle tried to ransom the poor prisoner, as likely to be such a guide as he wanted, but he could offer no inducement equal to the joys of torturing. Through the same interpreter the French got new descriptions of a broad prairie land to the south, which stretched a long distance without trees; and they heard, as Galinée's journal tells us, of a people who lived in a warm and fertile country, hard by a river which flowed so that it must run ultimately, as was thought, into the Mexican Gulf or the Vermilion Sea. Such were the reports of the yet undiscovered Ohio.

Among the Senecas. Hears of the Ohio.

The feasts, in which the visitors shared, resulted in drunken orgies, and the Frenchmen began to be alarmed at the possible dangers of inflamed passions. They had heard, moreover, that there was farther to the west a better way of finding this river. All this easily moved them to return to the lake, which they did without mishap.

Once more afloat, the little flotilla moved on towards the setting sun. They passed the Niagara River without entering it, and noted the sound of the distant cataract, and Galinée's account of it is perhaps the earli-

Hears the sound of Niagara.

est we have, except from Indian sources. They reached at last
the extreme western end of Ontario, and found welcome at an
Indian village. Here La Salle came in contact with a prisoner
from the Shawnee tribe held by these villagers, and this man
told the French that it was a six weeks' journey from where
they were to the great river, and that he could lead them there.
It was contrived to make this fellow's captors offer him as a
gift, and La Salle gladly accepted him.

Just at this juncture, word came from a neighboring village
that two Frenchmen had arrived there from the west. We
must go back a little to account for their appearance.

In February, 1669, Talon, who was then in France, informed
Colbert that he had brought with him from Canada a young
voyageur who felt confident of finding a way from Lake Huron either to the South Sea or to Hudson's Bay, and that the
man had already gone to a greater distance west than any one
else, and was ready to go still farther. This was Peré,
a frequent figure in these western explorations, and
when Talon shortly after returned to Canada, Peré was with
him. With Colbert's countenance, the intendant was prepared
to make new efforts to probe the secrets of the west. Plans
were soon made, and Joliet, then at the settlements, together
with Peré, was sent with the chief object of discovering
the deposits of copper near Lake Superior, of which
there had been many stories afloat. He was also expected to
discover if there was not a way of bringing the ore to Quebec
better than that by the Ottawa route, with its laborious portages. Colbert had not failed to make Talon understand that
to discover and make merchantable at a profit such copper deposits was of more importance than to find any passage to the
South Sea, and for some time after this Talon fed the minis-
terial cupidity with such stories as he could gather of huge
lumps of copper lying exposed on the shores and islands of
Lake Superior.

It now turned out that the Frenchmen whom La Salle found
to be in his vicinity were Joliet and his companion,
on their return from this copper-seeking expedition.
La Salle and Joliet were not long in establishing friendship,
and the young explorer, who was not far from the age of
La Salle, had much to say that interested the other. Joliet

Peré and

Joliet sent west.

They meet La Salle.

told these new friends about his journey, and though, as it seemed, he was not to carry back to the intendant any extravagant hopes about copper, he could tell him of a new way which he had opened for the growing communications with the west. He had descended the strait which led from Huron to Erie, and had for the first time followed eastward the northern shore of that lake. Fearing if he continued to its outlet by the Niagara River that he would encounter the Iroquois, Joliet had turned up the valley of the Grand River, — an affluent on its northern shore, — and by this route had struck the shores of Ontario near its western extremity. He exhibited to La Salle a map which he had made of his route, extending in its most western limit to the land of the Pottawattamies and other more remote tribes, which the missionaries had not yet reached. This map appealed more to the Sulpitians than it did to La Salle, who was little inclined to abandon his purpose of finding a more direct southwestern route.

So it was resolved that the party going west should be divided, and the two divisions parted company, not without some sarcasm on Galinée's side, who would have us believe that La Salle's determination to stay behind was *La Salle separates from Galinée and Dollier,* quite as much due to an illness brought on by the sight of some rattlesnakes as by any choice of route. Before separating, however, they all joined in the celebration of mass, and then the Sulpitians took the trail to the Grand River and Lake Erie, as they had learned it from Joliet.

On reaching the lake shore, Dollier and his companion found a sheltered place for a winter's sojourn, and built their bark huts and closed in their solitary altar. The *who winter on Lake Erie,* months passed quietly. They found food, and suffered nothing from intruders. They had looked during these weary weeks across the great lake, and gazed wistfully upon its limitless waters, gentle or in turmoil as the storms came and went. But not an object along that southern horizon helped them to picture that distant unseen shore of the lake where, as yet, no white man had trod. It was to remain, as it proved, for many long years, almost unknown to the explorer, if for no other reason, because a passage following it westward is thirty leagues longer than the route which skirts the northern shore.

As the spring approached, these solitary wanderers made

ready to move on ; but before departing they raised a cross and
and take
possession of
the country.
formally took possession of the country in the name of
the French king.   The instrument which they sub-
scribed is still preserved, and is printed by Margry.

This ceremony over, they bade adieu to what had been to them
on the whole a fortunate retreat, and, packing their altar service
and munitions in their canoes, they paddled to the west, facing
1670.
the balmy air of the spring.   This was on March 26.
But a mishap overtook them.   One night, landing
for their rest, they failed to secure their canoes properly, and,
the wind rising while they slept, one of their boats was washed
out into the lake, and disappeared.   It contained their religious
symbols and their store of powder.   The dilemma of being in
the wilderness without sacred vessels and with no defense was
enough to make it apparent that they must abandon their purpose of establishing missions, and seek to return as best they
could.   The obvious course was to make their way to one of
the western posts and seek an escort of the annual flotilla down
the lakes.

If Joliet had been the first white man to pass the Detroit
River, going east, Dollier and his companion, taking that track
in a reverse way, were the earliest to paddle by the same river
from Erie to Huron.   They now passed to the Sault Ste. Marie,
and reached its mission in May, 1670.   Here they found two
priests, Dablon and Marquette, in a palisaded inclosure, with a
chapel within.   These missionaries had started a garden close
at hand, and were thus the earliest to begin to develop the
agricultural resources of that region.   Laval's commendations
of the new-comers to the Jesuits seemed likely to produce no
better welcome here than in the Seneca country, and the Sulpitians hardly cared to tarry in order to make larger trial of
their hosts' hospitality.   So, securing a French guide, they did
not wait for the annual flotilla, but followed at once the Ottawa route, and by June 18 they were again in Montreal.
Galinée took this first respite from his labors to prepare a plot
of the region which he and Dollier had traversed.   It is the
earliest map which has come down to us of the upper lakes,
constructed a year before St. Lusson, as we have seen, made
his ceremonial at the Sault.   One of the marked features of
this Galinée map is a sketch of the northern shores of Lake

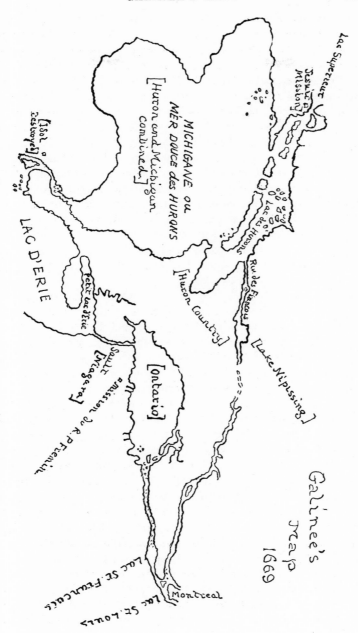

Galinee's
map
1669

Erie, never before comprehended, and henceforward the narrow river of Champlain was to give place to something like an adequate conception of this last of the Great Lakes to be mapped. It is somewhat surprising to find an entire absence of the Straits of Mackinaw, and apparently Michigan and Huron are made one expanse. It is also clear that Galinée had not yet surmised what the Jesuit map of Lake Superior was so soon to make clear, that the great water beyond the Sault Ste. Marie was larger than the Mer Douce, on the hither side of that strait. Dablon and Marquette, during the stay of Dollier and Galinée at the Sault, had apparently been reticent as to what had been done towards developing the outline of the larger lake. This map of Galinée is supposed to be the one to which reference is made in the *Relation* of 1670–71, as showing the missions among the Ottawas, where it is described as " very curious and very exact, inasmuch as they have set down nothing but what these two fathers, who made the journey, had seen."

We need now to try to discover what was done by La

La Salle's   Salle after he parted with the Sulpitians, and after
movements.   he had had his interview with Joliet at the western
end of Ontario. It is not quite certain that his particular companions stood by him in what subsequently happened, and some of them at least are supposed by Faillon to have deserted La Salle, returning to Montreal, perhaps, with Joliet. It is not easy to account for the lack of definite information as to the way in which La Salle, with what following he kept, now turned, unless it be supposed that his maps and journals for the next two years have never come to the knowledge of those who could use them in making a record of his movements. There are somewhat vague statements as to such papers being in existence about the middle of the last century ; but the tale is shrouded with doubt. Indeed, every statement which we have about La Salle's wanderings at this time is open to suspicion.

1670.   Perrot says that he met La Salle on the Ottawa in
1670 ; but there is nothing known to corroborate such an assertion, and it seems improbable. What purports to be a record of talks, which La Salle later made at Paris, in 1678, referring to this obscure period of his life, is found in a *Histoire de Monsieur La Salle*, which Margry prints. Who La Salle's

interlocutor was is not known, and this and other doubtful aspects of the paper have caused divided opinions as to its trustworthiness, and there is strong tendency among careful investigators to give it scant credence.

Margry, who does not waver in his trust in the document, used it, to his own satisfaction at least, in presenting a claim for La Salle to have found the Ohio in 1670, reaching the Mississippi by it, and in 1671 to have gone by Lake Michigan to the Chicago portage, and so to have reached the "great water" once more by the channel of the Illinois. This, if true, places to La Salle's credit the discovery of both the Ohio and the Mississippi. It is noteworthy that this claim for La Salle, a Norman, has found its chief supporters in Margry and Gravier, both natives of the same part of France. Some other writers, like Butterfield, have given it a qualified adhesion. It has not, however, been accepted by most of those entitled to be heard, and indeed Margry's reputation has been pretty severely handled in general by those who have tracked his historical methods. Suspicion has more than once arisen both as to his honesty and official fidelity as a keeper of records held for the public advantage. Eminent assailants like Major and Shea have not been tender in their blows.

Margry's view is that he reached the Mississippi.

Margry's character.

This *Histoire* makes La Salle leave the spot where he parted with Dollier, and return to the Iroquois country, and pass thence south by Onondaga. It is not easy to discover what water route through the wilderness could have taken him by Onondaga, and various conjectures have been advanced to open a probable way for him. Denonville, at a later day, says that La Salle had been at Niagara in 1668, and this has been supposed to refer to his passage by the portage of the great cataract at this time. There is also the route which we may conjecture he took by French Creek, and that by Chautauqua Lake, both known later to the French; or possibly, as Gravier holds, he may have gone up the river from where Cleveland now stands, and so reached the Muskingum River, — any of which would ultimately have led him to the Ohio. The truth, it is to be feared, is likely forever to elude search.

Doubts about La Salle's course.

The document to which we have referred states in addition

that at the farthest point which La Salle reached, his men deserted him, and left him to wend his way back alone.   Where
was this point of desertion ?   Margry contended for a while
that La Salle had reached the Mississippi when he was thus for-
saken.   Parkman thinks, for various reasons, that it might have
been at the rapids of the Ohio opposite the modern Louisville,
but it is difficult to suppose the descriptions of the *Histoire*
could apply to those rapids, or that he could have
viewed the country below them as the morass which
that narrator declares it to be.   The account says of the descent
of the water, " Ou elle tombe de fort haut dans de vastes ma-
rais."   This presents two difficulties in view of the conditions,
as now understood.   The fall at Louisville is only twenty-seven
feet in two and a half miles, and those who would reconcile the
statement prefer to render " de fort haut " by " after a long
course."   As to the vast marshes, it has been suggested that a
high state of the river may have produced " drowned lands."

Stopped by falls.

In Marcel's additions to Harrisse's *Cartography of New
France*, General J. S. Clark — one of the most assiduous of
our students in this field — is quoted as believing that La
Salle's course was in the first instance by Lake Michigan and
the portage to the Wabash, which La Salle called the Ohio,
and that the falls which stopped him were those of the Wabash
at Logansport, while in 1671–72 he went by the Chicago portage to the Illinois, descending it to Peoria, still calling it the
Ohio.

In what is known as Joliet's larger map, made four years afterwards (1674), there was originally no Ohio River laid down ;
but a later hand has apparently sketched its course, and marked
it as the river " by which the Sieur La Salle had gone to Mexico."   This addition, if authentic, would confirm La Salle's discovery of the Ohio, but would not settle the extent of his traversing it.   But the alteration in the Joliet map is awkward,
and General Clark is not alone in supposing that the change
was fraudulent, in order to make good the claim for La Salle.

Since 1862, when Margry first formulated the claim for La
Salle, he has found some supporters and more detractors.
Under the pressure of adverse criticism, Margry has ceased of
late years to claim that La Salle reached the Mississippi by the

Ohio, but is content to assert that he did nothing more than to follow the latter stream for some distance.

That La Salle reached the Ohio and pursued it for a while is conceded by Parkman and others, and it is contended that La Salle's later memorial to Frontenac (1677) carries a certain confirmation of the claim. Dr. Shea's latest judgment left the question thus: "La Salle by way of Lake Erie reached the Illinois or some other affluent of the Mississippi, but made no report and made no claim, having failed to reach the main river." This decision of the learned author of *The Catholic Church in Colonial Days* puts the conclusion very fairly.

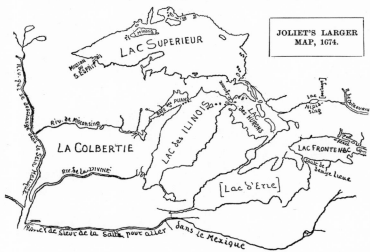

JOLIET'S LARGER MAP, 1674.

If Margry has wavered in his position as respects the Ohio route of La Salle, he has persistently contended for La Salle's passage to the Illinois by the Chicago River, and thence to the Mississippi. That he reached the head of Lake Michigan is not unlikely, but it may

Margry makes La Salle descend the Mississippi.

be a question whether it was the Chicago or St. Joseph River which he entered; and it is still more debatable whether he reached by either route the Mississippi itself. Margry claims that he did, and that he descended it to latitude 36°, which was far enough to satisfy him that its course thence was south to the Gulf of Mexico, and not southwest to the Gulf of California.

There are some embarrassing facts for Margry and his adherents to surmount in any endeavor to put La Salle before Marquette as the actual discoverer of the Mississippi. It was notorious at the time when this *Histoire* purports to have been

JOLIET'S

written (1678), that Marquette had first reached the great river in 1673, and in the intervening years there had been no denial of the fact. If this paper produced by Margry is genuine, it is strange that La Salle's brother and other kindred, when making, after La Salle's death, a memorial to the king for compensation on account of their kinsman's services, do not mention any such expedition of 1671.

The inference is hardly to be avoided, either that the questionable document has deceived Margry, or that he knows more

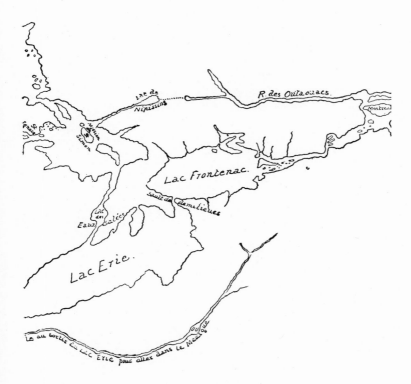

SMALLER MAP.

of its history than he cares to disclose. It is unfortunate that there is any suspicion attached to any paper in the important collection of documents which the United States government has assisted M. Margry to publish.

That La Salle's projects had failed of fruition in the opinion of those who knew the man at Montreal seems to be indicated by the mocking name of La Chine, which they were induced to apply to the estate he had parted with, in derision of his abortive attempt to find his way to China.

CHAPTER X.

THE MISSISSIPPI REACHED.

1673.

THERE have been opinions at times entertained, but upon no recognized authority, that the Jesuit fathers, Deguerre in 1652, Drocoux in 1657, Allouez in 1668, and Pinet in 1670, as well as a priest of the seminary of Quebec, Augustine Meulan de Circe, also in 1670, had visited the Illinois and the Mississippi previous to the expedition of Joliet and Marquette. The late Dr. Shea, who was for many years an ardent student of everything connected with the fame of Marquette, long ago, in the *Collections of the Wisconsin Historical Society* (vol. iii.), set such stories at rest. They apparently originated in the confused brain of a comparatively recent and irresponsible chronicler of Catholic missions in the west.

Early alleged visits to the Mississippi.

There is also a story (referred to in the preceding chapter) of some explorers going from Virginia beyond the Appalachians, in 1671, sent by Governor Berkeley, under the direction of General Wood, "for the finding out the ebbing and flowing of the water on the other side of the mountains, in order to the discovery of the South Sea." This account is in a diary, beginning September 1, 1671, which was first printed in the *New York Colonial Documents* (vol. iii.). It was originally sent to the Royal Society in London, and read before it in August, 1688. The explorers reached their most westerly point on September 17, where they marked some trees with the king's name. From an eminence they then saw "a glimmering light as from water," which they supposed to be a great bay. A certain Mohican Indian informed them of a very large number of Indians living thereabouts upon a great water. Mr. Clayton, who communicated this journal to

Alleged explorations from Virginia, 1671.

the Royal Society, said in a letter dated August 17, 1688, that Colonel Byrd declared the glimmer seen by the explorers not to be a bay with ebb and flow, but a lake then (1688) possessed by the French, who had " seated themselves in the back of Virginia," where there were several large lakes " betwixt that and Canada." John Mitchell, the later geographer of the continent, in some remarks on this story in 1755, made no doubt of its truth, saying that it had already been mentioned, but with less distinctness, by Robert Beverly in his *History of Virginia*, and that the water seen was probably Wood River, as it was later called, or the Great Kenawha, as it is now named.

This same journal records that initials were found cut on trees; and it is assumed that these traces were left by earlier explorers, who had been sent out by the same General or Colonel Wood, as early as 1654, and that their visits were continued till 1664. It is fair to say that the whole story has no sufficient attestation, and is open to a suspicion that the incidents were simply intended to give color to English claims beyond the mountains, of earlier date than the French. It was used certainly for this purpose in tracts by the English at the time of the treaty of 1763.

Mitchell also adds in much the same spirit that a party of New Englanders in 1678 coursed down the Ohio, and crossed the Mississippi; but he produces no proofs, though he asserts that it was the fruit of such exploit which sent La Salle to the Ohio in 1680, certain Indian guides of the English party having later gone to Canada, and accompanied the French explorer. Somehow he ignores the explorations of La Salle in 1669, which he might well never have heard of. We have seen that there is the best of reasons for believing that Nicolet had at least heard of the Mississippi as early as 1634, and that it is not unlikely that Grosseilliers, in 1659, had come in contact with the stream in its upper courses.

Parkman seems to credit a map which does not indeed show the Mississippi, but gives the Ohio to a point a little below Louisville, that stream bearing the legend, " By which La Salle descended." This historian considers the map to have been made before the voyage of Joliet, and that a small section of the upper waters of the Illinois which it shows stands for the exploration which La Salle made of them, in the year following his visit to the Ohio.   This would place the map, if Parkman is right, early in 1673.   There is a legend on it, which shows that the maker of it believed the Mississippi to flow into the Mexican gulf.   Parkman's conclusion as to such priority is disputed, however, by Shea, who claims that a similar map found in the Paris archives was drawn by Joliet himself, after his own exploration.   His inference consequently is that La Salle's exploits were simply added at a later day.   This objection has not induced Parkman to change his views, as they are repeated in his revised edition.

We come to more certain ground when we reach the indubitable expedition of 1673.   There was no cavil heard when the State of Wisconsin placed, in 1885, in the capitol at Washington, a statue of Marquette, as the first explorer of that affluent of the Mississippi which gives a name to the State.

Talon had determined to signalize his administration before it closed by the settlement of two geographical ques- Talon and tions.   He had sent, as we have seen, Father Albanel, ^{discovery.} in August, 1671, to find an easy route north by the Saguenay. On September 17, the priest and his party had reached 1671. Lake St. John, and there the Indians told them of Albanel goes north. two English ships trading in Hudson's Bay.   When the spring opened, the explorers pushed on, and soon found an English trading-house on the shores of the bay.   Avoiding contact, they erected the usual pillar of possession.

Charlevoix tells us that it was the chief ambition of the intendant to solve the problem of the great western river, The search and this was Talon's second geographical problem.   In for a western river. June, 1672, Colbert had written to the intendant that there was no more important movement to be started, after all efforts had been made to insure the increase of the colony, than to make it certain that this great river of the west flowed into the Gulf of California, so that a passage could be opened to the South Sea.   At the same time, this French minister was sending threatening messages to Spain, that the French flag in the Gulf of Mexico could not be disregarded without hazard, as if there might yet be a conflict over the mouth of this same river, should it prove to flow more directly south.   The English, as yet, were hardly observant of this ambitious aim of the French, and, as

Colden tells us, they accounted the pushing energy which carried the Canadians so far west as only the yearning for more productive soils than Canada had been found to possess. While the urgency of Colbert and the hopes of Talon were thus planning for the future, Father Dablon returned from the upper lakes and rehearsed his glowing descriptions, and they were not without effect in giving shape to the skirring notions of the hour.

But there was a new and vigorous spirit just come to the ripening task. Louis de Buade, Comte de Frontenac, had been appointed governor in April, 1672, even before Colbert was sending to Talon his renewed instructions about western explorations. Frontenac did not arrive till the autumn, and Talon soon discovered that he was not a man to his liking, and had time to transmit his adverse criticism before the government named a new intendant, and Talon was recalled. Talon was not alone in feeling the dislike which Frontenac soon succeeded in evoking on all hands.

Frontenac governor, 1672.

Talon recalled.

The new governor was too marked a character every way to make things easy. He was now fifty-two years old, and a successful life as a soldier with honorable wounds made him imperious. His blood was good, with a strong dash in it of Basque virility. His estate was ruined, and he had made an unfortunate marriage. If he could not endure his wife, she never ceased to have a certain pride in him. He by no means gave her the exclusive effects of his prejudices. If thwarted he grew red and chafed, and he made, if he did not find, opportunities for his anger. His will was headstrong. His habits of life were extravagant; so he had sometimes little scruple about using his position to make money. He was consequently continually confronted with disagreeable allegations against his official conduct. He knew how to meet them unblushingly. His language could be at times as full of acerbity as his heart was, when he was aroused; and his conduct had a vindictiveness by which passion sometimes usurped the rights of foresight.

Frontenac's character.

Yet he had his merits, and he served New France as hardly another could at a trying time. He was vigorous, robust, hardy, and when necessary he could draw himself up in grandeur.

He was too liberal in his Catholicism to please the ascetics, but whether this was because he was impelled by wider sympathies, or because he saw some gain in it, may be questioned. He certainly hated the Jesuits, and they bore no love towards him. He was like Talon in one respect, — he would have packed the fathers off to France summarily, if he had dared to do it. The last of their *Relations* which was printed announced Frontenac's arrival in Canada, and that the publication of these annals then ceased has been charged upon his influence. His quarrels with the governor of Montreal and with the Sulpitians were quite as violent as his hate of the Jesuits, and it was only towards the Recollects that he was tolerant, and that perhaps for the reason that he could play them off conveniently against the Jesuits. This enmity of the Jesuits he never quieted, and it played a fateful part in his sustaining the ambition of La Salle. He could be an Indian with the Indians, and the priests never forgave him when he divided with them a control of the savage nature, and welcomed native children into his household.

The Jesuit Relations no longer published.

Frontenac began his administration with an act that drew upon him the reproof of his king. He held a convocation of the three estates, the clergy, the nobles, and the commons, and sought to mete out their powers in a community of government. The king was prompt to disapprove, and the whole machinery of the government, under royal coercion, fell back into the old ruts. Never was there a more fatal infraction of the rule that colonies, to succeed, need to be let alone. The new life of a colony can only become virile by self-reliance and self-assertion. That ancient policy, always lurking in church if not in state, has successfully cultivated respect for absolutism in French-speaking Canada even to the present moment.

The site of Quebec had impressed the new governor, as he approached it for the first time, as fit to be the lordly seat of an empire of courageous men. He found he must make the colony under his master's wand one of subservient subjects. The rebuff turned his thoughts from the scenes around him to distant fields, and he set his heart on the success of exploration.

Frontenac turns to exploration.

Talon already, before the arrival of Frontenac, had selected Joliet for the new task, — a choice which Frontenac confirmed.

This leader was now a little less than thirty years old. He was
Joliet's character. a Canadian by birth, a son of a wagon-maker. He
had been educated under Jesuit influences. A passion
for trade had led him into a roving life, and we have seen that
the government had selected him a few years before to discover
a new route to Lake Superior. In this work he had proved intelligent and useful. His whole career showed that he could be
faithful to his charge, without evincing in any way exceptional
powers of command. Frontenac, after Joliet had started on his
mission, wrote to Colbert that the man had had great experience,
His aims in discovery. and that he promised to find the Mississippi by way
of Green Bay, and that he would probably make it
clear that its outlet was in the Gulf of California. Dablon at
the same time, in reporting to his superior in Paris, counted
upon the expedition opening a way to China and Japan.

La Salle was absent at this period on his somewhat obscure
La Salle's doings. errand in the direction of Lake Michigan. It has been
claimed that he had traversed the Chicago portage,
and had coursed the upper affluent of the Illinois, if he had not
actually, as Margry would have us believe, descended to the
Mississippi itself. As he did not return to Montreal till September, 1672, and as Joliet had left a month before, the latter
could not have known anything of La Salle's efforts, unless
1672, Dec. 8. Joliet at Mackinac. they had met on the way, and of this there is no
record. Joliet, by December 8, had reached Mackinac
(Michillimackinac, as it was then invariably called),
and here he passed the rest of the winter in preparing for the
undertaking and deriving what information he could from the
Indians who hung about that post. He found in the priest
Marquette. Marquette, who kept the mission there, a prompt and
natural sympathy. This Jesuit was eight years the
senior of his companion, and had come of a good family in the
north of France. He had at this time been two years ministering to the vagabond Hurons, who were still trying to keep together under all sorts of adverse circumstances. For five years
before he began his work among this tribe, he had had divers
experiences at other missions. While at St. Esprit, he had come
in contact with wandering bands of the Illinois, and he continued
ever after to harbor the hope that he might at some time find a
way to settle among them, as they had expressed a wish to have

him. Joliet's project therefore appealed strongly to the Jesuit's inclination, as the intended route must lead to the Illinois coun-

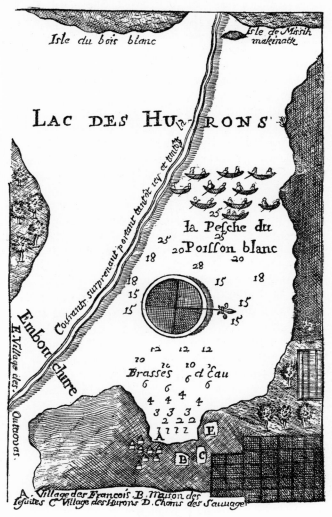

MACKINAC, 1688.

[From La Hontan's *Nouveaux Voyages.*]

try, of which so much had been heard in pleasant contrast to the deadly heat and forbidding monsters that this people insisted on apportioning to the lower country beyond them. Dr. Shea holds that there are reasons for believing that before Joliet left the settlements, Laval had picked out Marquette for the explorer's companion; but the evidence is not clear. That Marquette did decide to join Joliet seems to imply that some higher authority had permitted his leaving his post at Mackinac. Marquette's own assertion to that effect is explicit enough; but any conclusion must certainly leave Joliet as the recognized official head of the expedition.

During the winter, the two drew from the Indians information enough to enable them to map out their route prospectively, but this map is not preserved, unless indeed we have it in some one of the several maps ascribed to Joliet, which are known. All these maps have usually been placed after his experience of 1673.

It was not till May 17, 1673, that the party set out in two
1673, May. Joliet and Marquette start. canoes, — Joliet, Marquette, and five companions. It was nearly forty years since Nicolet had started on the same course, and had been the first to enter what is now known as Green Bay. Late in 1669, Allouez had opened a mission on its west shore, in the midst of a motley population of Indians, a strange mixture of the three great stocks of the Dacotahs, the Huron-Iroquois, and the Algonquins.

This " Grand Baye," perverted by the later English to Green
Green Bay, *Baye des Puans.* Bay, was not inviting in the name it then bore, for from the earliest knowledge which the French had had of it, they had in the *Baye des Puans* associated it with what to an inland Indian was an odor far from agreeable, that of the salt sea. In a then recent *Relation* of the Jesuits, the writer had thought to account for the appellation through the fetid effluvia from the marshes which bordered the bay in some parts. Marquette says he hunted for salt springs, to see if their existence could have suggested the name; but he could find none, and came to the conclusion that the name was given because of the slime and mud " constantly exhaling noisome vapors, which cause the loudest and longest peals of thunder " ! The violent and almost oceanic storms which sometimes swept across it might possibly have been sufficient to suggest the name.

By the end of the first week in June, 1673, the adventurers had ascended the Fox River, and found themselves in the country of the Mascoutins, the Miamis, the Kicka- poos, and the Foxes, — the latter, of all tribes which the French encountered, the most averse apparently to Christian influences. From among these tribes the party secured guides to lead them across the portage. It is another proof that Nicolet had not passed to the Wisconsin, that Marquette believed he had now reached the limits of the early French efforts. The carry they found an easy one, through a level region, and somewhat less than two miles across, through marshes and ponds filled with wild rice. The Fox, indeed, at the point they left it, was but five feet lower than the Wisconsin, and in high stages of water the current of the latter was sometimes diverted towards Green Bay. Once over, and parting with their guides, they launched their canoes on that affluent which the Mascoutins had said would conduct them in a west-southwest course to the great river. Following an obscure and devious channel through a growth of wild oats, they only extricated themselves from its mazes to find their canoes grating upon the sandbars which perplex the navigation of the Wisconsin. If such were their perplexities, there was much about them to command their praise. They soon ran into a region of rich bottom lands, diversified by undulations that were topped with trees. Festooning vines hung from branches which here and there flecked the gentle current with their shadows. Now a dense copse of walnut and oak, as well as trees that were new to them, stretched along the bank. They swept round islands in the stream as it broadened, and saw tangled climbers bearing down the imprisoned bushes. In the opens they espied the roebuck, and encountered singly or in herds " the Illinois oxen clothed in wool," for the buffalo had been more or less familiar to the French for ten years, and now roamed in this region, though destined to be pushed beyond the Mississippi, where the mature man of to-day can remember how they stopped by their surging masses the progress of railway trains, and compelled the steamboats to slow up as they swam the waters of the Missouri ; and where the child of to-day may possibly never see them more.

As the canoes went on, the sun glinted upon fluttering wings

Side notes:

1673, June. On the Fox River.

On the Wisconsin.

Buffaloes.

among the wild rice in one place; and a rocky scarp made shadows in another, where cedars caused a jagged bristling edge to run along the sky. Marquette calls the stream the Mesconsing, for so he had caught the Indian utterance, but the name was later made more liquid in the Ouisconsin of Hennepin, out of which our modern Wisconsin was naturally evolved, and fixed at last by legislative sanction.

It was the 17th of June when their canoes shot out into the parent current and they were afloat on the Mississippi. They sounded and found nineteen fathoms of water, and they might well have believed, had they suspected it, that this mighty channel poured to the sea a greater volume of water than all the united rivers of Europe, if the Volga be omitted. Not forgetting the haughty man at Quebec, whose fortunes he felt he was bearing, Joliet named the river La Buade, in recognition of the governor's family stock. The devotion of Marquette to the great dogma of his church scarcely allowed him to recognize any but the religious motives influencing his share in the adventure, and he fulfilled a promise which he had formed in giving the great river, on his part, the name of Conception, — with something of the fervor which had warmed the Spaniard a century and a half before, when he bestowed upon it at its mouth the name of the Holy Spirit, — a name, however, which had some latitude of application along the gulf shore. Marquette at the same time records its native name as " Missipi."

On the Mississippi.

It must have been with strange and swelling sensations that these wondering men saw the night fall about them. On the one hand a range of high hills lay darkening the declining day. On the other the light of the dropping sun rose from the variegated meadows, and gleamed upward from cloud to cloud; and when all was dark and the stars shone, one may well imagine the immensity of the hope which animated them, and a sense of the uncertainty of the future upon which they had entered.

Neither Joliet nor the priest could have had, in the then existing geographical conceptions of the interior of North America, any adequate idea of the vastness of the valley which they were aiming to acquire for France. The latest geographical conjectures were shown in the map which Sanson published in 1669.

Lake Michigan was depicted in this as of uncertain extent, and from a large bay on the north side of the Gulf of Mexico a group of radiating streams drained the southern part of the valley, while all else was void.

The proclamation of St. Lusson two years before, seeking to embrace a region that stretched between bounding oceans, north, west, and south, was simply audacious and not based on knowledge, — the immensity of the area would have appalled them, had it been suspected. Frontenac, with the inheritance which had officially come to him, had attained perhaps some idea of the half million square miles of territory which afforded two thousand miles of navigable water from the east to the west, in the St. Lawrence and the lakes. He knew that its dividing ridges bordered upon the great interior valley beyond the country of the Iroquois, and again at the head of Lake Michigan, and at no great distance from points which missionaries and traders had reached at Lake Superior. But even Frontenac's imperial eagerness had little conception of a water-shed five times as large as that whose waters flowed before Quebec, and whose central streams could conduct a canoe to the sea over a course three thousand miles in extent from the country of the Senecas; and over another of more than four thousand miles from the head of its greatest affluent, far in the northwest. Thirty-five thousand miles of navigable waters converging into one in the midst of this great valley, and seeking the sea, was a wonder that exceeded even the imagination of Allouez in his astounding speech to the Indians at the ceremonial of St. Lusson, when he was picturing the magnificence of the Grand Monarch. There was a vastly disproportionate extent in it for the paltry six or seven thousand Frenchmen whom Frontenac ruled from the rock of Quebec, and who were to be made the people of this magnified New France.

It was an easy matter for the adventurous explorers to go with the current as they sped downstream by day, and anchored away from shore by night. Each morning early astir, they were prepared with freshened energies to come, as they leisurely paddled along, within the range of new surprises. Now they saw a formidable fish. Now the current swept them round bluffs or between divided islands, fresh in the early summer's diversity of verdure.

They had been a week or more on the great river, observing deer, elk, bison, and turkey, but they had not seen a sign of man, when on June 25 they espied human footprints on the western bank. A well-used path conducted the two leaders to a native village of the Illinois, where they were welcomed and made to feel safe. They saw French cloth on some of the savages, and learned that intertribal traffic had probably passed it along from the French traders on the lakes. This people told them the same stories of demons and dangers to which a persistence in going farther would subject them; but neither the trader nor the Jesuit could be intimidated by such rehearsals.

1673, June 25. They see human tracks, and see the Illinois tribe

Once more on their way, they passed the mouth of the Illinois (to be better known a few weeks later), and wondered at the mocking castles which Nature had made of the stratified rock, and gazed upon the rude strokes of pigment which the Indians had combined into a demoniac figure on a rocky scarp above them.

and the Illinois River.

After some days, their canoes were tossing in the broken water of a muddy current, which poured into the clear Mississippi with such a volume that they naturally looked to the northwest, from which it came, as to some large water-shed. It was clear that the divide which held it was towards the great ocean of the west, the bourne of the hopes so long delayed.

They pass the Missouri

They learned from the Indians near at hand what seemed a confirmation of their belief. "I do not doubt," says Marquette, "that this other ocean is the Vermilion Sea, and I hope some day to be able to follow this inviting channel."

It was the commingled currents of the Missouri and the Mississippi which they had reached, and this flood of water from the west convinced Marquette that the united streams must find an outlet in the Gulf of Mexico. It was to be a hundred and thirty years and more before the wonderful interlacing of the springs of the Missouri and the Columbia, and of the La Platte and Colorado, was to be discovered. The Indians called this singularly intrusive and polluting stream the Pekitanoui, or the muddy river; but a little later, when more was known of the tribes which lived on its banks, it was generally known as the river of the Osages.

The adventurers were all the way on the watch for other indications of some such western passage, for it soon became more and more evident that the general direction of the Mississippi was towards the south. A little later on, Joliet says, he heard of a tribe lying only five days away to the west, which traded with others from the coast of California.

They passed by the site of St. Louis, then covered with forest, and as they went on they occasionally held out the calumet to Indians whom they saw, but as yet there was no hostile action in any of them.

They came to the mouth of the Ohio, which Joliet calls on his map the Ouabouskigon, — a name apparently al- *and the* lied to the later Ouabache, or as we have it in an *Ohio.* English guise, Wabash, for this stream and the Ohio below the other's mouth continued to be accounted one during the long interval yet to ensue before the placating of the Iroquois permitted the French to follow the upper reaches of the true Ohio.

The low and marshy shores which bound the mouth of this branch of the Mississippi allow it to mingle its waters with the main current with less impressiveness than is suited to its importance, and add a sort of mystery to the sources of its capacious flow. If La Salle had followed it from the Iroquois country some years before, there is nothing in anything that Joliet or Marquette say of it now to lead one to suspect that they connected it with any exploit of an earlier discoverer. Indeed, in their maps, they fail to associate it with any previous knowledge. The stories which had come to the French of the savage onsets of the Iroquois in this direction were vague, but the unavoidable inference was that the river whose mouth they now were passing was the theatre of these rancorous wars, in which wandering Shawnees and the confederates' bands met *Iroquois* in deadly struggle. Joliet, we know, had seen a Shaw- *raids along* nee prisoner in the hands of the savages at the end *the Ohio.* of Lake Ontario, when he met La Salle there in 1669, and he knew that the prisoner's country lay in this direction; but since then the implacable Iroquois had driven the Shawnees from both banks of the river, and forced them back into the valley of the Tennessee. It was within a very few years that the Iroquois had thus successfully raided this tributary valley. The Arkansas, whom Joliet was soon to meet lower down the Mississippi, had also fled before these savage confederates. The Illinois, whom he had visited, as we have seen, in their villages west of the great river, had been pressed along before the same inveterate enemies, who had used this valley of the Ohio as the main channel of their approach. Our explorers could now have little suspected what risks this same channel was to open to their successors in these western parts, when their Indian allies were hounded to the death by those same tireless foes.

July.

June passed into July, and the French canoes were still passing on with the current, by marsh and wood. The Indians, who now and then confronted them on the banks were more inclined to be hostile, but the calumet never failed to appease them, though it sometimes looked as if the hazards were great. Some savages whom they saw on the east bank had guns and wore European cloth, and it is surmised that they had got these articles directly or by intermediate traders from the English of Carolina or Virginia. At a village on the east bank, opposite the mouth of a river which Joliet named the Bazire after a fur trader in Montreal, but which we know as the Arkansas, they found a young Indian who could make himself understood in the Illinois tongue. From him they learned that the tribes farther down the river were enemies of his people, and had firearms from Europeans. They raised, he said, three crops of corn a year. When asked if they had ever seen the Europeans who supplied the guns, they replied that they had not, as the intervening tribes were always able to prevent their reaching them. This savage interpreter represented that the outlet of the river which they were following was a ten days' voyage farther on, but with extraordinary speed they might shorten the task by half. This led the French to think it nearer than it really was, for it was still seven or eight hundred miles away. Their almost unvarying southerly course — for the bend of the river one way had always been met by a corresponding reverse — had rendered it now hardly susceptible of doubt that it was neither to the Atlantic nor to the South Sea that they were tending, but to the great gulf of middle America, which, if their infor-

Mouth of the Arkansas.

mation was correct, placing its northern shores in latitude 31°
40', was not far distant. They had thus in effect, by an inference which was unavoidable, solved the problem of the great
river's course. If they went on they could scarce do more than
confirm their belief, and they would do it at the risk of losing
the fruits of their discovery, should they fall into the hands of
the Spaniards. A resolve was accordingly taken to stop at this
point (which Marquette calls 33° 40'), and return.
It was therefore on July 17 that they reëmbarked at _{1673, July}
Akamsea, as the friendly village was called, and be- turn back.
gan their arduous ascent.

It is not worth while to follow their laborious journey back
in detail. On reaching the mouth of the Illinois, they yielded
to the representations of the neighboring Indians, that it would
lead them more directly to Mackinac, and turned into Ascend the
its alluring current. It was a pleasant change for Illinois.
the weary voyagers, for the stream was placid, there was attractive shade under its umbrageous banks, and rich plains opened
between the hillocks, dotted with bison and deer. They tarried
awhile at Kaskaskia, — not the modern town of that name,
but an Indian village of the Illinois tribe, whose country it is
not always easy to designate at different periods, but which lay
in the main, after they came back from over the Mississippi,
between the Wabash and the banks of the great river. This
people were now very friendly. They tried to propitiate Joliet,
in the hopes of securing French aid against the Iroquois, of
whose ravages they were in constant dread, and towards Marquette they turned with wishes that he might abide with them
for their spiritual comfort. Joliet, with that policy which had
actuated him in naming the great river after Frontenac's family, now complimented the governor's wife with naming this
tributary stream as the Divine or the Outrelaise, which La
Salle later was to supplant with the name of the French colonial secretary, Seignelay.

Going on, the weary voyagers turned into the Des Plaines
River, and passed the elevation which the trader Des Plaines
named Mont Joliet, and which alone of all the names River.
bestowed by Joliet preserves his memory in that region to-
day. This eminence lies near Joliet city, forty miles The Chicago
southwest of Chicago. The stream led them to the portage.
Chicago portage.

The cutting of the gorge at Niagara had opened in pre-historic times a channel for the outflow of the upper lakes, in place of the older channel by the Illinois from the head of Lake Michigan, where there is scarce eight feet of rise at the divide in ordinary seasons. In wet seasons, even since the present century came in, heavily laden boats have floated from the lake to the Des Plaines. In the days of Joliet, the branches of the Chicago River and the headwaters of the Illinois interlaced so nearly that in ordinary springs the portage was scarce a mile and a half, and was obliterated in the actual waterway which, in very wet seasons, existed in the shape of an expanded lake. It was for a while in ordinary seasons dead water on either side, rippling as the paddle stirred it, when the spreading cir-cles broke against the crowded stalks of the wild rice. In very dry weather it was sometimes necessary to carry the canoe to the confluence of the Kankakee, thirty miles below.

There is no clear proof that any white man had preceded Joliet and his party in the passage of this portage, when now its practicability readily suggested to him the ultimate making of a canal. One cannot be sure, however, that some adven-turous trader had not preceded them; and we certainly find such traders at no great distance in Joliet's rear. The theory of La Salle's passage of it the year before has already been mentioned.

Once on Lake Michigan, the returning canoes found their way to Green Bay by the end of September. The adventure had cost them four months and more, and they had traversed a route of something like twenty-five hundred miles.

Leaving Marquette at Mackinac, in much need of rest, for he had been grievously ill on the return trip, Joliet passed on to the Sault Ste. Marie.

At Mackinac, 1673.

The following summer, Joliet took his way to Quebec. His last opportunity of showing his papers was probably at Fort Frontenac, where he briefly tarried, and where he found La Salle. At least such is Dr. Shea's belief, though Harrisse sees no satisfactory evidence that La Salle could have been at Fort Frontenac at this time. That the interview, if allowed, produced any results, is far from clear. La Salle at this juncture was engrossed with his trading tours and with the care of his Seigneury of Cataraqui. If Denon-

1674. Summer.

Joliet and La Salle.

ville's memoir is to be believed, La Salle in these expeditions
was accustoming himself to some of the affluents of the Ohio,
acquiring that knowledge of this approach from the Mississippi
to Ontario which was later in his mind when he was himself
on the great river in 1680. It was only at this later day, when
his mercantile speculations were at a low ebb, that he had
begun to raise visions of a traffic in buffalo skins on the Mississippi.

Joliet passed on to the St. Lawrence. All went well till
he reached the rapids above Montreal, where his canoe upset.

Two of his men — one an Indian from the Mississippi — were
drowned, and a box containing his journals and other Joliet's
papers was lost. He himself barely escaped with his papers lost.
life.

Joliet did what he could to repair the loss of his journals
by reviewing his recollections, and Frontenac later sent, apparently without success, to the Sault Ste. Marie to recover the
copies of the lost papers which Joliet had left there with the
priests. Dablon tells us that Joliet had also given a copy of
his journal to Marquette before parting with him, but no such

transcript has come down to us. Dablon himself, at this time in Quebec, had apparently talked over the adventur-
Records of the expedition.
er's experience with Joliet himself, and on the 1st of August he embodied what he learned in a communication to his superior in Paris, and later, in an amplified form, it was included in one of his annual reports, which was first printed when Martin gave it in his *Mission du Canada* (1861). The narrative as Joliet fashioned it upon his recollections is also to be found in two forms in Margry's collection, and Har-

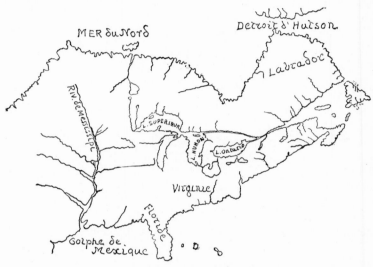

JOLIET'S CARTE GÉNÉRALE.
[Sketched from a copy in the Parkman collection (1681 ?), and signed by Franquelin.]

risse gives us a brief summary which the explorer offered in a letter dated October 10, 1674.

Joliet had been back three months before Frontenac drew up (November 14, 1674) an official report upon the trader's discoveries, and it was doubtless with small expectations that he forwarded it to France, for during the summer he had had a pretty sharp intimation from the king that he had better let projects of discovery alone.

Both Frontenac and Dablon, however, made the most they could of the new hopes which the expedition had created, — Dablon with a more intelligent appreciation of the case than the governor seemed to possess. The Jesuit alleged that it was now proved that if a bark was built on Lake Erie, there would only need to be a cut or canal made at Chicago for one to sail through to the Mississippi and the sea; and if it was not for the falls at Niagara, the vessel could start from Fort Frontenac. The governor was apparently most impressed with the possibility of a way being discovered to the South Sea by some of the western valleys of the Mississippi; but he was also struck with the ease with which one could pass from the St. Lawrence to the Gulf of Mexico with only the portage of half a league at Niagara! He urged, in consequence, that a settlement should be formed near that cataract, and that a vessel be built on Lake Erie, which he thought in ten days could reach the gulf. It seems clear that Frontenac had not quite understood what Joliet had communicated, or that explorer's enthusiasm had spirited away the obstructions at Chicago. The governor at the same time sent a map which Joliet had constructed with such observations as his memory supplied, and this has come down to us, being first introduced to scholars about ten years ago by Gabriel Gravier at Rouen. It is probably the earliest map to define the course of the Mississippi by actual observation, although Joliet connected it with the gulf merely by an inference which he felt he could not avoid. Marquette's contribution to our knowledge is more important on the whole, and not so dependent on recollection as what we learn from Joliet. His recital is in two forms as given by Margry, but it was originally sent by the priest to Dablon in Quebec. Dablon used it in his *Relation*, and sent a copy to Paris, while the original seems to have remained in the Jesuit archives at Quebec till, some time after the dispersion of the order, it was deposited by Father Cazot, the last survivor of the order in Canada, in the Hotel Dieu, not far from 1800, whence it was transferred, apparently about 1842, to the College of Ste. Marie in Montreal. From its nuns, Martin, a returned Jesuit, received it and committed it to Dr. Shea, who published it first in English in his *Discovery of the Mississippi* (1853), and two years later separately and in the original tongue (New York, 1855). It had been prepared for publication by Dablon, apparently in 1678; but had remained unedited in its complete form till Shea secured it. The *Mission du Canada* has since

Joliet's earliest map.

Marquette's narrative.

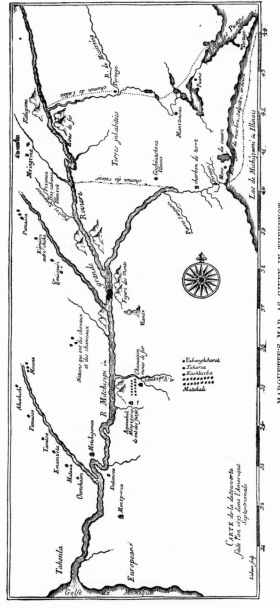

MARQUETTE'S MAP, AS GIVEN IN THEVENOT.

given it in a somewhat changed form, very likely as it was received in Paris, whither it was sent by Marquette at Frontenac's request. Thevenot in 1680 included an imperfect form of it, with curtailments and omissions, in his *Recueil de Voyages,* and also issued it separately, and it is in this shape that it has been used before the present generation, and was made familiar to English readers by Hennepin (1698) and at a later day by Sparks.

There was one feature in Thevenot's publication that deceived scholars for a hundred and seventy years, and that was the map which he gave as Marquette's. That editor had somehow got hold of a contemporary Jesuit map, now well known, and supposed it Marquette's. It may in fact have been that which J o l i e t h a d drawn from recollection, as Dr. Shea suggests. The genuine plot was discovered by Shea with the original manuscript, and has since been repeatedly reproduced.

Marquette's map.

Marquette, who had for some years dreamed of a missionary field among the Illinois, and who had welcomed the opportunity which the companionship of Joliet gave him, was not destined to enjoy a long fulfillment of his hopes. He had lingered at Green Bay on his return till, finding himself in the spring of 1674 in better condition of health, he organized a party of Indians, and with ten canoes started for the Illinois country. He followed up the western shore of Lake Michigan, which he describes in his journal in the oldest account of this shore which we have ; but at the site of the modern Chicago, or near it, he grew sick, and found it necessary to remain for the winter. He

MARQUETTE'S GENUINE MAP.

1674. Marquette returns to the Illinois country.

was cheered in his weariness by the kind attentions of everybody about him. Indian and trader passing that way, and hearing of his prostration, turned aside to give him any comfort in their power. The spring restored his strength enough to give him courage, and on the last of March, 1675, 1675. At Kaskaskia. he passed the portage and went on to Kaskaskia. The savage community gathered at this point welcomed him as a missionary would like to be received, and he turned in his ministrations from hut to hut amid such interest as he had never found before among Indian converts. But his frame was not equal to his spiritual energy. His strength failed, and it became evident that he should get back if possible to more civilized care. He started on his way with some companions. The party crossed the portage and followed the eastern shore of Lake Michigan. On May 19, in a quiet spot, they bore the prostrate May 19. Dies. man ashore and left him to his devotions, as he requested. In a short time they sought him, and found him dead. They dug his grave on the spot, and went their way, bearing the sad tidings to Mackinac. The next year (1676), some Ottawa Indians exhumed the body, and 1667. Finally buried at St. Ignace. a melancholy procession of thirty canoes accompanied the holy remains to St. Ignace. Here, beneath the chapel of the mission, they gave him a last resting-place. Two hundred years later (1877), some excavations were made on the spot where the chapel is supposed to have stood, and a few fragments of a skeleton were found and gathered for a new burial; but the pious act was not consummated without doubt being thrown upon the identity of the bones, inasmuch as the uncertain descriptions of the position of the mission which have been preserved do not render it clear beyond doubt whether its shrine was on the north or south shore of the strait, or on the intermediate island. Father Jacker, who performed the act of reburial, felt that he had sufficient ground for his belief.

Allouez was appointed (1675) to succeed Marquette in the 1675. Allouez succeeds Marquette. Illinois mission; but interest in the new discovery had largely ceased with the death of Marquette and the withdrawal of Talon. The petition of Joliet to be allowed to establish a trading-post on the Mississippi was promptly negatived in a letter of Colbert to Duchesneau, written on April 28, 1677. But events were already shaping for new scenes and new actors.

CHAPTER XI.

CATARAQUI AND CRÈVECŒUR.

1673–1680.

FRONTENAC had conceived the plan of establishing an advanced post on the northern shore of Ontario. It was partly with the expectation of intercepting the Indian trade with the English at Albany, and partly to bring a mart for skins nearer the sources of supply. The project disturbed the merchants of Montreal as likely to affect their own interests, and it was by no means satisfactory to the Jesuits, who dreaded its influence on the Indians. These priests were even accused of starting ill-omened rumors, such as an intended attack by the Dutch, — now temporarily in possession of New York, — in the hope of keeping Frontenac's attention occupied nearer home.

The governor was not a man to be intimidated; and he soon sent La Salle, between whom and Frontenac much cordiality had arisen, to visit the Iroquois, and to invite the confederates to send delegates to a council near the site of his intended fort. Frontenac was aware that the recent successes of the Iroquois in diverting the western trade to the factors at Albany rendered some attempt to propitiate or alarm the confederates highly necessary. _{1673. Frontenac invites the Iroquois to council.}

The governor had made many preparations for his journey to the rendezvous. With a large array of guards and a parade of staff officers, Frontenac left Quebec on June 3, 1673. His reception at Montreal was hearty enough to conceal the real feelings of opposition which pervaded that settlement, and when he left that place to move forward, on June 28, it was with a considerable increase of retinue. He had about four hundred men in his train, manning or occupying a flotilla of one hundred and twenty canoes and two flatboats. The procession had hardly passed into Lake Ontario when an Iroquois _{June 3. At Montreal.}

canoe was met, bringing letters from La Salle, with guides to lead them to the spot on the northern shore which had been selected for the council. It was the 12th of July when Frontenac disembarked his followers at Cataraqui. It was done with a pageantry which animated with delight the assembled Iroquois. On the next day, July 13, Raudin, the engineer, was set to work in laying out the fort, which in a few days was ready for occupancy. La Salle, who had meanwhile arrived, was put in command. Frontenac, who knew how to gratify the Indian pride, made everything pleasant for the grand council, which was held on the 17th. In his speech, which formed the principal feature of the convocation, the governor said everything to them that was agreeable, and promised them in the storehouse, which they saw in progress, the opportunity of getting everything they wished. He did not forget to remind them of their Great Father's power to punish as well as to reward. When, a few days later, the parting came, and the Iroquois started to cross the lake, they carried with them the conception of a white man quite different in his dealings from any they had hitherto known. Frontenac had vividly impressed his sturdy and emphatic personality upon them, and it did much for some years to hold them in check.

The governor was back in Montreal on August 1, and he had time to consider whether the 10,000 francs which his display had cost — a draft upon a treasury far from full — was to produce an equivalent return. To insure what he hoped for, he had formed plans of still another fort at Niagara, and the building of a vessel on Lake Erie. He had written to this effect to the king in November, and if allowed to carry out his plans, he had hopes to bar the Dutch and English effectually from the waters of the upper lakes. He had already ordered the construction of a vessel on Ontario to be used as an auxiliary force to Fort Frontenac, as the post at Cataraqui had been named. La Salle, at the same time, was informing his friends (November 13) that they would not be disappointed in his efforts to carry out all that Frontenac had looked for.

It was not long, however, before Frontenac's powers of controlling the Iroquois were put to a test. The Dutch on the Hudson were thought to be instigating them afresh. Frontenac wrote to Colbert that only his flatteries and presents

Margin notes: July. At Cataraqui.   Fort Frontenac.

to the Indian chiefs could keep the confederates quiet. The prospect was not better when, in February, 1674, the treaty of Westminster restored New York to the English.

1674. New York again English.

Grosseilliers and Radisson, who, as we have seen, had been serving the English at Hudson's Bay, had not found a compliance with the rules of the new company agreeable, and had returned to France discontented, and quite ready to reënter the service of Colbert, if he would pay their debts and provide for the future. Both returned to Canada, but Frontenac was not in a temper to dally with renegades. He had raised up too large a number of recalcitrants among the 6,700 inhabitants which Canada now showed, to open careers for others. He had leagued the whole body of bushrangers against him by his endeavor to break up their wild and independent systems of trade. He had an active quarrel with Perrot, the governor of Montreal, who was their avowed abettor. The Sulpitians had been provoked by him, and thwarted him when they could. The Jesuits, if their accusers may be believed, did not look with complacency upon any system of organized traffic which shut them off from a participation, clandestine it may be, in the profits of a trade which their missions might bring to them. But Frontenac got some relief from all these bickerings by reverting to other thoughts. He had taken Perrot into custody, and had sent him to France for the king to decide upon their differences; but he had sent over quite another sort of man, with other aims, in La Salle, who had sailed in the autumn of 1674.

Frontenac's enemies.

1674. La Salle goes to France,

It is said that La Salle had been pondering of late on Joliet's reports, and had made up his mind that the Mississippi must find an outlet in the Gulf of Mexico. He had formed this theory not without some ambition to prove it fact. On November 14, Frontenac wrote to Colbert that La Salle was a man worth his listening to, and so the king heard from that aspiring adventurer a proposition that Fort Frontenac and the adjacent lands should be granted to him as a seigneury. On his part, La Salle offered to reimburse Frontenac for the outlay already made on the fort, and to maintain a garrison in it. In recognition of the service which he proposed to ren-

and obtains a grant.

der to New France, he also solicited a patent of nobility. Colbert acquiescing, all went as well as La Salle had wished, but it became necessary that he should agree to rebuild the fort in masonry. This was settled, and the weight of debt which this undertaking drew upon him was not an unimportant factor in later obstructions.

The tide of emigration towards the St. Lawrence was already beginning to grow slack, and Colbert suspected that the six months in which the river was icebound had something to do with it. Accordingly, he had already informed Frontenac how desirable it was that some ingress to the interior of the continent should be opened in a warmer region than Canada. If such intimation gave Frontenac some heart for further exploration, the king's adjudication in the dispute between him and Perrot was not equally comforting. This tormentor was sent back to his post at Montreal, and both he and Frontenac were given some sharp reproof, and told to be friends for the future. They equally deserved the censure.

In September, 1675, a ship arrived in Quebec, bringing four notable persons. The conjunction was an unhappy commingling of incompatible natures. One was Laval, returning to the episcopate, and full of his headstrong devotion to what he believed to be his duty, — not unused or disinclined to a militant churchmanship, which Colbert and the governor must soon deal with. Another was Duchesneau, Talon's successor as intendant, and a stickler for his rights, the more vigorous when these rights collided with what Frontenac conceived to be his own. A third was Louis Hennepin, the Recollect friar, a man to be played off against the Jesuits to Frontenac's content. This restless priest had been smitten with travelers' tales from his early youth. He had recently been an army chaplain, but was now eager for a life as hazardous and as uncertain as he could make it. There were on the same ship a company of girls, coming to seek husbands and homes. They grew at times merry, and were not very complacent when the priest, to prove his holy vigilance, sought to check them. The fourth of these strange companions sided with the girls against the Recollect's austerity, and Hennepin certainly, in telling us of it, does not expect us to doubt his own sincerity. This defender of the merry damsels was the austere La Salle

1675, September. Laval, Duchesneau, Hennepin and La Salle at Quebec.

himself. Perhaps the buoyancy of his hopes, now that he had gained the royal recognition, had softened his temper, and he was not averse to making the bishop and the Jesuits hate him more than ever, since he knew the governor to be his friend.

In 1676, we find La Salle at Fort Frontenac, deeply engaged in increasing its efficiency as a trading-post. He built new walls to the fort, planted other palisades, brought cattle from Montreal, and laid the keels of the vessels which he depended upon to frighten the English. *1676. La Salle at Fort Frontenac.* Neither he nor Frontenac was quite clear yet as to what they might venture to undertake to the westward. The king was not willing to weaken the older settlements by such western schemes, and he did not hesitate to enjoin upon Frontenac his duty of being mindful of the royal wish. Frontenac, though he had been warned not to carry on any trade of his own, was known to have much sympathy with La Salle, and to have sent Raudin to Lake Superior with presents for the Sioux. No such transaction could escape the Jesuits, and what the Jesuits knew they shared with Duchesneau and, in turn, with the king. Frontenac, on the other hand, did not let the court remain in ignorance of the service that La Salle was doing. This faithful subject, the monarch was told, had spent 35,000 livres on Fort Frontenac, and was gathering settlers about its walls. The two or three small vessels which he had launched on the lake were bringing him in something like 25,000 livres yearly profit, as many believed.

Hennepin had found occupation in ministering to a colony of Iroquois, who had come across the lake and had set up their huts near the fort. It was not long before the priest felt enough at ease with their language to make a winter pilgrimage over the lake into the confederates' own country (1677). He found them not altogether dissatisfied *Hennepin among the Iroquois, 1677.* with the neutrality they were now maintaining with both French and English. They had recently subdued the Andastes, and there was no neighboring foe to fear. Their two thousand warriors were recuperating. Their raids as far south as the borders of Maryland and Virginia had harassed the whites equally with the Indians who were assailed, as such incursions always do. Representatives of those colonies had come to Albany to induce the Iroquois to fetter such roving bands of their young men; but the treaty proved little more than one in name. La Salle was perhaps induced to believe that his command of Lake Ontario and this wavering of the Iroquois meant a stay to English scheming, but he counted too surely. There is some reason for supposing that by this time La Salle had come to expect it easy to open a channel to the Mississippi valley by the Maumee and Wabash, and to extend his trade beyond Niagara in that direction. To appease the Iroquois and keep them quiet was particularly necessary if a portage so accessible to the confederates as that of the Maumee should be made a channel of commerce. It proved that nearly forty years were yet to pass before the enmity of the Iroquois was assuaged enough to permit that portage to be used.

La Salle's plans of trade.

With such dreams floating in his mind, La Salle once more, in November, 1677, embarked for France. His purpose was soon manifest, and Margry preserves for us the paper in which he outlined his aims in a memorial to the king. He professed in it that his work at Fort Frontenac was intended to form a base for a western trade that should extend to the Mississippi, — and he seems to have believed that this river flowed into what at this time stood for Mobile Bay in the Spanish maps, — where buffalo, wool, and skins would make the staple of a new traffic. These peltries he represented as being so exceptionally heavy that it would be much for the advantage of the trade if he could be allowed to pursue exploration along the route which Joliet had opened, and find the mouth of the great river. That being done, the transporting of this heavy traffic could be carried on directly by ships from the Illinois country. To this end he asked to have his seigneurial tenure of Fort Frontenac confirmed, and to be allowed to establish other posts towards the south and west for the space of five years. On May 12, 1678, his wishes were complied with in a patent signed at St. Germain-en-Laye. By this he was allowed to build forts in the coveted country, " through which," as the patent ran, " it would seem that a passage to Mexico can be found." A reservation was imposed in that he was forbidden to engage in trade with such tribes as would naturally carry their furs to Montreal. All this enterprise was to be carried on without expense to the

1677. Returns to France, and memorializes the king.

1678. And gets a patent.

crown. La Salle seems to have called successfully upon his relatives in France for capital. What was more important to him, he secured the fealty of a remarkable man. This was Henri Tonty, the son of an Italian refugee domiciled in Paris, whose fame is associated with the system of Tontine insurance. No man ever had a more faithful servitor than Tonty was to La Salle, and it is one of the proofs that the discoverer of the mouth of the Mississippi had something in him for a loyal and courageous man to respect, that Tonty became and remained his fast friend. For La Salle had not learned to make as many friends as a man of his ambition needed, and he was often found insupportably harsh and haughty. This want of tact, fatal in great enterprises, as La Salle found to his cost, has given some warrant for the opinion, which, for instance, Dr. Shea has zealously entertained, that La Salle was an incapable leader, and has been prodigiously overrated for his services. Such opinions are, it must be confessed, not wholly free from the prejudices which have been sent down to us by Jesuit antipathies. La Salle on his part was no lenient judge of that order, and he was prone to find ulterior and sinister purposes in all they did. He supposed their zeal in thwarting him in his projects was a wish to bar all laymen from having influence among the Indians, and to establish such an exclusive system in New France as had been formed by them in Paraguay.

Henri Tonty joins La Salle.

La Salle's nature and Jesuit antipathy.

It was in August, 1678, that La Salle sailed from Rochelle. He was accompanied by Tonty, and they took with them shipwrights and mechanics. Their shipments included anchors, sails, and cordage for a vessel which was to be built on Lake Erie. They reached Quebec in September, and there found Hennepin awaiting their arrival. The priest was soon sent ahead to prepare matters at Fort Frontenac, and after an interview with the governor La Salle followed. During this interval, it was arranged that a party should go in advance to trade and collect food in the Illinois country, and prepare for the reception of La Salle, who might be expected the next year. La Mothe and Hennepin were at once dispatched in a small vessel to Niagara, and a fort was planned at the mouth of that river. It was soon apparent that the neighboring Senecas

1678, August. La Salle sails for Quebec, and reaches Fort Frontenac.

Niagara and the Senecas.

felt uneasy at such signs of occupation. They were carrying on a lucrative trade as middlemen between the more distant tribes and the English at Albany, and they saw in the movements of the French an attempt to prevent such commerce. Therefore La Mothe and his companion visited the nearest Seneca village to make explanations. They were kindly received, and an Indian prisoner was burned for their enjoyment. They in turn outlined a plan of opening communication with Europe through the great river, so that goods could be brought with less expense, and could be sold cheaper than it was possible with the English. Their argument availed little, and the Frenchmen returned to camp with small encouragement. Meanwhile La

La Salle among the Senecas. Salle was coasting along the southern shore of Ontario, and on his way he visited the same village, which was, in fact, the identical one where he had in vain sought a guide ten years before. He was more successful than his precursors had been, and succeeded, as he thought, in making the tribe content with his projects, So with better heart he went on to Niagara and joined La Mothe, whom he found encamped near the Niagara rapids. La Salle, accompanied by Tonty, was soon on his way to discover beyond the cataract a suitable

Selects a shipyard on the Niagara. spot to lay the keel of his intended vessel. There has been some diversity of opinion as to the precise spot which he selected, but there is little doubt that it was just within or possibly on one side of the mouth of Cayuga Creek, where an island lying off the shore diverts part of the current towards the easterly bank of the river. Mr. O. H. Marshall of Buffalo, whose name is connected with many careful studies of the history of the Niagara region, first pointed out (1845) this spot as answering best the conditions of the contemporary narratives. Schoolcraft gave Mr. Marshall's views currency two years later, and they are now generally accepted. Though there is some disagreement as to the precise spot, there is none as to the general location.

It had already been found that the portage around the cata-

January, 1679. Plans for building the "Griffon." ract was not so favorable on the western side, and in the latter part of January, 1679, the party began to carry the material which they had brought from Fort Frontenac up the steep which leads to the plateau of the Niagara gorge, and to bear it along the portage track for

HENNEPIN'S DRAWING
OF A BUFFALO.

twelve miles. It was not all the material they had hoped to have, for after La Salle had left his vessel on the lake to make by land the latter part of his way to La Mothe's camp, the craft encountered bad weather and was wrecked. Fortunately, they saved the anchors and cables intended for the new vessel, and it was under the burden of these, with some rejoicing over their good fortune in saving so much, that the party now struggled along the portage of the falls. The new vessel was planned to be about fifty tons burden, as we should now reckon, and the keel being laid, La Salle himself drove the first bolt. Putting the charge of the construction upon Tonty, La Salle returned to the mouth of the river, where he began the construction of a block-house. This well started, he undertook with a few companions to find his way back to Fort Frontenac by land

La Salle at Fort Frontenac. through the Iroquois country. He had to cross the eastern end of the lake on the ice, and reached his destination exhausted and famished. He was in poor condition to encounter the aggravated attacks which his creditors were making upon his character, and to avoid the embarrassments with which his enemies sought to entangle his projects. It has been said that La Salle's creditors had already seized his property, but Kingsford, the latest Canadian investigator, can find no evidence of actual seizure.

NIAGARA RIVER.
[The " Griffon " was built near the mouth of Cayuga Creek.]

While La Salle was gone, Tonty pushed the ship well on toward completion, but with constant apprehension that the Senecas might burn her on the stocks. These Indians hardly concealed their hostility, and could not be induced to supply the camp with food, so that two Mohegan Indians whom the French had with them were kept out to hunt for game. By May the vessel was ready to launch. Once afloat, she was towed into the stream and anchored. It was the first moment her builders had had when they felt secure from possible mischief on the part of the

Indians. The savages could now prowl about and look on with wonder without exciting apprehension. Frontenac bore as supporters to his arms two griffins, and the workmen had carved the figure of one and placed it at the prow. They had given, indeed, to the ship the corresponding name of "Griffon." She was pierced for five guns, and the little pieces grinned ominously from their ports.

1679, May. The "Griffon" completed.

The fitting and rigging of the vessel went on, and when it was nearly complete Tonty started ahead (July 22) with a small party to the outlet of the Detroit River.

July. Tonty goes ahead.

HENNEPIN'S VIEW OF NIAGARA FALLS.

[From the *Nouvelle Découverte*, Utrecht, 1697. The cut in this edition shows the "Griffon" on Lake Erie.]

A few days later, La Salle arrived from Fort Frontenac, where he had made the best arrangement of his affairs which was possible, and brought with him the priest Membré, whose journal is to help our narrative henceforward.

Early in August, the "Griffon" was made ready for a start, and amid a discharge of guns, and with the crew chanting the *Te Deum*, she was towed against the current till she could bear away with spread canvas

August. The "Griffon" sails.

upon the waters of Lake Erie. Three days later (August 10), La Salle saw the three columns of smoke which Tonty gave as a signal at the Detroit River, and took his staunch friend and companions on board. Passing up the straits, with green slopes and verdant groves on either hand, they crossed on Ste. Clare's day the expansion of the stream which now bears a similar but perverted name (Lake St. Clair), and on the 23d the " Griffon "

On Lake Huron. was bounding over the waves of Lake Huron. The wind was rapidly freshening, and the flying vapors drove in upon her course. It grew to a gale, and the green timbers of the ship creaked ominously. Vows were made to St. Anthony of Padua, and as the seas broke over them hope was nearly abandoned. The crazy ship, however, rode out the

At St. Ignace. storm, and on the 27th she rounded to under the point of St. Ignace, and dropped anchor in its quiet shelter. Here the strange community gathered within the palisades of the Jesuit's house, and scattered through the startled Indian village, poured out upon the strand. Presently a hundred canoes were hovering about the weird and appalling " Griffon." La Salle, robed in scarlet and gold, landed with his companions, and heard mass in the bark chapel of the mission. This over, he lingered long enough among the huts of the village to discover that mischief was brewing. Some of the party which he had sent forward, as we have seen, to trade among the Illinois, had preferred to linger hereabouts, and were scattered among the bushrangers, who were loitering away their time in the indulgences of this frontier life. These faithless pioneers had imbibed something of the distrust and enmity which existed in this wild community against any organized method of trade, and were plotting sedition against their leader. La Salle caused the arrest of a few, and sent a party to the Sault to seize some who had wandered thither. Such peremptory demands on La Salle's part might stifle, but they did not eradicate, the poisonous opposition which his presence created.

Arranging for the coming back of the " Griffon " from Green Bay to Mackinac, whence she was to return to Niagara with such furs as could be gathered, to satisfy the demands of his creditors, La Salle set sail once more on her for his destination. At Green Bay, he found other of his men, and they had secured a welcome store of peltries. He seemed to forget that the shipment of them would expose him to the charge of having traffic with the Ottawas, whose trade his commission warned him not to divert from Montreal. Hennepin tells us that in determining to send the " Griffon " back with these furs, La Salle did not deign to consult with any one. The act was sure to turn against him any traders at Mackinac who were not already estranged. But La Salle never looked far ahead for the effects of any indiscretion.

On September 18, La Salle saw the " Griffon," thus laden with an ill-gotten booty, sail out of Green Bay on her way to Mackinac and Niagara. There were a pilot, a business agent, and five other men on board. She directed her course to the northeast, and was seen no more. La Salle's mind was soon made uneasy when a gale arose and swept along the course of the ship. The people at St. Ignace felt it, and feared the little vessel might be buffeting its violence. The storm passed, and while the sun shone, priest and trader at Mackinac began to peer up the straits for the white sail that was never to come.

1679, Sept. 18. The " Griffon " sails from Green Bay.

In all probability the " Griffon " foundered in the gale, and no one survived to tell the tale. There were stories of foul play, of Indians boarding her and murdering the crew, and of a faithless pilot, who ran her ashore and endeavored to escape with his plunder, but only to be stricken down by the savages, — but there is no evidence to substantiate any of them. La Salle indeed, at a later day, by talking with a Pana Indian, whom he represents as coming from a region two hundred leagues west of the Mississippi, was satisfied that the youth had seen the pilot of the " Griffon," whom his people had captured while he was on the Mississippi, endeavoring to reach Duluth in the Sioux country. La Salle was led to believe that if the renegade missed Duluth he was intending to go to the English at Hudson's Bay. La Salle was confident also that to reach the spot where he was captured, he must have passed near the Jesuit stations on Green Bay, and its priests were accordingly not so ignorant of the fate of the vessel as they pretended.

The ill-fated ship out of sight, La Salle was soon on his way up Lake Michigan toward the southern portages. He sent Tonty and a party across the lake, with instructions to follow up the eastern shore of Michigan, and to join his leader at St. Joseph.

La Salle himself led a party of fourteen in four canoes, by the western shore. The way proved perilous. His canoes were too deeply laden with forges and tools to buffet easily the gales they encountered, and their food gave out. Unless the shore Indians had supplied them with corn they would have perished, and there was a village of Maskoutens and Outagamies at the river Melleoki (Milwaukee) which proved hospitable. They were glad at one point to feast on the carcass of a deer which they rescued from the crows. Their Mohegans hunted to keep them in food, as they had done at Niagara. They discovered some wild grapes, — an unexpected feast. They found sometimes that their camp was robbed by lurking savages while they slept. Occasionally, a band of native vagabonds would manifest a hostile air. Once they thought they must fight for their lives, confronted by eight or ten times their own number of capering savages; but the danger passed. When the assailants came to a parley, La Salle was advised that he would find implacable foes in the Illinois if he went on, for they had been taught to believe by the traders, who were already warning them against La Salle, that the raids which the Iroquois had made into the Illinois country had been instigated by the French.

It was November 1, 1679, when La Salle reached the St. Joseph River. He was some time ahead of Tonty, and he employed the interval in building a timber fort. It was nearly three weeks before his lieutenant appeared with only half his party, for the difficulties of feeding them all along one route had compelled him to divide his followers, and the two sections had taken different ways. Tonty brought no tidings of the "Griffon," as La Salle had hoped he would; and so two men were dispatched to Mackinac, to be there when she returned from Niagara, and guide her to the St. Joseph, where four men were left in the fort.

1679, Nov. 1. La Salle at the St. Joseph River.

On December 3, La Salle, with eight canoes and thirty-three men, started up the St. Joseph River. There was nothing to cheer them in the stretch of dreary fields and bare woods which lined the river's channel. His anxiety about the "Griffon" weighed him down throughout these seventy sad miles. For a while he despaired of finding the portage. At last it was discovered, and there was a severe haul over five miles of stiffened ooze. When they once more

December 3.

launched their canoes on the Kankakee, they slipped along with the welcome current through open prairies, which were the range of the buffalo. At last they shot out upon the Illinois. They came to a large village of the Ottawas, but the huts were empty, for it was the period of the winter hunt. They searched the spot till they found a store of buried corn, and took in their need fifty bushels of it. They had passed under the ribbed precipice of what was later known as Starved Rock, not yet suggestive of future trials. Around them lay the broad plains of the Illinois, stretching between its bordering ridges.

On January 1, 1680, they landed, and celebrated the feast of the Circumcision. On the 5th, they darted into the expansion of water now known as Peoria Lake. As 1680, January. they approached its lower end they discovered some thin films of smoke writhing above the woods, and, doubling a point in the contracted stream, an Indian village was before them. La Salle slackened his speed enough to draw out his little flotilla in line across the river, and floated on amid the shouts and cries of the disturbed savages. The aspect for a while was threatening, but La Salle boldly landed as if for conference, and the chiefs advanced with calumets. The peaceful pipe removed distrust, and tobacco and hatchets were soon exchanged for hospitality, while the rubbing of the Frenchmen's feet with unguents marked the savage civilities. The taking of corn from their village garners was explained and payment offered. With faltering interpretation the visitors tried to make evident that they had come to do their hosts a service. They promised to open a route by which to bring them the articles of European traffic, which were so acceptable. If they would generously allow the French to build a fort among them, such trade and reciprocity would be increased. The tribe, said the visitors, could not wisely deny such a privilege, for it would only force their guests to pass on to other more hospitable people. Such were, as Hennepin tells us, the persuasions the Frenchmen offered.

But the golden offers were not doing all that La Salle expected, and he thought he saw that the demeanor of the savages was growing more and more uneasy. He began to suspect that some of the disappointed and vagrant Mackinac traders who were determined to thwart his purposes had their Indian emissaries in the dusky throngs which surrounded him. Hennepin charges Allouez, the Jesuit priest who succeeded Marquette in the Illinois mission, and who had been a good deal among these people for the last two or three years, with having instigated these distrusts, and La Salle later professed himself confident of Allouez's intrigues. At all events, it was apparent that some evil purpose had possessed the savages, and was extending even among La Salle's own followers. Two of his best carpenters, upon whom he was depending for future work, deserted him at this juncture, and others less valuable had slunk away. It is even affirmed that some tried to poison their leader, but a good deal of caution must be exercised in interpreting the morose forebodings of La Salle. A certain rigorous silence which sometimes came over him was associated in the minds of the mistrustful savages with what they imagined to be some purpose to favor the Iroquois, and no thought could be more disquieting among them.

It was amid such mutterings that La Salle resolved upon boldly placing a fortified post among these lowering savages. He selected a spot on a knoll on the eastern bank of the river. This little elevation was flanked by ravines and marshes, and they easily dug a ditch to complete the circuit of defense. La Salle builds Fort Crèvecœur, Within this they threw up earthworks, protected by palisades. La Salle named his fort Crèvecœur, — broken heart! It has been commonly said that this name was given in recognition of cruel mishaps, which perplexed him, and none of which was more disheartening than the disappearance of the " Griffon," for his followers, left at St. Joseph, had never been able to send him the grateful tidings of her appearance.

It may well be doubted if any but a foolish leader could have so clearly emphasized his misfortunes, when his querulous adherents needed so much to be inspirited. Shea is accordingly forced to believe that the name was chosen rather in reminiscence of the Fort Crèvecœur in the Netherlands which had been captured by Louis XIV. a few years before (1672).

The fort well planned, La Salle laid the keel of a small vessel of forty tons, — she was to be forty-two feet long and begins work on a vessel. with twelve feet breadth of beam, — which was to serve with her high rails as a floating breastwork in his intended voyage to the mouth of the Mississippi. Though he was embarrassed by the defection of some of his carpenters, the work went bravely on. He kept his party as closely within his fort as the work permitted, for he could hardly feel that his position was a safe one. Membré, however, lived among the Indians, ministering his holy calling, and we owe to his journal some part of our knowledge of these precarious days. The story which Sagean told after La Salle's death of his participation in this expedition has little or no claims for belief. The Indians had not ceased to picture the horrors of the lower Mississippi, in their efforts to dissuade the French from going farther down ; but the construction of the ship showed that their intimidations were useless. La Salle soon had the opportunity to impress them with something like a miraculous prescience. He chanced to intercept a young Illinois, bound to the village, but yet some distance afield. From him he gleaned a sufficiently accurate account of the leading landmarks in the great river's southern course. With this knowledge La Salle sought an interview with the chiefs, and told them what he expected to find. His descriptions so closely corresponded with what they knew, rather than what they represented, that they were embarrassed, and acknowledged they had had the purpose to deceive him. This moral victory served to make matters more promising, and La Salle determined to return to his manor at Cataraqui, and secure equipments for his ship. But one thing was yet to be done before leaving, and that was to dispatch a party to explore the upper waters of the Mississippi, as complementing his own project of exploring the lower parts to the sea. To this end one Accault was put in command of a party, and Hennepin was detailed to accompany him. On the last day of February, 1680, La Salle saw the little expedition start on its way. A recital of its adventures must be reserved for another chapter. We must also omit for the present to follow La Salle himself, when a few days later, bidding Tonty good-by, and investing him with the command, he also left for his visit to the distant settlements. It is only necessary now to record that he had not gone far when his eye measured the natural strength of the eminence now called Starved Rock, and making an examination of it, he determined it was a better post than Crèvecœur, if a siege was to be withstood. Accordingly, later in his progress, he sent back instructions to Tonty to occupy it.

1680, February. Accault and Hennepin sent to the Mississippi.

These messengers delivered La Salle's instructions; but that was not all. They aroused the lurking spirit of sedition which La Salle thought he had quieted. They told stories of the financial ruin which had overtaken their leader's affairs in Montreal, and of his consequent inability to succor them. The pay of La Salle's men was long in arrears, and there seemed no hope. Tonty, very likely not aware of the feelings of revolt which these stories were creating, did not delay to carry out La Salle's commands about the Rock, and left with a few men to visit the spot and begin his occupation of the heights. He was no sooner gone than the smothered passions broke into fury, and the fort was gutted and abandoned.

Tonty at Starved Rock.

Word of all this soon reached Tonty at the Rock, and he dispatched two small parties by different routes to carry intelligence to La Salle of the ill luck which had befallen Crèvecœur. One of the parties, as we shall see, reached its destination. The sending of these messengers depleted Tonty's force so much that he was left with only three companions beside the two friars, to meet what seemed an inevitable fate. There was nothing for the solitary Frenchmen to do but to mingle confidently with the Indian community which surrounded the Rock, and disarm enmity by a seeming trustfulness. In these straits, and with recurring apprehensions, the spring and summer passed.

Early in September, a Shawnee straggler came into the village and reported a war party of Iroquois and Miamis not far off. The community was exasperated at the sudden danger. It was thought that this new attack of the dreaded confederates was set on by the French, and some scouts who had been out to watch the enemy's advance reported that they had seen La Salle and a black-robe among the approaching foe. The truth was that some leader among them was arrayed in European clothes, and the real secret of their renewed hostility was to break up the French plans of establishing traffic in the great valley. If there was any spur upon their movements, it was applied by the English at Albany, who looked to the Iroquois as middlemen in keeping up their peltry trade with these western tribes. The Miamis had an old grudge against the Illinois, and the confederates had readily enticed them into joining in the raid.

1680, September. Iroquois attack.

Tonty thus found himself unexpectedly put to a test both of

his audacity and tact. His apparent eagerness to join in the fray at last dispelled the suspicions of his Indian allies. The Illinois hurriedly embarked their women and children for an island retreat down the river, and gave the night to making ready for the morrow's fight.

With the day the Illinois advanced to meet the attack, and in the midst of the confusion Tonty stepped to the front, holding a wampum belt as an invitation to parley. On his being recognized as a Frenchman, the conflict was partially stilled about him, but it was not checked enough even then to save Tonty from a wound in the surging of the combatants. He succeeded at last in warning the enemy that in attacking the Illinois they were warring upon the French, of whom there was a force of sixty, as he professed, not far off, ready to avenge any disaster. This effrontery gained time, and the Illinois, suspecting the confederates' hesitancy to be only a disguise for something worse, set fire to their town and joined their women down the stream. The Iroquois immediately swarmed over the ground, and began to devastate what the fire had spared. Tonty's position was growing more critical. It was evident that nothing but a policy of peace with Frontenac, which the Iroquois were practicing, saved these appalled Frenchmen from the old fury of their former foes. Tonty soon yielded to the Iroquois advice, and saw that he must leave the Illinois to their fate. He embarked in canoes with his companions, and paddled upstream out of sight and earshot of the hideous revelries. *Tonty escapes.*

Tonty gone, there was no restraint upon the furious Iroquois, and they started down the river in pursuit of the flying Illinois. The savage demons fell upon their victims wherever they could come up with them, and left the revolting traces of their fiendish fury all along their track.

Tonty, the day after his escape, stopped to repair his canoe, when Father Ribourde, wandering off from the party, was murdered by a marauding band of Kickapoos. There were four Frenchmen now left beside their leader, and they pushed on, buoyed by a hope which promised little. They suffered hardships that there was no chance of escaping. They passed the Chicago portage and followed down the western shores of Michigan, little suspecting that La Salle was at the same time

following up the opposite shore to succor them. It was now
Nov., Dec., November, and early in December Tonty met a party
1680.   of Ottawas, who took them in their canoes. Famished,
and weakened almost to exhaustion, they found at last hospitable entertainment in a Pottawattamie village. Tonty was too ill
to go farther, and there happened to be some Frenchmen in the
village to nurse him. Membré was left to proceed alone to Green
Bay and report the horrible details of these tragic experiences.

We may turn now to follow La Salle after he had parted with
March, 1680. Tonty. It was in March, 1680, when, accompanied by
La Salle's his faithful Mohegan hunter and four Frenchmen,
movements. La Salle's two canoes glided out into the icy stream
and began to ascend the Illinois. It was dreary weather, and
nothing but severe hardship could be in store for them ; but it
was necessary to undergo everything if he was to launch his
new vessel at Crèvecœur the next season, since the anchors and
other equipments must be brought from the St. Lawrence.
They found in some places the ice in the river too thick to
break, and were obliged to sledge their canoes. The snow lay
deep enough to embank the buffalo, and they got some meat by
killing the struggling creatures. Towards the end of March
they reached the fort on the St. Joseph. Here they found
some of the men who had been left there, but they had heard
nothing of the " Griffon." Two of them were ordered to join
Tonty and carry the message about fortifying the Rock, to
which reference has been made. There now lay before them
270 miles of an unexplored path across the neck of the lower
Michigan peninsula to the Detroit River. They encountered
trials and dangers enough to make the stoutest quail. Shea,
who is much inclined to belittle and disparage all of La Salle's
acts, looks upon this fearful tramp as " the only really bold and
adventurous act " in his career. They waded through drowned
lands. They were obliged to thaw their stiffened clothes in the
morning before they could move. Where they found a path in
the open they burned the grass to destroy their trail, for warring
savages invested the country, little discriminating as regards
their human prey. They fortunately escaped them, or appeased
them if encountered.

On reaching the Detroit River, along which the Hurons were

now gathering into a permanent settlement, two of La Salle's men were sent to Mackinac to report his movements. The leader with his remaining men now made from elm bark a canoe in which the reduced party finally reached Niagara. He here found other of his men holding the post near the shipyard of the "Griffon." These dependants were equally without tidings of the ill-fated vessel, and had new misfortunes to report, for a ship which La Salle had expected with supplies had been wrecked in the St. Lawrence. Such was the dismal condition which confronted him at Niagara.

La Salle had borne up under the hardships of the march better than his men. He bravely stood all these failures of his hopes. Taking three fresh men in place of his prostrate com- panions, he again started for Fort Frontenac, and reached that post on May 6; he had traveled a thou- sand miles, and had been sixty-five days in doing it. May 6. At Fort Fron- tenac.

There was little to inspirit him about the condition in which he found his affairs. Inquiries disclosed that some of his trusted agents had appropriated the profit of his furs. He learned that others had deserted his interests and had taken his skins to Albany. Somebody had started a report of his death, and on the strength of it, a forced sale had been made of some of his effects. There was yet, however, something more than a reed to depend on. Frontenac was still his support, and La Salle found on going to Montreal that he could yet get credit and supplies. During the two months in which La Salle addressed himself to the improving of his affairs, he succeeded in accom- plishing much, and was on the eve of again departing for the Illinois when one of the parties which Tonty had sent off with the news of the revolt at Crèvecœur reached Fort Frontenac. These men also brought tidings of the later riotous conduct of the mutineers, plundering where they could, and that they were now on the way to Cataraqui, scattering reports as they came on of the death of Tonty, and harboring vengeance on La Salle. It was towards the end of July, 1680, when La Salle was awakened to these new dangers. His decision was prompt. He mustered some faithful men, and started to meet the vagabonds. He ambushed his party on the track of the marauders, and easily captured the two canoes which were in advance, and later he seized a third, and returned with all his prisoners to the fort. July.

La Salle had twenty-five men with him when, a few days later, he left the fort. He followed the Humber River, and thence crossing to Lake Simcoe, he tracked its outlet to Georgian Bay. Reaching Mackinac, he divided his party, and leaving La Forest, now his lieutenant, to follow with the rest, he pushed on with only twelve men.

1680, August. Starts west again.

October.

October with its variegated charms had come when La Salle was moving with his canoes along the eastern shore of Lake Michigan, — just at the moment, we have seen, when Tonty, faltering with his burdens, was being borne along the western. Neither was conscious of the movements of the other.

November. At St. Joseph's fort.

In November, La Salle was at the fort on the St. Joseph, which he found had been abandoned. He wrote here for Frontenac a statement of his belief in pursuing this western discovery. He left five men to repair and occupy the post, and went on with six others and a single Indian. The prairie, as they passed along the Kankakee, was dark in places with hordes of buffaloes. They killed twelve and dried the meat. They passed Starved Rock; it was silent. They came to the great town of the Illinois, but it was a scene of black desolation. Wolves and buzzards were feeding upon the half-buried bodies of its defenders. The skulls which were grinning upon poles here and there told the old story of Iroquois ferocity. In the Illinois fort they found a few bits of French cloth, — that was all. The skulls were examined, — they were all Indian. Where was Tonty?

La Salle left three men to conceal themselves near the town for the present, and with four others he went on. He found where the camps of the Illinois and the invaders had been on opposite sides of the river; but everything was abandoned. He reached Crèvecœur; it was demolished, but the vessel was still on the stocks, though the Iroquois had drawn out the iron spikes. He still went on, and reached the Mississippi. It was his first sight of it. Here he tied a letter for Tonty to a tree, and turned back. It was now the early days of December, 1680. He rejoined the men whom he had left near the Illinois town, and a great comet hung ominously over the scene of desolation, and with its baleful impressiveness following him, La Salle went back to the Miami country.

At the Illinois fort.

December, 1680. First sees the Mississippi.

CHAPTER XII.

DULUTH AND HENNEPIN ON THE MISSISSIPPI.

1678–1683.

DULUTH was a cousin of Tonty with the silver hand, as La Salle's friend was designated because of his metal member. There is preserved in the Archives of the Marine at Paris an account which Duluth wrote in 1683 of his experiences in the Sioux country. He was an adventurous young fellow, who had found, off and on, attractions in the Canadian wilderness, till on September 1, 1678, he was allowed to start on explorations to see what he could find among the Sioux. The priests and traders had known this people as wanderers and loiterers about the Lake Superior stations for several years. Duluth took with him three Frenchmen and three Indians, and wintered somewhere on Lake Huron. In the following spring (1679), he was in the woods not far from the Sault Ste. Marie, and on April 5 he wrote to Frontenac that he was preparing to forestall the English, and to get ahead of any Spanish who might come from the South Sea to explore the region west of Lake Superior. He also informed the governor that he intended to set up the king's arms among the Sioux who inhabited this country. This act he performed on the 2d of the following July, in the midst of the Mille Lacs region. In the autumn (1679), he was near the head of Lake Superior, using his good offices to establish a peace between the Sioux and the Assiniboines. This was about September 15, and the site of his mediation seems to have been the spot where later Fort William stood.

The enemies of Frontenac were not backward in insinuating that clandestine trade for the governor's advantage had not a little to do with this movement of Duluth; and it was not

[marginal notes: Duluth. · 1678. Among the Sioux. · 1679. · Near Lake Superior.]

unknown that a trader named Pierre Moreau, but commonly
called La Taupine, was at this time wandering about
this very region, perhaps with Frontenac's protection
in his pocket. Some years before, Joliet had found
Moreau in the Illinois country, and when afterwards in Montreal the fellow boasted of his success in trading for furs, and
the intendant sought to arrest him for illicit traffic, he produced
orders from Frontenac appointing him to secret service among
the Ottawas.

In the summer of 1680, Duluth was once more in this region,
and this time he sought to find a waterway to the
Sioux country, which he had reached before by land.
He had two canoes, and with him were an Indian
interpreter and four Frenchmen. He passed from Lake Superior into the Bois Brulé River, a narrow stream with an ob-
structed channel, and then crossing a portage he reached the
St. Clair Lake, and so descended by its outlet to the
Mississippi. Duluth had learned from the Sioux that
a party of their tribe had gone down the river to hunt,
and that some Europeans were with them. Duluth had
intended on this expedition to push on westward to salt water,
which he expected would prove to be the Gulf of California,
and he supposed it was distant only twenty days' journey. It
was the prevailing notion at this time that the line of the upper
Mississippi was from two thirds to three quarters across the
continent, when in reality it is about midway. This is the
geographical view which we find was cherished by Joliet and
Hennepin, and appears in the maps of Franquelin, who was
at this time living in Quebec, and embodying in his maps the
latest reports of the western explorers.

Who these Europeans were, thus following the hunting party
of the Sioux, was an interesting question, which Duluth was
anxious to solve, for it was possible that his planting of
the royal column amid the Mille Lacs was none too soon, if
English or Spaniard had penetrated to its neighborhood. So
leaving two of his men to guard his wares, and taking the
other two with him, Duluth started down the river.

We have seen that just before La Salle left Crèvecœur to go
back to Cataraqui, in the early spring of 1680, he had dispatched Michel Accault, a Picard man, whose name is variously

BUILDING OF THE "GRIFFON."
[Hennepin's *Nouvelle Découverte*, Amsterdam, 1704.]

spelled, with Hennepin and another Picard man, Du Gay, as companions. Their purpose was to conduct an expedition to the region where we have just parted with Duluth. The trip is mostly associated with Hennepin, because we depend on his account of their wanderings; but Accault, as the better linguist, seems to have been in charge by La Salle's appointment.

1680. Accault and Hennepin.

Passing down the Illinois, the little party turned up the Mississippi, and went on amid the floating ice. They paddled up beyond the Wisconsin, and when near the Black River, on April 11, they met a party of Sioux, a hundred and more in number, in thirty-three birch canoes. The savages came down upon the little exploring party with precipitation, and soon surrounded them. The Frenchmen seemed for a while in great danger, but the Sioux had already profited by the French trade, and whatever passions for plunder stirred them now, there was prudence enough in the savage leaders to check the murderous impulse. They therefore carried the captives to their villages. The whole flotilla struggled up against the current, till, coming to the widening of the stream below the modern St. Paul, their canoes were hidden, and the party made the rest of the journey by land, and found a halt at last, and relief from a march which proved weary and painful to the prisoners, on the shores of Lake Buade. Here the Frenchmen were detained for some weeks, being distributed to separate masters ; but all three were at last brought together, to accompany a party of their captors down the Mississippi on a buffalo hunt. Later, Accault preferring to stay with the Indians, Hennepin and Du Gay were allowed to depart in a canoe to try to join some French, who, as La Salle had promised, were to be at the mouth of the Wisconsin. They went off in the slumbrous air of summer, — for it was July, 1680, — and floated with the current till the falls near the modern St. Paul confronted them. This cataract owes the name of St. Anthony to Hennepin, who now first saw it. Carrying their canoe to the quiet water below, they still went on, wondering at the seamy towers of nature's architecture everywhere around them. At last they cast a longing gaze upon the festooned trees which marked the approach to Lake Pepin, and were smoothly floated out upon its waters.

April. Encounter the Sioux.

1680, July. Hennepin released.

In this neighborhood Hennepin encountered the Indian whose adopted son he had become during his stay at Lake Buade, and from him he learned that a band of the Sioux were not far off, hunting on a tributary of the Mississippi. The Frenchmen's ammunition was well-nigh spent, and they found it impossible to keep from one meal to another the game which they were fortunate enough to kill. With powder gone they would be in danger of famishing. The lesser evil was to join these hunting Sioux, which they did, and they found Accault among them. While in company with these Sioux, two squaws came from the east and reported meeting a war party of their tribe, accompanied by five white men. Henne- Soon hears of white men. pin was as curious as Duluth had been to know what other Europeans were so near him. They were in fact Duluth and his companions.

The party which Hennepin had joined, having now ended their hunt, started northward towards their homes, and it was not long before the two Sioux parties met, Hennepin meets Duluth. and Hennepin and Duluth encountered one another.

It was represented later both by Hennepin and Duluth that at the time of their meeting Hennepin was in forcible detention by the Sioux, and that it was Duluth's intervention which released him. The story is not altogether credible, and La Salle at least did not believe it. At all events, the two Frenchmen parted with the Indians in company, and with their companions, eight in all, they passed up the Wisconsin, where the traders which La Salle had intended to meet them were not to be found, as the reader might readily suppose from the evil fortune which had overtaken that leader. They passed unmolested by the Fox River to Green Bay, and win- 1681. Duluth at Quebec. tered at Mackinac. In May, 1631, Duluth reached Quebec, and was arrested for illegal trading at the west. The suppression of clandestine traffic had proved so difficult that the home government made a virtue of necessity, and sent orders that the treasury should profit from a freer distribution of licenses. It was directed that twenty-five such permits should be given annually, each covering a single canoe and three men. The spirit of the order was enough to establish greater leniency for such transgressions as had gone by, and Duluth was released.

In the same spring (1681), Hennepin appeared among his old companions at Fort Frontenac, almost as an appa-rition, for it was believed, as the report ran, that the savages had hanged him with his own waist-rope. At Montreal he met Frontenac and interested him in his story, and then sailed for France.

Hennepin at Fort Fron-tenac.

By the following summer he had prepared a manuscript of his adventures, and, September 3, permission was given to him in Paris to put it to press, and on Jan-uary 5, 1683, it was issued as a *Description de la Louisiane.* It is probable that at this time the priest was abiding in the convent at St. Germain-en-Laye. The book is accompanied by a map, which has some noteworthy features. One is that the southern shore of Lake Erie is carried so far south as to cover the proper latitude of the Ohio, of which river the map shows no sign. Indeed, Hennepin seems to have missed a true conception of that stream, for he says it is in the country of the Iroquois, and affords a passage to the Sea of Florida. It is surprising that Hennepin could have been the companion of La Salle and not have heard of the latter's visit to that river fourteen years before, unless, indeed, La Salle at this time had no conception that the river which he then followed flowed into the Mississippi. If the southern shore of Lake Erie had ever been tracked by explorers, equipped after the usual fashion of the time with astrolabes, it is also surprising that some record of its approximate latitude should not have been known, for Hennepin could hardly have failed of converse with Franquelin when he was at Quebec on his way to France, and that car-tographer studiously kept abreast of the increasing knowledge of these distant parts. That European axemen had been in this region just about this time has been claimed by Colonel Whittle-sey, because of the discovery in numerous places of trees show-ing the cuts of broad-bitted axes under the annual rings, which had begun as early as this period to overlay the wound. It is of course possible that such implements might have been wielded by the savages themselves, and procured through the Iroquois from the English mart at Albany.

1683. Pub-lishes his narrative in Paris, with a map.

Another noticeable point of the map is the representation of a mission station far north of the source of the Mississippi, where it is certain that none had been established, or at least there is no record of such. The placing of it there seems to have been a pretension on the part of the Recollect Hennepin

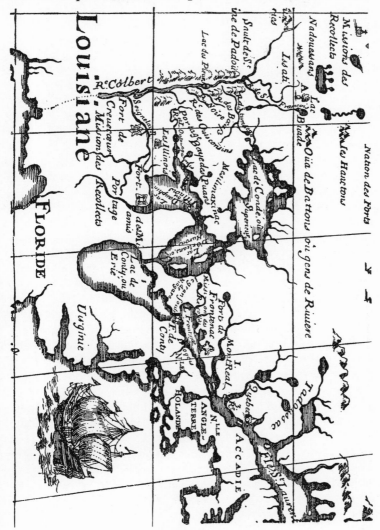

HENNEPIN, 1683.

that his order had outstripped the venturesome Jesuits, but he prudently removed it from his later maps.

In the book itself, Hennepin speaks of encountering four Indians on his route who had come from a place four hundred leagues farther west, and had been four months on the way, and they had assured him that there was no place like the Straits of Anian, such as was put down on the maps. Here was a reference to an old problem that had puzzled many generations of geographers. If Humboldt has correctly divined the origin of the mystery, — it is hard to be satisfied that he has, — the notion had arisen as early as 1500, when Cortereal had found the opening of Davis's Straits, that it was in some way the ingress to Asia, and was called the Straits of Anian. It is certainly a long time after that before we meet the name, or the passage itself, in cartographical conjecture, and, indeed, it was hardly possible that it could have existed on the maps before the substantial insularity of North America was established. It was then placed so as to prefigure the later-found Bering's Straits, only considerably farther south. Running in a general north and south direction, it was made to form a passage to the wide expanse of water which in the sixteenth century was generally believed to lie along the northern confines of Canada. It is found in this position in the map of Zalterius in 1566. The interval from the days of Cartier to the coming of Champlain, when almost nothing was done to clear up the geography of the northern verge of Canada, was when conceptions of the Straits of Anian, traversing or opening to this region from the Pacific side, were most rife. It got recognition from Mercator, Ortelius, Porcacchi, and Furlano, who were leading geographers of those days. It appeared in the maps of Sir Humphrey Gilbert and Frobisher, and the straits called after the latter were supposed to connect with it. Drake sought it in 1578; and six years later, when Gali made a northern sweep from the Philippines to Acapulco, he was thought to have disproved its existence by the breadth which he found the North Pacific to have. The tendency was to move the position of the straits farther north, and Wytfliet in the first American atlas (1597) reverted to the old notion, which was kept up later by Hondius (1613). Thirty years afterwards the explorations of De·Vries, the Dutch navigator, induced people to think for a while that where Gali had supposed a broad ocean, there was really a huge island, which the Spanish navigator did not go

Straits of Anian.

far enough north to see. This was thought to be of almost continental extent, barring access to the boreal regions except at its eastern and western extremities. The channel on the American side of this island thus became the straits so long searched for. This was perhaps the prevalent belief when Hennepin ques-

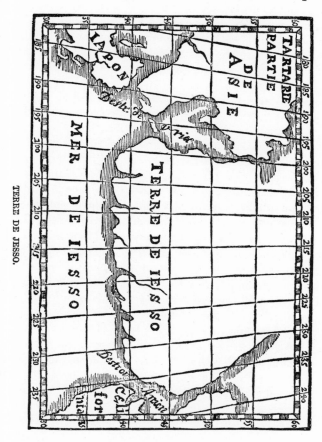

TERRE DE JESSO.

tioned these hardy wanderers from the distant west on the upper waters of the Mississippi.

While recording this denial of the straits' existence, Hennepin refers to the failure, as he understood it, of both the English and the Dutch to find such a passage at the north, but expresses a faith that by pursuing some of his own discoveries, a river would yet be found capable of floating large vessels to the South Sea, where without crossing the equator, Asia could be reached. " It is most likely," he adds, " that Japan and America are one continent," and such was not an infrequent belief in some form, before the severance of Asia and America was finally established by Bering nearly fifty years later. Hennepin wavered in his dissent, or perhaps his editor did for him, for when in 1697 his new edition appeared, he adopted the Dutch notion of Jesso — as the intervening island already mentioned was called — in a map of the north Pacific which is given in that book.

Hennepin's reputation with posterity has rested rather upon this later edition than upon his original of 1683, and not to his advantage. In this earlier book, excepting his forcible detention by the Sioux, which La Salle found it worth while to discredit, there is not much to question. Parkman calls it " comparatively truthful." It stands reasonably well a critical test, and the internal evidence is in its favor. It has been alleged by Margry that the correspondence in the text shows a closer relation to an account written by La Salle than is consistent with an independent relation ; but this correspondence extends to events of which Hennepin had personal knowledge, and La Salle had not. It is therefore reasonable to suppose that Hennepin may have acted as a scribe for La Salle, and that each used the same record for his own purposes. It is hardly worth while to go to the other extreme adopted by Shea in charging La Salle with pilfering from Hennepin.

The map which accompanied this *Description* omitted the lower parts of the Mississippi where it connected itself with the gulf, and this connection was only suggested by a dotted line. The *Nouvelle Découverte* of 1697 is the *Description de la Louisiane* of 1683, enlarged. It purports also to be a more truthful account of Hennepin's discoveries than he felt at liberty to make while La Salle, whom he looked upon as an enemy, was alive. These suppressed statements, no longer withheld, were to substantiate his new map, which boldly represented the Mississippi throughout its entire course to the gulf. There is some reason to believe that about the time of issuing his first book, he orally professed to have descended the Mississippi ; but that book contains only a regret

Hennepin's veracity.

Hennepin's Nouvelle Découverte.

that he had not the time to do so. The statement which he now printed represented that when he and Accault went down the Illinois to its mouth, they then turned downstream and proceeded to the outlet of the Mississippi. After this, returning to the starting-place, they went up, and pursued the course which had induced the narrative of the earlier book. This meant, provided the dates given in the *Description* were correct, that Hennepin had, within the thirty days which were allowed for the exploit, paddled thirty-two hundred miles, down and up stream, and that he had made sixty miles a day, when only an average of perhaps twenty to twenty-five was possible. La Salle, in one of his papers, says that a day's travel on the river means seven or eight leagues. It was certain this difficulty would be noted, as well as the remarkable secrecy which had been maintained in his first book regarding the undertaking. Some bluster was sufficient to meet the charge respecting the secrecy, and this was abundantly offered in the *Nou-* His *Nouvelle* *velle Voyage*, which was printed as a sort of supple- *Voyage.* ment the next year. In this a violent preface defended his claim to have gone down the Mississippi. To support his audacity, he had two resources: one was to assert that the distance was not what it was supposed to be, and the other was so to change his dates that he could make it appear that he had forty-three days instead of thirty for the task.

Curiously enough, he boldly in the *Nouvelle Voyage* shifted the charge of plagiarism — which followed upon its being discovered that the account of La Salle's own voyage to the mouth of the Mississippi bore a close resemblance to Hennepin's narrative — upon Leclercq, in whose *Premier Etablissement de la Foy*, Hennepin's text, with little change, had recently appeared, as a journal of Membré, the companion of La Membré's Salle. It was now asserted that Hennepin had left in journal. Quebec an account of his own experience while descending the river in 1680, to which Leclercq got access, and converted it to his purpose in describing the adventures of La Salle for the following year. Dr. Poole, who, in an address before the American Historical Association in 1888, was inclined to look charitably on the charges ordinarily preferred against Hennepin, frankly acknowledged that if he was the author of this statement, a defense of his reputation is hopeless.

Sparks, in his *Life of La Salle,* made a thorough exposure of the correspondences of Hennepin's narrative with the journal of Membré as given by Leclercq. From that day to Parkman's Hennepin has usually been held up to the modern reader's scorn. Shea, not long after Sparks's exposure, went so far as to

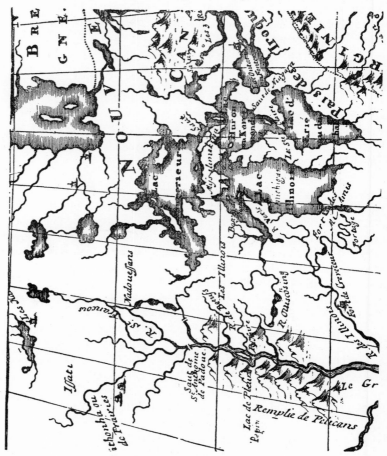

throw discredit upon what Hennepin says of the upper Mississippi, and to doubt if he ever went upon its waters at all.

Of late there have been persistent efforts to restore the good name of Hennepin, and Shea, to make amends for his early mistrust, has been the chief advocate of these

Defense of Hennepin.

later views. The argument which has been relied upon is this: Hennepin having prepared a new edition of his *Description*, the copy was left with the publisher, who, to add to the attractiveness of the book, and to give some surprises that would induce a larger sale, subjected it to further remodeling by an irre-

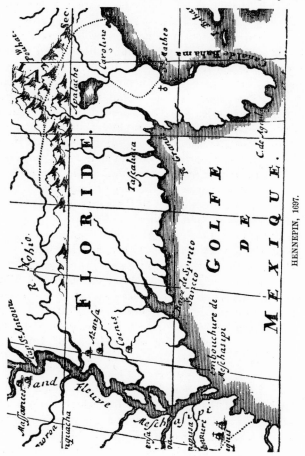

HENNEPIN, 1697.

sponsible editor. It was the work of this literary jobber who, it is claimed, interpolated the citations from Membré. He it was, too, who added to the book the parts which are relied upon to prove Hennepin's audacity. That there was such a mendacious editor is supposed to be shown in the passages which

Hennepin, as a Catholic, could not have written. This argument is not a strong one, for Hennepin was quite capable of writing, it is to be feared, much that one would not suppose him to write. The other argument is stronger, for it is founded on a comparison of type and other signs of the printing-office, to show that these questionable parts were not set up in the same office, or at least at the same time, with those which are not questioned. It does not certainly follow as a matter of course that Hennepin could not have done even this, though his defenders would fain think that he could not. It is reasonable perhaps to suppose, if Hennepin had found his name was used to inflict a wrong, that he would have in some way rectified the error, or at least have prevented the repetition of it in the numerous editions of the text which followed, or were transformed by translations. He certainly busied himself with no such purpose, and winced not a little under the imputations of fraud which early beset him. The *Nouvelle Voyage* of 1698 returned to the task of imposing on the public.

Nouvelle Voyage, 1698.

His defenders resort to the supposition that this book was under the same evil influences of a hireling publisher as the one of the previous year, and that Hennepin had no more to do with its impositions than with the earlier ones.

Meanwhile, pursued, as is represented, by the enmity of the provincial of his order in Paris, either through the influence of La Salle or because of some recalcitrancy of his own, Hennepin had thrown himself into the service of William III. of England, whom he had known in the Netherlands, and simultaneously a combination of the books of 1697 and 1698 was brought out in English at London, as *The New Discovery*, and the imposition went on.

The New Discovery.

Membré's journal is very like a *Relation* which is preserved in the Archives of the Marine at Paris, which Parkman suspects was La Salle's official report, drawn up perhaps by Membré, if indeed it was not written by La Salle himself, as some suppose. That Hennepin got access to this in the manuscript, and was not compelled to draw upon Leclercq's printed volume, is not unlikely, though it has been alleged that he more confidently used the book of Leclercq because the chance of detection was decreased from the suppression of that printed narrative. There is certainly room for doubt as to the authorship of this *Relation,* — it is given by Margry, — and just precisely what are the separate or combined connections of La Salle, Membré, and Hennepin with it is open to conjecture. It was very likely a compilation from various sources, made in Paris for presentation to Colbert, and perhaps put in shape by the Abbé Bernon, as has been alleged.

CHAPTER XIII.

LA SALLE, FRONTENAC, AND LA BARRE.

1681–1683.

A WEARY, disheartening winter lay before La Salle at his post in the Miami country. He had left the wreck of his fortunes on the Illinois. There were no tidings of his faithful Tonty, though a piece of sawn wood which he had seen on the Kankakee gave him hope that his friend had passed that way. La Salle knew how the story of his misfortunes would sap the spirits of his distant friends. Those who had risked money on his undertaking were to be appeased. He had, during the autumn, written to one such, assuring him that profits would surely come, if he would only be patient. " I am disgusted at being always compelled to make excuses," he wrote, " but I hope you will get other information of how things are going on here, beside what the Jesuits give you." He advised his supporter to send some one out who could take an intelligent view of the situation. He did not greatly encourage such a creditor, I suspect, when he acknowledged that he had little business skill of his own, and knew nothing about bookkeeping !

When he reached the fort on the St. Joseph, in January, 1681, he found La Forest with his party occupying it. They were getting out timber for a new vessel, and had repaired the defenses of the post. In the neighborhood there were a few New England Indians hutted for the winter. They were outcasts that had fled west after the failure of King Philip's war, and were mainly Mohegans and Abenakis. La Salle won a staunch friend among them, and his Mohegan hunter long merited his confidence.

Dethroned almost from leadership as he was, La Salle's steadfast spirit was planning how he might head a league of the

Miamis and other western savages, in the hope that it could roll back the tide of Iroquois success. Perhaps he could work upon them through his faithful Mohegans. In March, he started on towards the Illinois, full of this hope. 1681, March. Goes toward the Illinois. On the way, he met a band of the Foxes, and from them learned that Hennepin had passed through their country from the Sioux region, and that Tonty was among the Pottawattamies. These tidings hurried him on. He laid his plans before the Illinois, and then, coming back to the Miamis, endeavored to enlist their sympathies with those of the New England Indians that were scattered about the country. He felt that he had accomplished something, and, leaving the plot to ripen, he started from Fort Miami toward the end of 1681, June. Finds Tonty at Mackinac and returns to Fort Frontenac. May, and made his way to Mackinac. There he found Tonty and Membré, and spent awhile in talking over their varied mishaps. It was now June, 1681. Membré gives us a picture of La Salle bearing up, as he saw him, under his accumulated burdens. In this courageous frame of mind, he and Tonty left Mackinac, and undertook a thousand miles of canoeing to his seigneury at Cataraqui. Here he addressed himself to repairing his credit and getting a new outfit. He offered his creditors a lien upon his estate and discovered new resources, making his will at the same time in favor of one of his chief abettors, a cousin, for whom he seems to have had much consideration.

It was at this time (August 22) that he wrote a letter which Margry assigns to the following year, but its contents belong clearly to this period. The letter is given largely to complaining of Duluth, whom he accuses of boastfully claiming for his discoveries in the Sioux region what His claims for Hennepin and disgust with Duluth. La Salle thinks should be rather credited to his own agents, Accault and Hennepin. Just what La Salle had to depend upon for a knowledge of Hennepin's movements is not clear, for the priest had before this passed on to Quebec and France. It is possible that the priest left some narrative for La Salle. We know that he later left, or said he left, a duplicate statement with another priest at Quebec. Accault's account is thought to be embodied in the *Dernières Découvertes* (Paris, 1697) which Tonty, to whom it was ascribed, disowned. This narrative may at this time have been accessible to La Salle.

There was another grievance on La Salle's part, — he was seldom without such troubles, — in that Duluth, beside boasting, as he said, of his discoveries, was undertaking to open communication with the Sioux country through the Illinois region, over which La Salle claimed a prescriptive right, and with whose trade he could allow no one to interfere. La Salle claimed further to have established a right to kill buffalo on the Wisconsin, to the exclusion of any such interlopers as Duluth.

There was much in this arrogant spirit of La Salle, notwithstanding some validity in his claim, to make his enemies all the more clamorous. La Salle never succeeded in holding an easy mastery over other than his nearest friends. Charlevoix tells us that La Salle's enemies darkened his character beyond the power of his friends to lighten its traits. There was no La Salle and one upon whom La Salle bestowed severer objurgathe Jesuits. tions than upon Allouez and his Jesuit abettors. He charged all his adversities largely upon their machinations. He avowed that they did not hesitate to report false rumors of his own and Tonty's death.

It was in August that La Salle was once more on his way 1681, August. west. He had, according to one account, fifty-four Starts west persons in his train, and twenty-three of them were again. French. His Indians were wholly from New England. He may have gathered recruits on his way, for another statement, written by him to a friend, gives him thirty Frenchmen and a hundred Indians, some of them Shawnees, and all, Nov. 3. At he said, were handy with guns. On November 3, he Fort Miami. was at Fort Miami, and Tonty and Membré were with him. Here he divided his party. Tonty and Membré with most of the train pushed around the head of the lake, a hundred miles, to the Chicago River, and thence dragged their burdens over eighty leagues of the frozen streams to the Illinois. On 1682, Jan., January 4, 1682, La Salle himself joined them by the Feb. At Kankakee route. They found open water for their Crèvecœur and on the canoes when they reached the ruins of Crèvecœur, and Mississippi. on February 6 they glided out upon the Mississippi, known at this time as the Colbert River. Here they were entangled in the ice-floes for several days, but at last the channel cleared, and they went on. Passing the mouth of the Osage (Missouri), Membré records that beyond the mountains, where its sources are, "great ships are seen." They passed the Ohio, but La Salle does not seem to have comprehended that it was the stream he had found in 1669, for there is reason to believe that he supposed the river which at that time he followed made its way to the sea by some basin east of the Mississippi, and he had apparently communicated this belief to Hennepin. He was impelled to this notion by finding no large river south of the Ohio flowing into the Mississippi from the east, corresponding to the ample currents of the Red and Arkansas rivers on the west. He did not yet, and probably never did, comprehend the

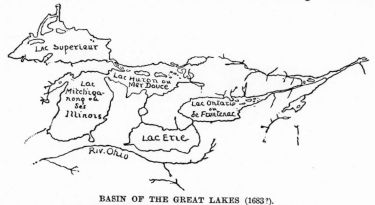

BASIN OF THE GREAT LAKES (1683?).

[Sketched from the Parkman copy of a map in the Archives of the Marine at Paris.]

river systems which drain the mountainous region west of Carolina and Georgia by channels which feed the Ohio and urge their waters on to the Gulf of Mexico. In a paper which he wrote about this time, given by Margry, he seems to have known of the Wabash as a northern affluent of the Ohio, but apparently confounds the Cumberland and Tennessee by making them a single southern branch.

Late in February, they were at the third Chickasaw bluff. Here one of his men, strolling off, got lost in the woods, and was for a while supposed to have been carried off by the Indians. They built meanwhile a stockade on the bluff, and, their companion being at last discovered, it was called after him, Fort Prudhomme. They left him in command February. At Fort Prudhomme.

of it, when they went on. By the middle of March (1682) they were in the region of the Arkansas Indians. One day they could see nothing for a thick fog, when through it came suddenly from one bank the cries of Indian revelry. Cautiously paddling to the other shore, they landed, and barricaded themselves on the river's edge. The fog, lifting, revealed to the revelers their unwonted visitors. The savages respected the calumet, and the wanderers coming among them were struck with the fine shapes of their naked bodies. They tarried awhile for feasts and merriments, in the midst of which, not forgetting a loftier ambition, La Salle set up a post, and hung upon it the arms of France. We have the official record of the transaction (March 14) in Margry, and thus see how the whole valley of the Mississippi was once more mortgaged to the power of the French. Father Membré erected a cross in the village. " Though he could not speak their language," says a trustful Catholic, " he succeeded in acquainting them with the existence of the true God! "

[sidenote: March. Among the Arkansas.]

[sidenote: March. Takes possession of the country.]

Two of the Indians offering themselves as guides, the party paddled on for three hundred more miles, and then landed to visit a town of the Taensas, situated on a neighboring lagoon. Tonty paid a visit of ceremony to the chief, and found the houses of his people built of sun-burnt clay, — the first they had seen. The little native potentate, in returning the civility, paid the Frenchmen a visit with such state as befitted a man who could have two bearers of white fans march before him. Passing on, they were after a while among the Natchez. In their ways of life and worship, this people impressed them more than any tribe they had yet seen. The French accounts speak of the religious caste among them, and of a building which they dignified by calling it a temple. La Salle confidently slept in their village, and with equal confidence set up another column of French authority. On the last of March they passed the mouth of Red River.

[sidenote: Among the Taensas.]

[sidenote: Among the Natchez.]

They were now among a people not so peaceful, and on April 2 they received a shower of arrows, but without disaster. On the 6th they found the river dividing into three channels, and separating their company La Salle led one party down the westerly passage, Tonty with Membré and others took the middle, while Dautray

[sidenote: April. Attacked.]

[sidenote: The party divides.]

conducted the rest along the most easterly current. Presently the water grew from brackish to salt, and they knew they were approaching the sea. On the 9th they all reunited, and just within one of the outlets they made preparations for a ceremony, long thought of. The customary column was set up, proclamation was made in the name of the king, and France assumed the kind of domination that comes of such ceremonies, over the entire water-shed of the great river. It was a confirmation of the lesser claim which La Salle had only recently made among the Arkansas, and which Duluth had made in the country of the Sioux, — a more definite assumption certainly than that which St. Lusson had proclaimed in so vainglorious a fashion at the Sault Ste. Marie eleven years before. The *Vexilla Regis* and *Te Deum* were sung as usual, the notary drew up the record, and a vast stretch of territory passed into history as Louisiana. A leaden plate, with engraved testimony to the act, was buried at the foot of the column. Membré tells us that La Salle took the latitude with his astrolabe, and the party supposed it to be between the parallels of 27° and 28° ; but their leader did not disclose the exact position. They thought that the Bay of Espiritu Santo lay northeast of them, and that vagrant name doubtless here meant the Bay of Mobile. The nearest settled post of the Spaniards was thought to be Panuco, ninety to a hundred leagues to the west. Just what was determined to be the limit of this vast territory appeared when Franquelin worked over all the evidence, and marked the extent in his great map of 1684. By this the French claim was bounded by the Gulf of Mexico westward to the Rio Grande, thence northwesterly to the rather vague water-shed of what we now know as the Rocky Mountains, with an indefinite line along the sources of the upper Mississippi and its higher affluents, bounding on the height of land which shut off the valley of the Great Lakes till the Appalachians were reached. Following these mountains south, the line skirted the northern limits of Spanish Florida and then turned to the gulf. Such dimensions disclosed a marvelous domain. At the north, the headwaters of the great river were still unknown, and were long to remain so. They were in a region where the mean temperature of the year was 40° Fahrenheit, and at the gulf it was 72°. This stretch

[marginal notes] 1682, April. Ceremony at the mouth of the Mississippi.

Limits of Louisiana.

of twelve hundred miles ran from corn to oranges, from syca-
mores to palmettos.   The flood that coursed this enormous basin was one of the world's largest, draining an area of more than

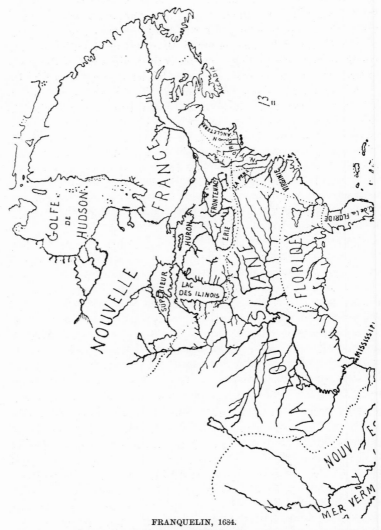

FRANQUELIN, 1684.

[Sketched from the Parkman copy of the original (now lost) in the Archives of the Marine at
Paris.   It resembles closely one in the Ministère des Affaires Etrangères of similar title, No.
7920.   If not by Franquelin, it was doubtless made from his drafts.]

twelve hundred and fifty thousand square miles, which sent twenty million of millions cubic feet of water annually into the sea. Below the Ohio, the rise and fall of the current was forty or fifty feet.

La Salle had been the first of Frenchmen to reach the mouth of the great river, and fifty years had passed since his countrymen on the St. Lawrence had begun to dream of this mysterious river and to debate about its outlet. A paper which Margry prints shows that La Salle was acquainted with the narrative of De Soto's adventures, opening to Spanish acquaintance the circuit of the gulf, a century and a half before.

After La Salle had passed on to the river's mouth, through forests of cypresses hung with moss, and when he experienced what a tremulous ooze its swamps and bayous afforded, he found it difficult to suppose the river which he had coursed was the one which De Soto had known. This unbelief was further reason for him to suspect that another great valley lay to the east of the Mississippi.

It is rather striking that New England Indians, outcast by their tribes' reverses, and sent as homeless wanderers to the west, should have looked on at this far-reaching act upon the delta of the Mississippi, for by it La Salle secured to France that "Acadian coast" as an asylum for that other luckless race of the eastern seaboard whom the struggle between France and England was destined to throw upon its banks, seventy-five years later. Agency of New England Indians.

At the time of the discussion which arose under the treaty of 1763, the fact of this attendance of New England Indians in La Salle's train was brought up as indicative — but certainly without proof — of earlier English knowledge of this outlet of the great valley, which had been gained in company with these same Indians. It was alleged that in revenge for the reverses at the hands of the English in the war which drove them from their soil, they now led the French to their great discovery!

La Salle started to return with gloomy prospects. Food was scarce, and some dried meat which they found proved to be human flesh. They put up instead with alligator steaks. They fought the Indians for something to sustain them La Salle returns.

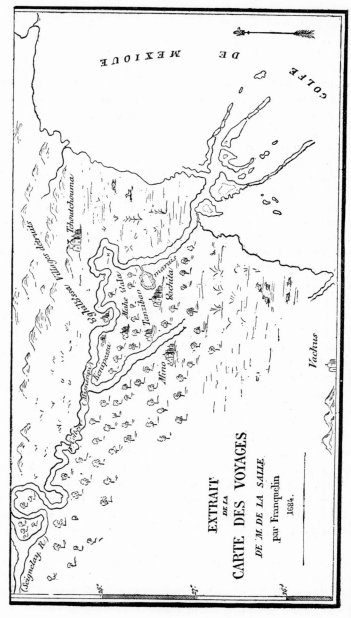

[From Thomassy's *Géologie pratique de la Louisiane.*]

in one place, and barely escaped a fatal encounter at another. La Salle represents that as he approached the country of the Arkansas, he took the west channel, where a large island divided the stream, because he had left some equipments on that side in going down. Here he pushed ahead of the others, taking two canoes with him. When he reached Fort Prudhomme, he fell ill, and for forty days his life was despaired of. Membré watched him tenderly through it all, while Tonty was sent ahead to carry the news of the discovery. By the end of July, La Salle had recovered sufficiently to start on. Passing by Fort Miami, he rejoined Tonty at St. Ignace, in September.

1682, September. La Salle at St Ignace.

La Salle was still weak from his illness, and he tells us that he was hardly himself for four months. He might have gone on and carried the details of his expedition to Quebec, but there was need of his returning to the Illinois. This necessity probably prompted him to write out what passes for his official report, preserved in the Archives of the Marine at Paris. A *Relation* which rendered the narrative in the third person, and which Thomassy was the first to publish, has apparently a pretty close connection with the paper in the Archives of the Marine. It may be that the Membré journal, as printed in Le Clercq, is derived from the same source. It was first given to the English reader in Shea's *Discovery of the Mississippi.*

His report.

It was not long before Tonty was sent back to the Illinois to found a colony, as the best way to secure and organize the possession of the country. In a letter which La Salle had just (October, 1682) dispatched to France, he had hinted at an expedition which he might yet make by water to the Gulf of Mexico, so as to establish a complemental colony at the mouth of the Mississippi. The two colonies would then be in proper correlation to one another, and trade could be carried on between these two extremes of Louisiana, and brought into easy communication with France, — more easy than could be possible by the uncertain and laborious passage by the Great Lakes and the St. Lawrence, closed as it was by ice during so large a part of the year. The proposed movement in turn fell in with the wishes of some in authority to secure the outlet of the great valley against both the Spanish and the English.

1682. La Salle's schemes.

A contingency very soon made it evident to La Salle that his presence was needed in support of Tonty's mission, for rumors had reached him at Mackinac that the Iroquois were again raiding westward and threatening the Illinois.

Frontenac in the last months of his power saw that his control of the Iroquois was slipping from his hands. He wrote to the home government that for ten years his policy with the Indians had been successful, but that a military force of some five or six hundred men was absolutely necessary if his control was to go on for another ten years. There was nothing incensed the confederates more than the movement which La Salle was making in the Mississippi valley. Scarcely a French trader could enter that country and escape the vigilance of the Iroquois. They even dared to ambush the French canoes on Lake

Iroquois and the English.

Ontario. Meanwhile the English allurements were growing stronger and stronger, and the savage confederates were entering into mutual obligations with distant settlers of that race in Maryland.

The king was fast losing patience with the way in which affairs in Canada, with a population that had grown to

Bad condition of Canada.

rising ten thousand, seemed to be going from worse to worse. Her trade with the West Indies had about come to a standstill, and home farming was in no better plight. If the government distributed seed, it was left to rot, and was not planted. If the church was paternal, it claimed for observances all but about ninety days of the growing season, which was short enough at the best. The passion of the young men for the woods was uncontrollable; and it was estimated that at least eight hundred youngsters, fitted to till the soil, were scampering wildly in the forests, doing good to no one, and destroying the regular channels of trade with the Indians. They were carrying brandy to the braves and debauching them, and the law against it could not be enforced. The girls who were left unmarried in the settlements were hardly less idle, and no one taught them to weave or to spin.

His royal master more than once wrote to Frontenac that everybody complained of him, and none more than the intendant. Affairs were no better when Colbert, who had always admonished Duchesneau as if he were a child, resigned, and his son Seignelay took charge of the colonial business. This change

in the ministry was not an auspicious one for La Salle ; nor for
Frontenac, for it gave new opportunities for crimination and
recrimination. Duchesneau lost no time in renewing his
charges against the governor. He intimated that Frontenac
and La Salle were conspiring together to keep up the war between the Iroquois and the Illinois, in order to further their
projects of trade. Frontenac wrote to the perplexed monarch
that it was the enemies of La Salle and the English who were
instigating these savage hostilities. In fact, there was little to
choose between these mutual accusers. The fur trade had
always demoralized the whole people, and there could be no
improvement so long as the government imposed impracticable
restraints. There was hardly a family in Canada that was not
interested in this illicit commerce and had not a member in the
woods, and the English traders at Albany were profiting from
it all. Nothing could be more natural, when, as Duchesneau
informed the king, beaver was worth nearly double in Albany
what it was in Quebec. Frontenac told him much the same
story, for he said that the English rated beaver at about a
third more than the French, and they counted the merchandise
which they used in exchange at not more than half the value of
the French. With this tax, how could Canada compete ? And
who could say that even the governor and his friends were not
using their position to trade with Albany ?

Duchesneau's remedy was to destroy their rival by buying his
country, and he urged upon the minister at home the purchase
both of New England and of Manhattan and Orange (Albany).
But it was not left for Frontenac to deal with the approaching
questions. Already, in May (1682), the king had
commissioned a new governor, and had given him his
instructions. These were to make a show of power to
impress the Iroquois, but to avoid a war if possible, and by all
means to preserve quiet among the Illinois.

It was August, and Quebec was trying to recover from the
horrors of a great fire in the town, which, in destroying fifty-five houses, had swept away half the property
of the colony. Just at this juncture, the new ruler, to replace
Frontenac, arrived. La Barre was a soldier, who had done good
service against the English in the West Indies, but he was no
longer young and agile in body or mind. He was sixty years

1682. La Barre governor.

Quebec afire.

old. He had been a lawyer once, and perhaps that rendered him timid in facing new problems and taking responsibilities. The Indians soon discovered that the vigor they had been accustomed to respect in Frontenac was gone. The king had warned La Barre that he must get on as best he could with the military force already in the colony, for he could spare him no more. The new governor was soon appalled at what he saw and learned, and wrote back that it was absolutely necessary to have an increase of his force. In October, the governor held a council, and it seemed to be the general opinion that the Iroquois were deceiving the French in order to pounce upon their western allies. Frontenac had called the confederates " Children ; " La Barre called them " Brothers," after the earlier
Change of habit. It betokened very well the altered relations
policy. with the savages which were taking place perceptibly. There was no less a change with those who had stood by the government of Frontenac. They now found themselves cast aside, and it was the enemies of Frontenac and of La Salle who came into power.

La Chesnaye, the richest merchant in Quebec, who just now stood well with all for his generous bounty to those who had suffered by the fire, readily got the ear of the new governor, and poured into it all the rumors which were afloat prejudicial to the absent explorer. La Salle's property at Cataraqui was after a while seized, on the ground that he had not kept his contract in maintaining it. It was not long before La Barre was throwing doubt on the pretenses of La Salle to discovery, and was writing to the king that the man was doing his best to bring on an Iroquois war. The king had no sanguine hopes in respect to western discovery, at the best. He had told La Barre that these western efforts were not as useful as was claimed, but that he might suffer La Salle to go on, just to see what would come of it.

For seventy years and more, and ever since Hudson's explorations at the north had disturbed Champlain and his associates, the French had kept an eye upon the English in the north, and
French upon their efforts to divert the Indian trade. Without
claims at the discovery or occupation the French had in 1627 pro-
north. fessed their right as far north as the Arctic circle by

the charter of the company of the Hundred Associates. They now professed that England recognized these boreal rights when in the treaty of St. Germain-en-Laye in 1633, Canada — whatever that may mean — had been restored to the French. There is no evidence that down to 1660 France had obtained any knowledge of this northern region except as the Indians had described it. As the result of Captain Gillam's venture, the English had in 1670 laid claim to the whole water-shed of the bay in the charter of the Hudson Bay Company. This and the earlier exploration of Hudson were much more than a fair offset for the paper claim of the Hundred Associates. We have seen that Talon sent Albanel by way of the Saguenay to get a glimpse of James's Bay, in 1672. Grosseilliers and Radisson, who had been in the English service there a few years later, had found it prudent to leave that service and seek restitution to French favor; and with the certificate that they had made their peace in Paris, they had appeared in Quebec in 1676, anxious to be recognized, but were not successful in the attempt. While they were still in an enforced disgrace, Joliet had been sent in 1679 from Tadoussac, and accomplished the feat of Albanel once again. It is claimed that the English tried to induce Joliet to join their interests, but he proved faithful to his race. He probably on his return prompted Duchesneau, in 1681, to ask to be allowed to undertake an expedition to drive the English out. The next year, 1682, the Company of the North, which had been formed to be some sort of compensation for the trade which was slipping into the hands of the English at the west, undertook to do what Duchesneau had urged. They put two ships under the command of Grosseilliers and Radisson, who were now restored to active participancy in their old field. The party attacked unexpectedly the English post at Port Nelson. The authorities on the wavering con- English and flicts between the French and English at Hudson's French conflicts. Bay during the rest of this century are difficult to use with satisfaction. The two sides differ constantly in their statements, and every effort is made by each to cast the stigma of unprovoked assault on the other side. Neither were the French the only adversaries which the Hudson Bay Company encountered. It had become much the habit for the New Englanders to carry on an illicit trade there by water, and the company constantly complained of such " interlopers." There is no occasion now to dwell upon the bewildering story, other than as it has some relation to the schemes of discovery at the west. English possession of these northern rivers, which led up to the sources of those that beyond the divide descended to the region of the Sioux, affected the French trade in that direction, and controlled French discovery.

We have seen that La Salle had taken exception to the attempts of Duluth to open this Sioux country by way of the Illinois territory, and it was La Salle's eagerness to be sure of maintaining his hold on the Illinois that made him give up his proposed visit to Fort Frontenac, when he started to join Tonty among the Illinois. It was in December when the two friends laid out the plan of a stronghold on the top of what is now known as Starved Rock and named it Fort St. Louis. The place was by nature unassailable except in the rear, while the river front arose in a beetling fashion from the water, and the sides were equally precipitous. The summit was a hundred and twenty-five feet above the plain. It was a conspicuous feature in the broad landscape. Intrenchments and palisades, the remains of which were seen by Charlevoix forty years later, soon encircled the open acre of the top. There was a neighboring community of savages who made a busy scene. About six thousand of the Illinois who had fled before the Iroquois had returned to their old homes, and their numbers were increasing. Other tribes were coming to settle near at hand. The map which Franquelin made a year or more later shows how the villages were scattered in the vicinity, and the count of the warriors which he gives foots up about four thousand, or an equivalent, say, of twenty thousand souls. It was this number which was shortly afterward gathered under the eye of the French commander. Upon this body of friendly Indians, and upon their intercourse with more distant tribes, the French depended for the traffic in peltries which was to support the colony, if, indeed, it could be maintained at all against the Iroquois.

Concerning the defense which could be made against those confederates, La Salle could make some estimate, and he was

Marginal notes:

1652, December. La Salle and Tonty at Starved Rock.

Starved Rock, Fort St. Louis.

preparing for the conflict if it should come ; but the enemies he had made on the St. Lawrence were a force that must yet display itself. It was later asserted that La Barre — whose superseding of Frontenac had not yet come to La Salle's knowledge — had told the Iroquois to respect only his own passes if

STARVED ROCK.

[After a Photograph taken by Bowman, of Ottawa, Illinois, and furnished by the Rev. C. M. Stuart, of Chicago.]

they encountered any French. Since La Salle's warrant in the Illinois country was not dependent on the governor's passes, the protection of the government was in effect withdrawn La Salle and from La Salle, if the story be true. It is fair to say La Barre. that La Barre denied it, but not perhaps till some of his own traders had been robbed by the Iroquois, on the supposition that they belonged to La Salle. The temptation to illicit trade had proved too great for any governor to resist. But an act which La Barre could not deny was his sending the Chevalier de Baugis to seize upon La Salle's post at the Rock. This seems to have been a part of a scheme to control all western posts so as to be prepared against any onset of the Iroquois in the English interest. To a similar end, at the same time, Durantaye was sent with thirty men to strengthen the force at Mackinac. La Barre justified such a movement against La Salle on the ground that his trading privileges were near expiring, and that some responsible power should control the exposed posts in the Illinois. He looked upon La Salle as a debtor for thirty thousand crowns, and likely soon to fall into the hands of his creditors. La Barre, meanwhile, was writing to Seignelay just as if he believed that La Salle's head was turned, and that he was unable to control his own men, — truth, doubtless, in some

1683, April.
La Salle
hears of La
Barre's suc-
cession.

degree. It was just about the same time, near the 1st of April (1683), that word had reached La Salle of the change of power at Quebec. He at once wrote to La Barre a propitiatory and somewhat piteous letter. He told him that his enemies would try to prejudice the governor's mind against him ; that his losses amounted to forty thousand crowns ; that his force was reduced to twenty men, and that they had only a hundred pounds of powder among them. He told him that the Indians were coming in under his protection, and that he should be obliged to send men to Montreal for supplies, and hoped they would not be looked upon as bushrangers, but be allowed to come and go ; for he intended to keep strictly to his instructions and trade with no tribe that

June.

was accustomed to go to the old settlements. Early in June, he again wrote to La Barre, complaining that the men whom he had sent down for supplies had been detained. With the Iroquois skulking about him, munitions were necessary, and he hoped that La Barre would officially direct him to protect the Miamis against the confederates, and give him a chance to eradicate from these western Indians the belief that he was in reality abetting the Iroquois in their raids. This appeal was a difficult one for La Barre to meet. He desired the western Indians should be protected, but he did not believe, or at least did not profess to believe, that La Salle had any purpose to do it.

Since the spring, the Senecas had been restless and seemed to be moving west. La Barre's efforts to check them by negotiation effected little, and he renewed his petition to the king for a military force to occupy his forts while his veterans took the field. He also appealed for farmers to till the ground while the experienced settlers were spared for a campaign. If the English and Dutch were not to capture all the western trade, he said, the Senecas and Cayugas must be crushed. In August (1683), La Barre got some of their chiefs to come to Montreal for a conference, but he could do little with them. They were determined, so they said, that the Illinois should die !

August.

If this was not encouraging, the tidings which the governor soon got from the king aroused hope that something active could be done in the north, for he was instructed to prevent the English occupancy of Hudson's Bay; and in pursuance of that plan La Barre soon dispatched Duluth to build a fort on Lake Nepigon and distribute presents to the Indians, so as to check the English trade in that direction. To the south it was not less encouraging, for the king informed him that Thomas Dongan, a colonel in the royal army, the son of an Irish baronet, and a Catholic, had been sent by the English king to New York as governor, with instructions to do nothing to disturb the interests of the French in Canada. This seemed to promise well; but Dongan proved a good Briton despite all the promises, and the authorities at Quebec soon learned that he was not a man to be trifled with. He had more faith, too, in what La Salle had done than the French themselves, and perfectly understood how French settlements along the river, " running all along from our lakes by the back of Virginia and Carolina to the Bay of Mexico," might prove " very inconvenient to the English." He had not been long in New York before he was asking permission to send a ship to discover the river of " Lassal."

Dongan,
Governor of
New York.

Meanwhile the Iroquois threats against the Illinois had not come to an outbreak. Straggling parties of Cayugas here and there cut off French or Indian, but nothing more alarming had happened. La Salle nurtured his hope of completing his plans by a voyage to the gulf, and, leaving Tonty to deal with the Iroquois if they approached the Rock,

La Salle
leaves Fort
St. Louis.

started for Quebec.   In passing up the east shore of Michigan, he met De Baugis on the way to Fort St. Louis to relieve him of command.   La Salle now comprehended, for the first time, the full effect of the change which the departure of Frontenac had occasioned.   He further understood how it had been deemed necessary to depose him in order that his presence among the Illinois might not prove a pretense for an Iroquois attack.   He accepted the disclosures with what equanimity he could, and sent

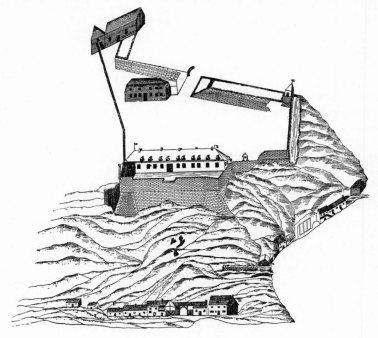

FORT ST. LOUIS DE QUEBEC.
[By Franquelin, 1683.   From Sulte's *Canadiens-Français*, vol. ii.]

word to Tonty to acquiesce cheerfully in the new rule.   He probably learned at Mackinac that La Barre had already planned to send his own traders to the Illinois country, and it was not long after that the Sieur de Beauvais and others, with such permits, were passing over the Chicago portage.

1683, Nov., Dec. In Quebec and Rochelle.   This outcome of all his efforts and trials had not much in it to inspirit the weary dreamer and discoverer, now on his way to encounter his creditors.   La

Salle reached Quebec in November, and embarked for France. On December 23, he landed at Rochelle.

Perhaps he gained new courage when he found how large a space in the public mind Canada was beginning to fill. If the king had not been much impressed with the importance of La Salle's discoveries, others had been. It all had served, says Professor Seeley, " to bring France into the foremost of colonial powers." The interest had in some part arisen from the attractions which Hennepin was offering to the ordinary reader, since the priest's first book, as we have seen, was just now creating a lively influence in what he had revealed, and the narrative was rapidly extending its circle of readers by translations into nearly all the western languages. A cataract five hundred feet high, as his story represented Niagara, and of enormous volume, was finding a place in popular regard among the world's great wonders.

CHAPTER XIV.

LA SALLE'S TEXAN COLONY.

1684–1687.

IT has been supposed that La Salle on going to France took with him the material which he had accumulated for a map of his discoveries. The data had probably been arranged by Franquelin in Quebec, and we have, it is supposed, the result as worked up by some Parisian cartographer, in what is known as the 1684 map of Franquelin. This production has already been referred to as defining what was then understood to be the bounds of Louisiana. If it was not upon the representations of this map, it must have been on such showing as La Salle could make from his own memoranda, that soon after his arrival he was at work framing a memorial to the king, in which he asked that he might be allowed to conduct an expedition by sea to the mouths of the great river which he had discovered. It was not an inopportune moment for such a petition. The relations of France with Spain suggested a blow at the Spanish domination in the Gulf of Mexico, if France could deal one. There was, moreover, an attractive field for conquests in the Spanish silver provinces of New Mexico, which La Salle was not slow to point out as a way for France to take revenge for Spanish insolence in the gulf. It would at the same time secure for a dutiful subject like himself some recompense for his loyal sacrifices. La Salle reminded Seignelay also that it was not to be forgotten that the expedition offered a great opportunity to reach the heathen, who were already, as La Salle represented, much incensed against the Spaniards for their treatment of them.

It was not only in generalizations of glory and Christian endeavor that La Salle urged his plans. He entered into particu-

[margin note: 1684. Franquelin's map.]

[margin note: La Salle proposes expedition to the Gulf of Mexico.]

lars of the way in which he proposed to proceed. He would fortify the Colbert (Mississippi) sixty leagues above its mouth, where the river could be readily defended by fireships. He could count, he said, on fifteen thousand fighting men among the river Indians. He asked for two hundred men to accompany him from France, and expected to pick up fifty buccaneers at San Domingo. He could bring down four thousand warriors from the Illinois country. He could advance on the Spanish province of New Biscay by the Seignelay (Red) River. All this he could do, if only he was allowed a vessel of thirty guns, with some extra cannon for land use.

This plan curiously accorded with that of another adventurer who had been hanging for some time about the French court. La Salle's needy abettor was Peñalosa, a former Spanish governor of New Mexico, who had his own reasons for wishing to get into the good graces of the French government. To strengthen his pretensions, he published an account of an expedition which he professed to have made from Santa Fé to the Mississippi. The Rio Bravo, which he named as the site of the colony which he proposed in the French interest, he and La Salle — for they were not long in getting into communication — evidently thought to be the same stream which La Salle had descended. It was in January, 1682, that this Spanish renegade had first proposed his plan, which involved an attack on Panuco, and then a march inland. There is some reason to believe that La Salle did not at first heartily accede to any joint arrangement, and Parkman and others contend that the peace with Spain which intervened prevented the intended coöperation. The subject is certainly surrounded with doubt, but Shea thinks we clear off all mists if we allow the joint scheme to have been accepted by La Salle and forwarded by the government. There is a good deal which is best understood in such a solution. Peñalosa was now a man of sixty, rather old for untried adventures, and perhaps not averse to letting a younger man like La Salle break the way. It was three and twenty years since this Spanish adventurer had been sent out to New Mexico. During his term in office he had had differences with the Inquisition, and had fallen into their net, from which he did not extricate himself for a long time. When he did, he went to Spain to seek redress, but getting none, he fled to France, in no spirit to suffer longer, and resolved to be revenged. In pushing his project at this time, he did not overlook the advantages which La Salle's establishments on the Illinois might be in the near future, and he told Seignelay that such benefit ought to be counted upon. All this helped La Salle, who at the same time was very likely instigating the public reports that in establishing those posts on the upper Mississippi he had not had the support which he deserved from the authorities in Canada.

These movements had all the effect on the king which La Salle could hope for, and letters were written to La Barre ordering the restitution of Fort Frontenac and the Rock to La

1684, Nov.
La Forest
sent to
Canada in
La Salle's
interests.

Salle. His lieutenant, La Forest, was dispatched in April, 1684, with such directions, being at the same time instructed to receive the fort and hold it for his master. La Forest apparently had some hope that he might be later directed to lead a force down the Mississippi to coöperate with La Salle, but no such orders were sent.

When the plans had ripened, La Salle received a new com-

La Salle
made gov-
ernor of
Louisiana.

mission, by which he was authorized to found colonies in Louisiana, and to govern the vast territory from Lake Michigan to the Gulf of Mexico. The king did his part in ordering to the service more than La Salle had dared to ask for, — one ship, the "Joly," of thirty-six guns, and another of six guns, beside two smaller craft. By the end of May, La Salle was in Rochelle, making ready for the embarkation, and his agents were going about the streets picking up recruits. He secured a force of marines, a hundred soldiers, and about two hundred and eighty other persons, including women and children; for it was to be a colony based on family life, whatever ulterior purpose it was to serve as a military rendezvous. Among the leaders of the party we recognize an old friend in Membré, and there were other priests, not without later fame,

His com-
rades :
Douay,
Leclercq,
Cavelier,
Joutel.

in Douay, and Leclercq, the *Etablissement de la Foy* of the latter being a book we must often turn to in our study of these times. Another Sulpitian was Father Cavelier; a brother of La Salle, and a fellow Rouennaise, Joutel, were also in the company. We know more of the story of the subsequent mishaps from the journal which Joutel kept of them.

Beaujeu, a captain in the royal navy, reported to take command of the principal ship, and his position was Beaujeu and La Salle. necessarily such as brought him into close companionship with La Salle. If they had been suited to one another, Beaujeu would not have had for so many years a bad reputation with writers as an obstructor of La Salle's purposes. The documents which Margry has of late published quite reverse the world's judgment of this naval officer, and lead us to believe that he did all that a sensible person should do to bring order out of the confusion with which such a visionary as La Salle was sure to swamp any business he undertook. Beaujeu, by his education as an officer, was very likely exacting in the requirements which he considered essential to the proper ordering of such an undertaking, and he could hardly avoid reaching the conclusion that La Salle's unbusiness-like ways were the signs of a wavering intellect, — as he did. It was natural for a vain, self-contained man like La Salle, who had no conception of how a well-ordered experiment should be tried, to grow jealous of any one who showed superiority in method. So the relations of the naval commander and the leader of the expedition were strained from the first, and we cannot but wish that Beaujeu had been left to his own head for this venture, and that La Salle had been sent back to Canada with La Forest. As it was, Beaujeu's position was most trying, and nothing but resources of tact on his part carried the project on at all. It was unfortunate that the wife of Beaujeu was a confidant of the Jesuits, for this was enough to disquiet La Salle's mind as to every motion of the naval commander. So there were imagined machinations of the Jesuits haunting La Salle, and causing distraction when he should have been forming plans. Beaujeu constantly complains that he never knew where to find his associate. This seaman was a Norman himself, and he thought he knew his countrymen's failings. " Never a Norman was so much Norman as La Salle," he said, " and Normans are always stumbling-blocks." It is curious to see how Margry, another Norman, in printing the damaging testimony against La Salle, is anxious to break its force as much as he can.

La Salle kept even from Beaujeu the secret of his destination, until it became necessary to engage pilots, the result of which was that when Beaujeu discovered he was going to the gulf, he found he had not made all the provisions for the voyage which were necessary.

Thus the period of preparation was filled with vexation and dispute. At last, on July 18, just as everything was nearly ready, La Salle wrote a final letter to his mother in Rouen, telling her that, with four vessels and nearly four hundred men, he was about to sail. The fleet finally put to sea on July 24; but the "Joly" soon breaking her bowsprit, they had to put back for repairs, and did not finally get off till August 1. The counsels of the two leaders were still at variance. Beaujeu thought it necessary to put in to Madeira for water; but La Salle opposed it, on the ground that the Spaniards might divine their aim. They were two months in reaching San Domingo, and many fell sick on board, including La Salle himself. They were further unfortunate in having Spanish cruisers capture the smaller vessel of their fleet; and when La Salle was informed of it, he was still ill at San Domingo. With the principal leader off duty, the company on the fleet fared badly in that port. The men gave themselves over to unrestrained dissipation, and the more reckless among them succumbed to the enticements of the buccaneers and deserted. Beaujeu observed it all, but could do little beyond controlling his crew. He gave pretty bad accounts of it in his letters which he sent home, saying among other things that the Spaniards had six ships scouring these waters, each one of which was more than a match for the "Joly."

On November 25, the expedition left San Domingo, La Salle and his immediate adherents shifting their quarters from the "Joly" to the "Aimable," the larger of the remaining vessels, leaving Beaujeu in undisputed charge of his own ship. The ships followed along the south side of Cuba, and were soon separated in a fog. On December 28, a sailor at the masthead of the "Aimable" saw land. They took it to be Appalachee Bay, three hundred miles east of the Mississippi, while in reality the vessels were a hundred miles west of that river, and in the neighborhood of Atchafalaya Bay. It was later believed, when it became known that La Salle had his thoughts upon the New Biscay mines, as Coxe, for instance, held in his *Carolana*, that La Salle had purposely overshot the mouth of the Mississippi.

1684, July–August. The fleet sails.

November 25. Leave San Domingo.

December. Make land.

It is difficult to believe this; for though he had taken the latitude of the mouths of the Colbert, it was only the merest guess which he could have made regarding their longitude. 1685, January. Off the Sabine River. Here, at the beginning of the new year (1685), he lay at anchor, hoping for the "Joly" to appear. He was probably off the mouth of the Sabine River, with a marshy stretch of shore in sight three leagues away. It is not easy to settle beyond doubt the landmarks of this cruise of La Salle along the Texas coast, and investigators are not agreed in their identifications. It was on January 6 that they discovered an opening, which was very likely Galveston Bay. La Salle did not like to enter it for fear Beaujeu would not discover him, though he thought it was one of the Mississippi mouths. He lingered off the shore for several days, but the "Joly" was not seen. At last, supposing Beaujeu must have passed beyond him, he steered in pursuit. After a while some Indians came off, but he could not understand them. He saw breakers and, beyond, what appeared to be a vast plain with buffalo and deer roving upon it. He made a landing, and found the country barren, and lined with flats of mud. He could find no fresh water. The coast stretched south, and perhaps the best supposition is that he was near Matagorda Island. A fog came on and he anchored. When it lifted, the "Joly" was in sight. The two leaders met, and charged each other with the blame of the protracted separation. Beaujeu evidently thought that La Salle had no conception where he was. La Salle professed at any rate to believe he had struck another mouth of the Mississippi. He was persuaded that the open water which he had seen at the mouths in 1682 was what he now found to be lagoons, separated from the sea by long stretches of narrow, sandy islands, which extended up and down the coast. There were delays on making ready for landing, and Beaujeu and La Salle had continued disagreements. It seems at this time to have leaked out that La Salle had some purpose to attack the Spaniards, and that Peñalosa was expected to join him, after he had established his foothold on the coast. Cavelier says that they did not despair of this relief till near the end of the following year. It is stated that one of the priests in the company was so disturbed at the idea of attacking his countrymen — for the priest was a Spaniard — that he withdrew from the expedition and determined to return with Beaujeu.

It was now February, and Joutel was sent along the shore to explore, since La Salle determined on disembarking. The entrance to the bay, close at hand, was difficult on account of sandbars, but they marked out the channel by sound-

1685, February.

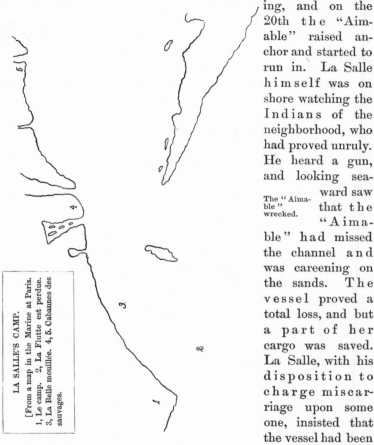

ing, and on the 20th the "Aimable" raised anchor and started to run in. La Salle himself was on shore watching the Indians of the neighborhood, who had proved unruly. He heard a gun, and looking seaward saw that the "Aimable" had missed the channel and was careening on the sands. The vessel proved a total loss, and but a part of her cargo was saved. La Salle, with his disposition to charge miscarriage upon some one, insisted that the vessel had been

The " Aimable " wrecked.

LA SALLE'S CAMP.

[From a map in the Marine at Paris.

1, Le camp.   2, La Flutte est perdue.
3, La Belle mouillée.   4, 5, Cabannes des sauvages.

purposely stranded, in order to embarrass him. Joutel certainly shared this opinion with him.

The "Joly" and a small messenger vessel were now all the ships they had, and it was necessary to make some lodgment before Beaujeu's time for leaving came. So the company was landed, and they began to intrench a camp as best they could, for some essential tools had been lost in

A camp begun.

the wreck. Some defense was necessary, for the natives grew more and more troublesome. The savages stole what they could, and even killed some of the French. Disease was doing sad work, and the colony was soon burying five or six a day. The prowling foe fired the prairie, and La Salle feared for a while that the conflagration might approach his powder. They had nothing but a barricade of tree stumps, which they had picked up on the shore, to keep the devastation off.

La Salle w i s h e d Beaujeu to take the " Joly " and explore the coast farther, and settle some of their geographical p r o b - lems, but that officer said he was not pro- visioned for any long search, but would go to Martinique f o r supplies, if La Salle thought best. F o r some reason nothing was done.

Later in February, Beaujeu was prepar- ing to leave. Stowed in the hold of the " Joly " were the can- non and balls, which La Salle needed ; but in the rolling sea, Beaujeu declined to

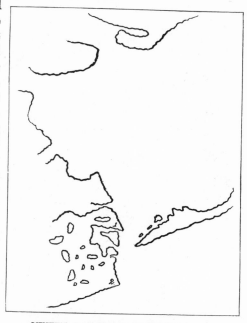

MINET'S SKETCH OF MATAGORDA BAY.

[KEY: 1, Cabanne des Sauvages. 2, Campe de M. De la Salle. 3, Where we left Mons. De la Salle. The original is in the Archives at Paris.]

risk removing so much ballast, but promised to do so when he could find a quiet harbor. On March 12, he sailed, March. taking with him such as had lost heart. Among these Beaujeu sails. was Minet, the engineer, who on the voyage made a map, which has come down to us. He placed the outlet of the Mississippi apparently at Matagorda Bay, with the mouths as La Salle had mapped them in 1682, but with also a sketch of them according to Minet's own observations.

Beaujeu intended to stop at Mobile Bay and get out the cannon for La Salle; but he missed the opening and went on to France.

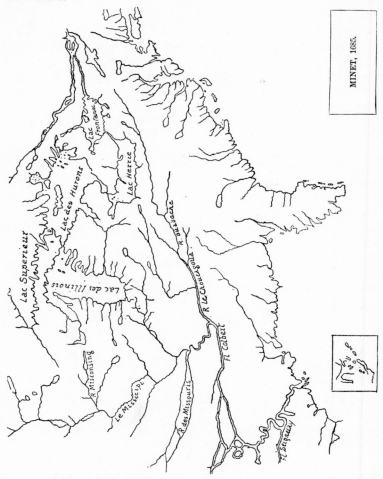

NOTE. The sketch in the small square shows the mouths of the Mississippi " comme nous les avons trouvez." The map shows it as " Le Salle le marque dans sa carte."

It was a discouraging prospect before La Salle. He had written, only a few days before, to Colbert that he had reached the western mouth of the Mississippi, and should soon begin the ascent. The main channel, he supposed, was twenty or thirty leagues to the east. He did not, however, hold to this opinion long, for he grew distrustful of his position, and made up his mind that he must seek elsewhere for that stream. But first it was necessary to get into a healthier and more defensible spot; and so, fixing upon a site for a fort on a river a little distance up from the head of the bay, he constructed, largely out of the wreck of the " Aimable," his Fort St. Louis. General Fort St. J. S. Clark, a recent investigator of the topographical Louis. features of the region, is confident that the camp first occupied was on Mission Bay, near the Espiritu Santo Bay, and that the Fort St. Louis was on the Garcitas River five miles above its junction with Lavaca Bay, while the adjacent river of that name has usually been considered the site of the fort. General Clark represents that the ground of his supposed site still bore, at a recent day, remains of the fort, and was marked by other relics. To most inquiriers the evidence has been sufficient that the vicinity of Matagorda Bay — and Espiritu Santo is not far off — was the scene of these fearful experiences, though Kingsford, the latest historian of Canada, inclines to place them in Galveston Bay.

There were now only a hundred and eighty souls left on land of all that had started from Rochelle. The small crew which navigated the little " Belle," the sole vessel now remaining, was additional. It was the middle of July when La Salle was able to occupy this new stronghold and 1685, July. to lay out his garden beds. The construction of the fort had severely tasked his weakened comrades. They had to cut trees for the work three miles away. They mounted some cannon upon the palisades; but as their balls had been lost in the " Aimable," they loaded the pieces with bags of bullets. They had occasionally to make a demonstration against the hovering Indians, in order to remind them of the force which was in reserve for any hostile act. Since Margry has printed Joutel's journal in full, we can trace their daily doings with more minuteness than the earlier published abridgments of it rendered possible. This somewhat abridged and altered text, edited by De Michel, was printed in 1713 as *Journal historique*, accompanied by a map. The story abridged or at full length is one of anxiety, dread, and misery. Thirty died in a short time, their head carpenter among them. By the close of October, La Salle was ready to set out on an expedition of

1685, Oct.
La Salle's
explora-
tions. discovery. He left Joutel in command of the fort, with thirty-four companions. He ordered the "Belle" to follow the shore, so that he could communicate

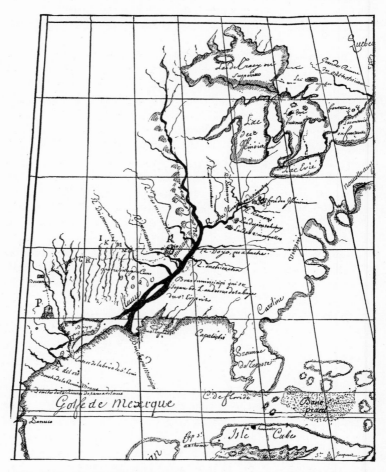

NOTE. This map by Joutel is reduced from the upper portion of the map in a MS. of the nar-which the book of 1713 was printed, and its map engraved. Mr. A. P. C. Griffin, of that library, verbal changes, apparently made in conformity with the requirements of the censor expressed in Archives and printed by Margry) used for the press.

with her when necessary; but he was not always within sup-porting distance of the craft, for some of her crew, at one point, landed and wandered off to meet their deaths at the hands of lurking savages. It was rather an aimless march, so it seemed. His men wandered, and one of them, 1686, January. Duhaut, appeared at the fort in January, 1686, in a

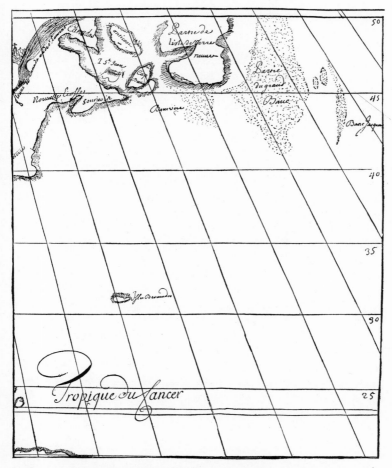

pitiable guise. He had lost the trail, and came back to bring Joutel tidings of their miserable experiences, and of the loss of the seamen from the " Belle." Two months later, near the end

March. La of March, La Salle himself returned. Joutel espied
Salle returns. him afar off one day from the roof of his fort, approaching with seven or eight others. La Salle's story was that they had found a river, which they had supposed the Mississippi; and in a palisade which they had built on its banks, they had left some men, — none of them were ever heard of. He had detached a small party on his way back to carry a message to

The " Belle " the " Belle," which had been ordered to wait in a little
lost.   bay. She was not to be found there, as the messengers reported when they reached the fort the day following La Salle's return.

This was the severest stroke which fate had yet leveled at the leader's plans. The little craft had on board his ammunition and his papers, and he was depending on her to transport his colony to the Mississippi, if ever he could find it. Under the blow La Salle fell ill; but when he recovered a little, — he never needed anything more than time to restore his courage, — he began to cast about for some plan of rescue. Nothing was so promising as to get through, if possible, to Canada, and send word thence to France for naval help.

A new party to make the trial of reaching the Illinois country was now made up, including, beside La Salle, the two priests,

April. New Cavelier and Douay, and a score of others. They
futile at- started across the prairie on April 22, laden down
tempt to with provisions and camp fittings. Joutel was again
reach Can- left in charge of the fort, and a few days later (May 1)
ada. he was cheered by the arrival of six men who had been saved from the wreck of the " Belle." It was not long before La Salle and eight of his men once more came back to tell a fearful story of suffering and disaster. Death and desertion had made sad havoc, and less than half of the company had returned with their leader. They reported having found illimitable prairies, with herds of roaming buffaloes. They had got five horses of some Indians, which told of trade or plunder either among the Spaniards or the Comanches, nearer neighbors of the Spanish posts. They had met delays at broad rivers, and, finding their powder gone, La Salle had led them back. The colony was now reduced to forty-five souls. All hopes of succor by sea were now gone. They had watched in vain for signs

of Peñalosa, and nothing was to be done but to make another trial to reach the Mississippi, and ascend to Canada.

Again a forlorn-hope was made up. Twenty men were to stay behind. Those who were to go included, beside La Salle, his brother Cavelier, Moranget his nephew, Joutel, Douay the friar, Duhaut and his servant L'Archevêque, Liotot the surgeon, Heins, a German bucca-neer picked up at San Domingo, a boy of the Cavelier family, beside two Indians, one a Shawnee, and others, — seventeen in all. They were a sorry set in appearance, clothed in draggled finery and in such garments as they could patch up out of the sails of the "Belle," which had been saved. It was early in January, 1687. We follow their march in the journal which Joutel has left, — much the best of all the accounts, — and it is supported by the story as Douay tells it, so far as it goes. The narrative of Cavelier is confused, but he says that La Salle's purpose was to reach the Mississippi and dispatch him (Cave-lier) up to Canada, while the leader himself returned to his colony. Their course lay northerly, in the main. The horses which they had secured on the previous expedition now relieved them of much of the burden, and they packed upon them a bull-hide boat, to use in crossing the streams. It was the hunting season, and they found wandering bands of Indians everywhere. It rained often, and this forced them to live much in camp, and such inactivity conduced to discontent and plotting.

It was the middle of March when La Salle found himself within a few miles of a spot, on the southern branch of Trinity River, where he had concealed some corn on his previous expedition. He sent a party to recover it, while he with Joutel and others remained in camp. Those who were sent found the corn spoiled, but they soon killed a buffalo, and sent back for the horses to take the meat in. The nephew of La Salle was in the party, and in making a division of the carcass high words had arisen between him and Duhaut. Those who sustained the latter now plotted to kill Moranget, as well as the Shawnee and La Salle's servant, who were sup-porters of the nephew. That night the plot was extended, and the death of La Salle himself was decided upon. The occasion soon offered. The party not returning, La Salle took Douay

[marginal note:] 1687, Janu-ary. Last attempt to go north.

[marginal note:] 1687, March.

with him and went to discover the cause. Approaching the conspirators' camp, he fired his gun to attract attention, which gave them time to arrange an ambuscade. L'Archevêque, the servant of Duhaut, was placed as a decoy to guide the approaching
La Salle
murdered. victim, who no sooner got within close range than two shots from the tall brakes laid him dead. Duhaut called out to Douay not to fly. The murderers stripped the body of La Salle, and left it a prey to the wolves. The shots were fired by Duhaut and Liotot. The latter had harbored a revengeful spirit ever since a kinsman among the colonists had died, as he thought, under the responsible act of La Salle.

Duhaut was now master of the camp, and no one of those not implicated in the assassination knew what to expect. The party moved about under his direction in a listless way, buying food of the Indians and feasting in their lodges. In their wanderings they met a Frenchman who had deserted from one of La Salle's earlier parties. They learned from him that there were two other such deserters in the neighborhood. These they found living as the savages did.

It was not long before the assassins were quarreling with
The assas-
sins divide. each other, Heins, the German, heading a faction against Duhaut. When it came to violence, Duhaut was struck down by the German, and one of the barbarized Frenchmen killed Liotot. This broke up the party. Heins and the six guilty ones divided the spoils with the others, and gave themselves up to a career in the woods.

The party which adhered to Joutel were given six horses,
1687, June.
Joutel's
party. and thus equipped, they started to find the Mississippi under the conduct of three Indian guides. It was in June when they got started, with feelings of relief. They went towards the northeast, found friendly reception among such tribes as they encountered, and reached the Arkansas River not far from its outlet. They saw on the opposite bank a house of European construction, with a tall cross standing beside it. Its occupants discovered the wanderers and ferried them over. It seemed that Tonty, reinstated at the Fort St. Louis of the Illinois, had heard of Beaujeu's arrival in
Tonty's
search for
La Salle in
1686. France, and of the tidings which he had taken of La Salle's landing and misfortunes. This was in the autumn of 1685, and in February, 1686, he had

started with twenty-five Frenchmen and eleven Indians to descend the river. In holy week he reached its mouths. It was a solitude, not broken by human sign for thirty leagues east or west, where he searched. Tonty wrote a letter for La Salle and committed it to an Indian chief, and fourteen years later Iberville found it in the savage's hands. The dejected searcher now turned back. Six of his men volunteered to stay with the Arkansas and hold a post, and it was two of these who now welcomed Joutel and his friends, and listened to their story, which as Couture heard it is rather unsatisfactorily set forth in a paper printed by Margry.

On the 1st of August, Joutel's party went on once more, and, passing into the Mississippi, struggled slowly upstream, bearing their sad story, just a year after Tonty, on his return to his post, had communicated to the minister the story of his luckless efforts to succor La Salle. In September, they were 1687, September. paddling up the quiet Illinois. By the middle of the month, they were at the Rock. They were received at the fort by Belleforest, then in command, for Tonty had gone east at the summons of the governor, to join an expedition against the Senecas. A *Te Deum* was sung in the chapel, but Allouez, the missionary, lay ill in the fort. Joutel tells us that this priest was uneasy when they told him that La Salle was on his way to join them, being conscious of many efforts to thwart La Salle's purposes, and that it was a fear of meeting one whom he had wronged that induced Allouez shortly after to leave the fort. It is fair to add that the Jesuit writers deem such a story an injustice to a devoted missionary, long resident among the Illinois.

Why were Allouez and all the other occupants of the fort given to understand that La Salle was still alive, and was soon to appear? There is no wholly satisfactory reason why such a misrepresentation was practiced. The truth was not long after to be known, when Couture came up the river with the tale as he had learned it from those who were now falsifying its particulars. The only reasons which have been offered for the deceit are that Joutel and the rest dreaded to abate the joy which their coming created ; that in getting supplies to go on, they could not have got the same credit with La Salle known to be dead, and that for La Salle's relatives, at least, there were reasons why they should get to France in advance of the news of his death, to secure some property rights.

Leaving this deceitful story behind them, Joutel and his party pushed on to Lake Michigan, where, being overtaken by a gale, they found it prudent to return to the fort in order to recover for a new start. In the interval, Tonty had come back, and March– ʾhe, too, was kept in the same ignorance of the truth. April, 1688. He fitted them out with new supplies, and they passed on and reached Mackinac in safety. Here some furs which Cavelier had received from Tonty were sold on La Salle's account. With the burning burden on their conscience, they at last embarked at Quebec. The truth was not disclosed when they reached France in October, till after a delay which caused suspicion; and then when the worst was known, the king did nothing to rescue the poor colony on the gulf shore. It was at last determined by the government that the murderers should be apprehended if they appeared in Canada, and such an order was sent to the governor ; but no one ever suffered at the hands of the law.

The fate of the colony is not unknown. The vessel which the Spaniards had captured near San Domingo revealed to them the object of La Salle. During the next three years, four expeditions were sent by Spanish authority to discover the French, but without success. They surmised something of disaster when they found the wrecks of the " Aimable " and " Belle." It is probable that one of La Salle's deserters finally tried to destroy the colony, for an overland expedition from Mexico at last discovered their fort, and this party was thought to be led by a Frenchman. It was too late, however, for rescue or revenge. Three dead bodies lay on the ground. It was otherwise a scene of devastation and solitude. A crowd of savages hovered around, but gave no sign. A few days later, two men presented themselves to the Spanish force. They were in native guise, but proved to be two of the colony, — L'Archevêque and Grollet. This was in May, 1689, and according to their story, the remnant of the French had been attacked three months before by Indians, and all were either killed or carried off. It has been said that these two Frenchmen were sent to Spain and thrown into prison ; but Bandelier claims to have found in the records of Santa Fé traces of L'Archevêque's later career among the Spaniards, and says that his descendants are still living in that region. The same investigator affirms that he has discovered traces in the archives of New Mexico of two others of La Salle's colony. We learn from a report of the viceroy of New Spain that measures were taken about 1690 to occupy the Texan country against the French, and that missions were established there by the Spaniards, who afterwards succeeded in rescuing the few survivors of the French who were found among the native tribes.

A few years later (1693), when Tonty was living at Fort St. Louis, he prepared the *Memoirs* relating to his own and La Salle's discoveries which is now accessible in the Margry collection. It is an excellent guide to the historian ; but the same cannot be said of the *Dernières Découvertes*, published in Paris in 1697, and in the next year in an English version at London. This publication was charged upon Tonty, but he disowned it, and well he might. Whoever compiled it doubtless used the memoir which Tonty prepared in 1693, but other less trustworthy material was embedded in it. The putting of it together was done without close knowledge of the events, and manifests, moreover, no skill. With Tonty's own narrative preserved, the book has little value.

CHAPTER XV.

DENONVILLE AND DONGAN.

1683–1687.

WITH La Salle gone to France and the governor's emissaries
1683. La Barre. in possession of what that projector had left behind
him, La Barre closed the year (1683) with a pros-
pect of doing something; at least, so people thought before he
had time to show his timidity. The next year (1684) opened
with renewed activity on the part of the Iroquois. War parties of the Senecas were moving west, and there were suspicions
that English packmen were following in their rear and making
trade among the Shawnees and Choctaws. By March,
March, 1684.
some of La Barre's agents on their way to the Illinois were robbed on the Kankakee, and before the month was
over a party of Senecas broke upon the Indian camp near the
Rock, and Tonty and De Baugis worked together successfully
in defending their stronghold for nearly a week, before the
assailants retired. When La Barre heard of this, the exigency
seemed for a while to arouse him, and he sent off messengers to
the upper lakes to ask his lieutenants there to come and help
him punish the Senecas in their own country. At the same
time he wrote to Dongan, asking him to prohibit the sale of
firearms to the Iroquois. The English governor reminded him
that the Iroquois whom it was proposed to chastise were British
subjects, and that he was quite willing to make recompense for
their misdeeds, if the French had any charges to prefer against
them.

If the French armed the Illinois, why should not the English
put guns in the hands of the Iroquois? Dongan knew that
English firearms were seen almost everywhere through North
America, carried by these same confederates. He was at this
time writing home that the Iroquois, having no beaver in their

own country, sent parties, both for trade and war, as far as the
northwest passage, on the one side, and to the South Sea, —
wherever he supposed that to be, — and even to Florida, on the
gulf side.   Only recently Lord Effingham had come from Virginia to make the Iroquois agree to spare the frontiers of that
colony, and by treaty Dongan himself had been hanging the
armorial bearings of the Duke of York in the villages of the

RUINS OF THE INTENDANT'S PALACE IN QUEBEC.

[Originally built, 1684 ; reconstructed at different times, and finally destroyed in 1785.   After
a sketch in Lemoine's *Quebec, Past and Present*, p. 105.]

Mohawks and Oneidas.   Father de Lamberville, at this time,
writing from the Onondaga mission to La Barre, said that the
governor of New York had sent a shabby flag with the English
arms on it, to be hoisted among the Mohawks, but that people
had shut it up in their treasure-box.   Dongan had nevertheless
arranged with the confederacy to take the country south of Lake
Erie under the English protection.   The Canadian intendant
knew well enough what all this meant, and wrote to the king
that La Barre would bluster, but would not fight.   Perhaps

some of the lookers-on thought differently when La Barre in July set out for Fort Frontenac. The Jesuits had already recalled Father Milet from the Oneida country, where he had kept a mission for seventeen years. The governor's bluster ended as the intendant had predicted. The French leader went very peaceably across the lake, and accepted a truce, in which the Senecas would not abate one jot of their purpose to destroy the western allies of the French if they could. This was the news which reached Niagara when Durantaye, Duluth, and Perrot arrived there with a hundred and fifty bushrangers and five hundred Indians, whom they had led down from the upper lakes for some savage work, as La Barre had proposed. This western rabble turned back indignantly, and La Barre's lieutenants had no easy task to hold them together.

In October, the intendant, who had no confidence in the peo-

October, 1684. ple, could boast to his government that he had not misjudged their governor. The king, who was just at this time looking forward to La Salle's successes over the Spaniards on the Mississippi, was prompt to decide that a different leader must be given to the Canadians, if the English were to be restrained on the lakes. Dongan in New York had proved an adversary that no common man could wrestle with, and the French were beginning to understand that their movements beyond the mountains were now watched by a man who

1685. Denonville governor. had a decided western policy for his government. It was to struggle with such a man that Denonville, in the autumn of 1685, came to Quebec as governor, followed by a fresh accession of troops, not all of whom, however, survived the tumultuous voyage.

With a vigilant antagonist in New York, the commandant at Quebec was not in an enviable position. The town was but a nest of inflammable tenements, and had not a gate that would shut. The revocation of the Edict of Nantes had just taken place (October 18), and there was no hope in a resuscitated strength through immigration, while the Huguenots were instilling new and vigorous blood throughout the English colonies.

The new governor, in the midst of this condition of affairs, was writing home of the dangers. He wanted Fort Frontenac strengthened, the vessels on Ontario repaired, and new ones put on Erie. "These precautions," he said, "are necessary, if we are to keep the English from securing the western fur trade."

It was the belief in Canada that Dongan was inciting the Iroquois to further strife. He himself denied that he followed any clandestine methods, and it seems quite clear that the French Jesuits, who were still among the Onondagas, did not have any such suspicions. Denonville, as a devotee of the Jesuits, may perhaps have known what these priests thought. As representatives of their respective royal masters, Denonville was far more fortunate than Dongan. The French governor had behind him in Louis XIV. a potentate whose ambition he could share. The timidity of James II. in every way in which he was brought to measure capacity with his neighbor across the channel left his American representative with only the shadow of support. In his own province, Dongan had a population half as large again as that of Canada, to say nothing of the moral support of a much larger preponderance of numbers in the adjacent English colonies.

Denonville and Dongan.

Dongan was the only governor along the Atlantic slope who was a constant source of anxiety to the French. The Canadians knew that the Iroquois dealt their strokes at the Illinois with greater security because these English of New York were their allies. Denonville felt that by the instructions which Louis had given him (March 10, 1685), it had become his duty to dispell the disquiet which La Barre's abandonment of the Illinois had occasioned. He was expected to show that the power of France must and could protect her Indian allies.

The English intentions were always a doubtful quantity. " We have always the English to warn us both on the north and on the south," said Duchesneau a little while before, " and the Iroquois are a constant threat. Perhaps we can placate the Indians ; perhaps destroy them ; but a great deal of uncertainty would be cleared up, if we could only buy the region dependent on Albany." And this wish remained as constant as the troublesomeness of the English and Iroquois. Denonville expressed the tiresome uncertainty of the situation when he declared it impossible to know just what to expect of a neighbor who was, as he phrased it, both lawless and infidel. He could see no remedy but in an increase of the Canadian population, and bringing into more compact settlements what they already had. The mischief lay in everybody trying to advance his little trading-post into the wilderness to catch the fur trader all the sooner.

It was clearly a part of the English policy to confront the French traders at the west wherever they could, and to outbid them in offers for the Indian fur. They even went to Mackinac, and were known among the Foxes near Green Bay, and were successful in diverting a good deal of trade from the French. Dongan did not hesitate to give English passes to Frenchmen and send them among the Ottawas, who, in the main, were middlemen in the peltry trade, having few beaver in their own territory. In May, 1686, Denonville was complaining to Seignelay that French renegades were leading English parties across Ontario. This was in defiance of the royal order, issued in April, 1684, which made it death for a Canadian to emigrate to Albany or Manhattan.

1686.

To frustrate this audacity, the French governor tried to interpose armed posts in their way. He ordered Duluth to the Detroit River with fifty men, and Durantaye built a stockade at the Chicago portage. Nothing disturbed Denonville more than the reckless and abandoned dispersement of the woodsmen, — bandits he called them, — who under some organization might become a help, but in their lawlessness were only a mischief. It was not always they could be forced to offer resistance to an enemy. When by combination they could have protected the region of their trade, their wanton independency left the Iroquois to raid the country about Lake Superior so effectively that the marts at Montreal were without peltry from that district.

Bush-rangers.

It was to remedy this that the government instituted some active movements on the one side toward Hudson's Bay, and on the other toward the upper waters of the Mississippi. In the last direction, they had in the field a vigilant leader in Nicolas Perrot. He had been in command at Green Bay, and thence with a small party he struck across the country which Duluth and Hennepin had traversed, and planted the French flag on forts and stockades. He built one such post just below the mouth of the Wisconsin, and another on the shores of Lake Pepin. He kept his ears open for reports of more remote regions, and heard of a distant people to the west, who wore ornaments of stone in their ears and noses.

Nicolas Perrot at the west.

When he heard that there were others among them who used horses and looked like the French, he knew them to be the Spaniards of New Mexico, whom the French might yet encounter in the southwest. Hearing of some Iowas up the river, a tribe which the French had not yet met with, he went to seek them. From this direction there came stories of men in houses which walked on the water, and he knew that the English were still pressing their trade in Hudson's Bay. Duluth, meanwhile, was directly facing this impending danger. He had been among the tribes which sought the English of the great bay, giving presents, and alluring them to the French posts. He had written to Quebec that in two years he could break up this English trade. At last an overland expedition from Montreal set out in March, 1685, going from the Ottawa River, along a route which some hardy bushrangers had found the year before. The force was placed under the command of the Chevalier De Troyes, and with him, as his lieutenant, went Iberville, an indomitable spirit, in whom New France and Louisiana were to have much confidence for some years to come. Troyes scoured the shores of James's Bay with great alacrity, capturing Forts Hayes and Rupert. He completed his round of devastation at Fort Albany. The Canadian Company of the North had got its revenge on the Hudson Bay Company, and it was by no means certain that this success was not as gratifying to the Catholic king of England as to the grand monarch himself. When the specious treaty of neutrality was signed between the two powers at Whitehall (November 16, 1686), Troyes was back in Quebec. The few survivors of the captured garrisons, crowded in a single small vessel, entered English waters to learn how they had been abandoned by such a peace. The Bay Company had ground enough for redress, and petitioned the crown; but as long as Louis was keeping James on his throne, there was no remedy. There must, however, be some show of resentment, and the French busied themselves with proving before a commission that the English were but interlopers in the great bay, and were properly expelled. The controversy ended as might have been expected. The French remained in possession till the vexed question of priority could be settled, and the Eng-

Marginal notes:

The Iowas.

Duluth tending toward the north.

March, 1685.

Troyes and Iberville at Hudson's Bay.

1686, Nov. Treaty between England and France.

lish king warned the American colonies by a circular letter
(January, 1688) not to mar the prosperity of the French meanwhile. The war which followed the expulsion of James, the

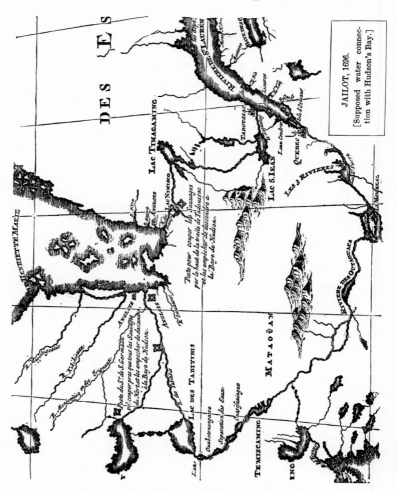

next year, threw this vast territory of the north once more, as
we shall see, in the scales of contention.

Meanwhile this success under Troyes found a contrast less
pleasant for the French to the south of the St. Lawrence.

Louis could bid the English king to instruct Dongan to keep
the peace, but there was no commission to be intrusted with
settling the question of interloping in the Iroquois   Rival claims
country; indeed, Denonville soon found that the   to the Iroquois coun-
documentary registry of the evidences of early French   try.
expeditions to the country south of Ontario was nowhere to be
discovered in the archives of Canada, and he informed Seignelay that Talon must have taken such papers to France. He
affirmed, too, that Talon had carried off the agreement, signed
by the Iroquois in 1667, to put themselves under the French
king's dominion. All this was embarrassing in his correspondence with so wary a diplomatist as Dongan. The best that
Denonville could do was what Vaudreuil and Begon did at a
later day, — to search the *Jesuit Relations* for such unofficial
records as could be found on going back for forty years. Dongan had something better vouched in the various recorded trea-
ties which the English had made with the Iroquois, by which
they succeeded to their rights of dominion.

Denonville, aware that he was expected to make the Iroquois
feel the French power with little delay, had soon discovered
that it took many months to bring the forces scattered throughout New France to bear upon any one point. Durantaye and
Duluth, whose assistance was necessary, were too remote to be
communicated with for any concerted action during   November,
1685.
the next season, and it was in November, 1685, that
the governor was thus looking ahead. The long interval, however, could be employed in provisioning the fort at Cataraqui
and making needful preparations. In the spring of   1687.
1687, events were moving forward. The governor's
messengers had long since departed to his lieutenants in the
west; and by this time Dongan, who learned of the plan, had
warned the Iroquois. It was by no means certain, after the dis-
appointment which had been felt at La Barre's recusancy, that
the western Indians could be brought again to the task. The
French were pretty sure to have to confront, if the confederates
combined, about two thousand of the best warriors that the red
race could produce. These fighters were not indeed   Iroquois
braves.
all of the old stocks of the confederacy, for debauch-
ery had checked their natural increase, and the losses of num-

bers in their incessant wars had been largely repaired by the adoption of their prisoners. But the prestige of the Iroquois name was such that the aliens grew to the work imposed upon them. It was supposed that about twelve hundred Mohegans could also be brought against the French.

It had been a provision of the treaty of neutrality between Louis XIV. and James II. that the colonies should remain at peace, however the native tribes should be impelled to war. Notwithstanding this, the French government had been sending over more regular troops, and something like sixteen hundred soldiers were at Denonville's disposal. He expected to use them largely in garrisoning posts, while the more experienced militia were to be used in the campaign. It was June 13, 1687, when he left Montreal, at the head of eight hundred troops, and he found he had two thousand with him when he reached Fort Frontenac. Here he gave himself to a fiendish act, and it has been alleged, not, however, by proof which the Catholic historians accept, that the bishop approved it. A number of unoffending Iroquois who were living near the fort were seized to prevent their sending tidings across the lake, which act was defensible ; but they were tied to stakes and tortured for the amusement of the neighboring mission Indians, which was certainly indefensible, even if in dying they kissed the cross to save their souls.

June, 1687. Denonville's campaign.

Iroquois tortured.

Lamberville. Denonville had not recalled the missionary Lamberville, who was among the Onondagas, for fear of exciting suspicion. This proceeding meant abandoning him to his fate. If Charlevoix is to be trusted, the Iroquois took no advantage of their opportunity, but suffered him to depart. He soon appeared at Cataraqui, to look with horror, let us hope, on the inhumanity of a higher race. It was July 4 when the imposing flotilla of four hundred canoes and bateaux moved away from Fort Frontenac. Three days before, Denonville had heard from Niagara — this form of the name was just now coming into vogue, and was to be made popular shortly after in Coronelli's map — that the contingent from the west for which he had hoped had reached that point. With this rein-

Tonty, Duluth, and Durantaye join Denonville. forcement was Tonty, who had come from the Rock with sixteen French and two hundred Indians. He had struck across the country to Detroit, and there

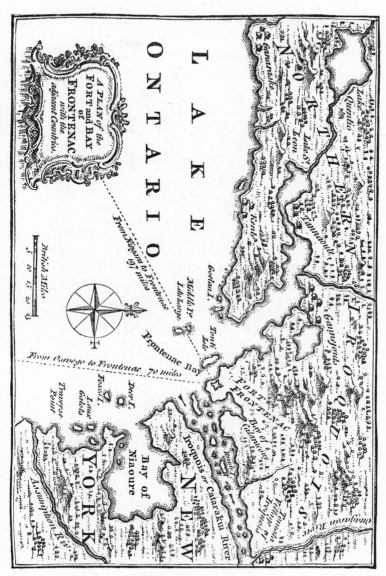

[From the *London Magazine*, 1758.]

he had met and joined Duluth, coming with a large body from
the upper lakes, and Durantaye, who led a force from Mackinac.
On Lake Huron, their lieutenants had met and captured a trad-

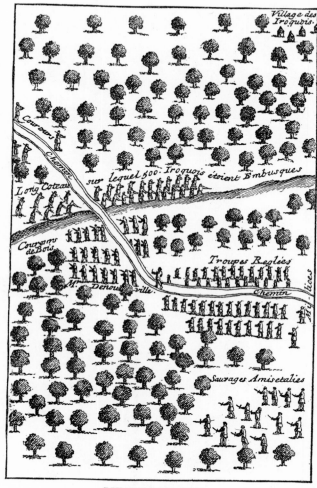

DENONVILLE'S MARCH.
[From La Hontan's *Nouveaux Voyages*.]

ing party of Dutch and English, who were seeking traffic under
permits from Dongan.   On Lake Erie, a second party fell into
their hands.   Their prisoners were sixty in all, and the plunder

of their canoes was valuable. Towards the end of June, they had all assembled at Niagara, when the word was sent on to Cataraqui. They numbered about one hundred and eighty French, and four hundred Indians. By the return of the messenger, they were ordered to join Denonville at Irondequoit Bay. On July 10, these two sections of the invading force, coming from opposite directions, met at that rendezvous, being together not far from three thousand men. One day was spent in building a fort, in which four hundred men were left to protect their canoes. On July 12, they began their march inland, carrying provisions for thirteen days. There *1687, July. The Seneca country invaded.* were twenty-two miles before them, and on they plodded, Callières leading a vanguard of bushrangers and Indians, Denonville following with his regulars and Canadians, while a body of savages and a force of white men almost as savage brought up the rear. The day was one of sweltering heat. Suddenly the van found itself in an ambush of three hundred Senecas. There was some loss on both sides, for the enemy, unaware of the nearness of the main body, were over-bold. The defenders at last yielded. The French were glad of a halt for the night. The next morning, the van advanced with caution, and was unopposed. The Senecas had sent off their women, hid their treasures, and burned their chief town. The invaders came to the blackened ruins, and made everything wherever they went blacker still. They uprooted gardens and cornfields. They leveled everything that stood. There were ten days of havoc, but the marauders were not spared a misery of their own. They ate immoderately of green corn and fresh pork, — for the hogs of the villages were running wild, — and sickened. The wild riot maddened their Indian allies, and they scattered in crowds. On the 24th, such of the bewildered force as had kept together returned to their canoes. Re- *The French retire.* embarking and coursing alongshore to Niagara, Denonville built there a fort on the site of the one constructed by *Fort built at Niagara.* La Salle. He left the Chevalier de Troyes with a hundred men to hold it, and then the flotilla started down the lake, and on August 13 Denonville was at Montreal.

The governor had inflicted a chastisement, but only upon the Senecas. The other tribes of the great confederacy were unhurt. He had done nothing, in fact, from which the Senecas

themselves could not readily recover. He had killed but few
of them. He had destroyed their villages and ruined their
crops, but their habitations were easily replaced, and English
corn was to be had for the asking.

We have Denonville's own account of these proceedings. It
Denonville's was found by Brodhead in the Archives of the Marine
narrative. at Paris, and Mr. O. H. Marshall published it for the
first time. It can be supplemented by a variety of minor

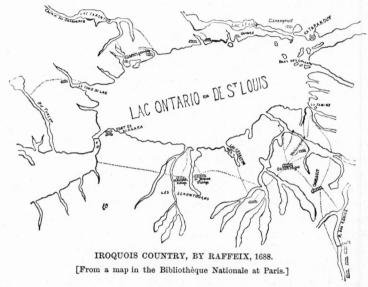

IROQUOIS COUNTRY, BY RAFFEIX, 1688.
[From a map in the Bibliothèque Nationale at Paris.]

sources, so that we are not at any loss in telling the story.
Marshall has succeeded best in identifying the sites of the cam-
paign, and he places them by his map near the modern town of
Victor.

It was on his return to the Rock, on October 27, 1687, that
1687, October Tonty met Joutel and heard the false stories about La
Tonty goes Salle. A few weeks later, when Couture came up the
back to the
Rock, and river and Tonty learned the truth, he started down
descends the
Mississippi. to the gulf with five Frenchmen and three Indians,
to do what he could to rescue the poor lingerers at the Texan
fort. He was not without some hope, too, of banding the
river tribes and attacking the Spaniards; for Couture had suggested the practicability of doing so, and the plan had a certain

opportuneness in it, since he had just heard from Denonville of war with Spain being declared. It was early in December

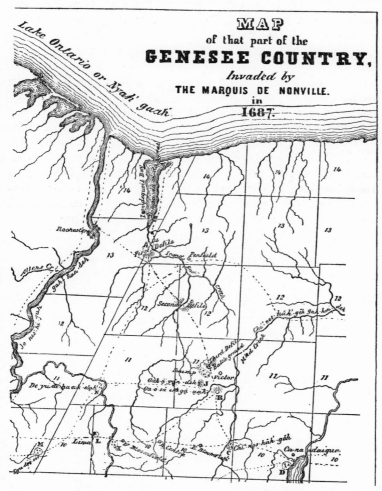

[A section of the map given in O. H. Marshall's *Historical Writings*. The dash-and-dot line is Denonville's route; the dash lines show Indian paths. *A*, Indian fishing station. *B, C, M, N*, the four principal Seneca villages. *D*, Indian village. *T*, the fort.]

when Tonty left his fort. Late in March (1689), he was at the Red River. Here he got tidings, as he thought, of Heins, one of La Salle's conspirators, and resolved to find him if he could.

His men revolted, and only two would accompany him further. He lost his powder while crossing a river, and when he reached the village that he sought, he found nothing of the German, but suspected by the bearing of the Indians that they had killed him.

Tonty had no courage, perhaps no strength, for further trial. His life as a trader. He turned his canoe upstream, and after many tribulations reached his Illinois fort. The next year, in consideration of his unselfish services, a royal grant made him master of his stronghold, and he lived on there for a dozen years, trading with the Indians who came to the post. The government regarded him kindly, and when it stopped other unofficial trading, it suffered his to go on; and year by year two of his canoes and twelve men brought his peltry to a market as long as the fortress on the Rock was permitted to exist. In 1702, a royal order caused it to be abandoned, and Tonty sought Iberville at the mouth of the Mississippi.

CHAPTER XVI.

FRONTENAC RECALLED.

1687–1698.

It was said at the time that in his devastation of the Seneca country, Denonville had destroyed the wasps' nest, but the wasps were unharmed. As always results from such a success, the victorious party was more alarmed than the beaten one. There was trepidation throughout the St. Lawrence settlements. The noise of axe and beetle betrayed the work of palisading on every hand. There was a cessation of the fur trade, for the prowling Senecas were too numerous to be evaded.

1687. Trepidation in Canada.

On the other hand, Dongan was not intimidated, but he was anxious. He had promptly protested against the occupation of Niagara, — Onygaro as he called it, — and was not quite sure but some movement against Albany was hatching in Quebec. There was ground for the suspicion, for Callières was sent to Paris to present a project of invading New York by way of Lake Champlain and capturing Manhattan, a scheme that always came to the minds of the Canadian leaders when matters grew unbearable. There were French spies in Albany that were not easy to discover; but Dongan expelled the Jesuits from the Iroquois villages, and stopped any revelations through that source. In November, (1687), it seemed as if there was to be an end to the prevarications of the English king, when word reached Dongan that he must protect the Iroquois against any repetition of the recent raid; but the feeling that some sort of a stand could at last be made did not continue long. James yielding to the exactions of Louis, Dongan was recalled, and the English colonists were deprived of the ablest leader they had had in their contention with the French. This was some

Anxiety in New York.

November.

Dongan recalled.

relief to Denonville, but he was not so content with the rumors which came from the west. The old antipathy against La Salle was perpetuated in the suspicion entertained of his successors, and Denonville was by no means sure that mischief was not brewing in the Illinois country. He feared that the young men in Tonty's company valued the profits of trade more than loyalty to France, and that they only awaited an opportunity to carry their interests over to the English. Denonville's recommendation to the home government was to change the governor in that region often enough to prevent the ripening of any mischievous plot.

Sir Edmund Andros, with more extensive power, covering
Sir Edmund Andros.
New England as well as New York, succeeded Dongan. He was soon made to understand that the English king had constituted the Five Nations as a part of his subjects. It was a renewed instance of playing fast and loose on James's part. Andros was quite of Dongan's spirit, and he had forbidden the Iroquois to yield to the temptations which the French were offering, under what they evidently supposed were better chances of success, now that Dongan had gone. To accept some advantage from the Iroquois, the Canadians proved willing to abandon the Illinois once more. They were ready to cause even the destruction of Fort St. Joseph in order to appease the confederates.

The sacrifice was premature, for on July 14, 1689, the flight
1689, July.
The English revolution known in Quebec.
of James II. from England was known in Quebec, and there was an end of French influence at the English court. War between the two countries was certain. Perrot had already been ordered to the western country, and in the autumn of 1688 he had passed with forty
1688–89.
Perrot at the west.
men, by Green Bay and the Fox River, into the region bordering upon the upper Mississippi. On the 8th of May (1689), on the Wisconsin side of Lake Pepin, he emphasized the French claim to the possession of all this region watered by the St. Croix, St. Peter, and the other afflu-
Pierre le Sueur.
ents of the great river, and took formal occupation, under the observation of a notary. Pierre le Sueur, whose name had been associated since 1683 with the early explorations on the upper Mississippi and in the present Minnesota, was with him at the time.

At this period, when England exerted herself to secure a Protestant succession, and France was under the most imperial of her kings, in the greatest amplitude of his powers, a political prophet, as Professor Seeley says in his *Expansion of England*, comparing the prospects of these two colonizing powers, might have been led, by observing what an advantage the possession of the St. Lawrence and the Mississippi French and English schemes and prospects. valley gave to France, to think that in the future North America would belong rather to her than to England, notwithstanding there were but about twelve thousand Frenchmen on the continent, to something like two hundred thousand English. La Salle had, it is true, failed at the mouth of the great river, but there was no one as yet to dispute the French sway along its banks. There had been danger at the north, but Duluth, Perrot, and Tonty were vigilant. The English, indeed, had threatened to extend their influence from Hudson's Bay by the attractions of trade rather than by occupying the soil. It was a struggle in which English mercantile thrift was set against the flexible adaptability to circumstances which characterized the French intercourse with the natives. The greater superiority of the English as colonists has usually been recognized by the French themselves, unless they limited the sphere of colonization to the pioneer work of the bush-ranger, as Rameau has done in comparing the two. At this very time a memorial was presented to Seignelay, setting forth the instability of trade and fur-hunting in comparison with the tilling of the soil, as conducing to colonial prosperity.

But the chief danger to the French lay nearer their main settlements, and did not diminish till the Iroquois, ten or fifteen years later, began to lose their prestige. The revenge for the devastation of the Senecas came suddenly, when a failure in investing Fort Frontenac set fourteen or fifteen hundred of the confederates free to fall (August, 4, 5, 1689) upon the settlement at Lachine. Death or capture 1688, August. Lachine attacked. came to three or four hundred unprepared victims. The suddenness of the attack seemed to paralyze Denonville, since he countermanded orders for pursuit, when Subercase, who had reached the scene from Montreal, was prepared to hunt the assailants down. Dr. Shea does not doubt English complicity in this movement of the Iroquois; and why should he, when

French and English were as barbarous as their savage depen-
dants?   There is little doubt that Governor Leisler of New
York had prompted them to the futile effort to capture Fort
Frontenac. If they failed in this, they succeeded in luring
Father Milet out of the stronghold, and ran him off to the

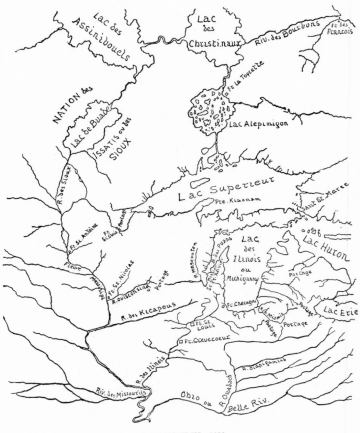

FRANQUELIN, 1688.

Oneida country. We have his own account of his captivity,
and the English at Albany did not profit much in the face of
the influence which he acquired in the savage councils.

It had earlier become apparent that if there was to be open
war along the frontiers, the French needed a better leader than

Denonville. Consequently there was general acquiescence in
the wisdom of the choice when Frontenac came back
to his old post. His remembered career gave ground
for hope, and the necessity for a man of his indomitable courage and unfailing resources had induced the king to

1689.
Frontenac
recalled.

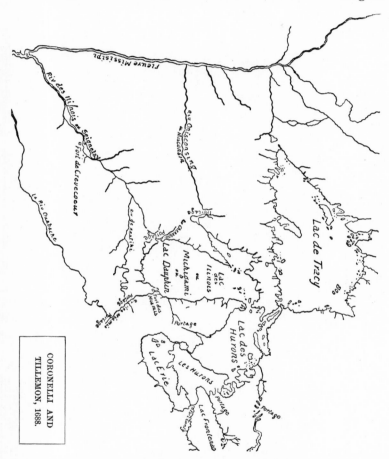

CORONELLI AND
TILLEMON, 1688.

forget all the charges which had compelled his recall seven
years before. Frontenac did not disappoint expectation, though
he was now a man of threescore and ten.

His instructions, which were dated June 7, 1689, had made
it imperative on him to attempt two things, — the expulsion of

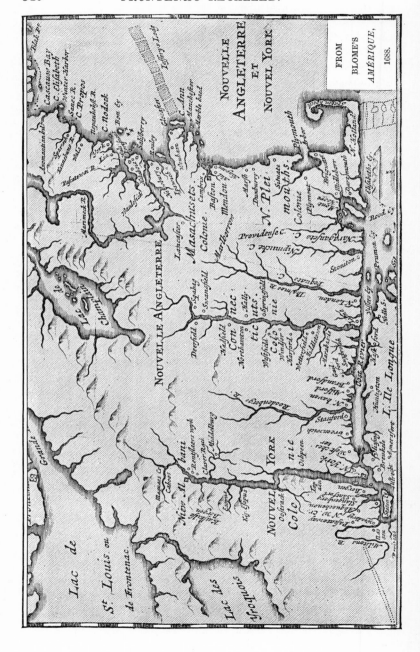

the English from Hudson's Bay, and the capture of New York.
The last did not contemplate Callières's plan of invasion along
Lake Champlain, except as subordinate to a direct naval attack
at the mouth of the Hudson. It is curious to see how widely at
variance with the geographical conditions of the problem were

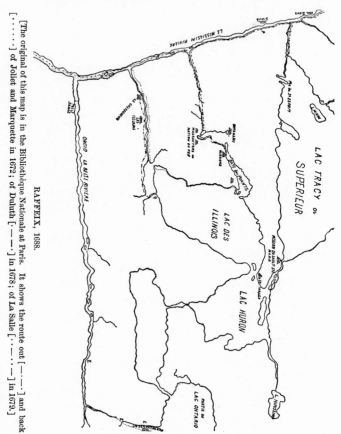

[The original of this map is in the Bibliothèque Nationale at Paris. It shows the route out [— . —] and back [. . . . . .] of Joliet and Marquette in 1672; of Duluth [— —] in 1678; of La Salle [. . . . . .] in 1679.]

RAFFEIX, 1688.

the current notions which prevailed even in Holland at this
time, notwithstanding the close intimacy which the Dutch had
had with this region. Official knowledge in France was of
course much better, but the Amsterdam edition of Blome's
America, which was just published (1688), makes the portage
between the St. Lawrence and the Atlantic at a divide which

separated the headwaters of the Connecticut River and the sources of Lake Champlain.

The scheme of invasion of the English colonies, as they understood it in the cabinets of Quebec and Paris, was a far-reaching one. It would isolate New England for the same end which Burgoyne and Clinton sought, when in 1777 they aimed at uniting their forces at Albany. It would deprive the Iroquois of their accustomed dependence on the English, and so check their western raiding. It would give to Canadian trade a harbor that was not blocked by ice a large part of the year.

It was hoped that the campaign could be consummated by

Failure of attempt on New York. October (1689) ; but that month had already come, when the fleet under Frontenac reached the Gulf of St. Lawrence. To perfect the strategical arrangements involved, and organize a land service, the governor, leaving the fleet in the gulf, had intended to go on to Quebec, and when all was ready to send back word to his naval associate in the gulf, who was then to proceed to New York. All this, to be effective, ought to have been done at an earlier season. Therefore it was not long before the French determined that the project must be abandoned for that year at least.

The demoralization which Frontenac found on reaching Quebec, as it turned out, gave no time to think of any such

1690, Jan. Troubles at the west. offensive undertaking. With the opening of the year (January, 1690), it was known in Quebec that conspiracy against the French had ripened among the tribes around Mackinac. They were known to be joining in the councils of the Iroquois. The Foxes were rendering the portage to the Illinois by Green Bay almost useless, because of their hostility, and all communication with the Mississippi valley was forced to find a channel by Lake Superior and the St. Croix, where we find Le Sueur, a little later, endeavoring to protect even this distant portage from hostile raids. Perrot was doing what he could to hold the Ottawas to their allegiance.

It was clear that Frontenac had no resources to meet these dangers where they lay. Louis in sending him to Canada had warned him that he must do the royal bidding with no further help than he could find in the country, for France had dangers enough at home to employ all her troops. It was also apparent that to paralyze the English support of the Iroquois, whose machinations had produced this western difficulty, these rivals must be kept busy at home. While there was a plan under consideration at Versailles to attack Boston, Frontenac thought

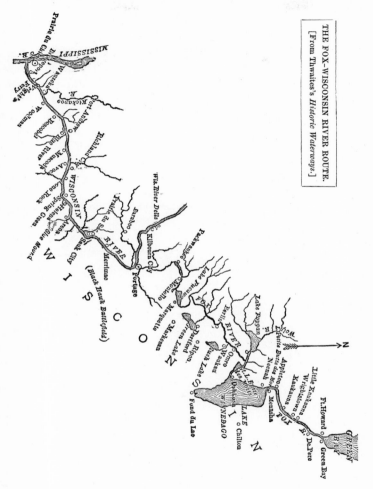

THE FOX-WISCONSIN RIVER ROUTE.
[From Thwaites's *Historic Waterways*.]

that it was left for him to set on foot the expeditions which led to the bloody work at Schenectady, Salmon Falls, and Fort Loyal (the modern Portland). In the spring of 1690, the English at Albany, aware of the natural result of any Iroquois defection, had warned the Boston government of

Bloody work at the east.

what they were to expect along the eastern frontiers. The New Englanders on their part, and at the same time, sought to keep the attention of Frontenac on the alert along the St. Lawrence, and so leave the western question to settle itself, confident that the Iroquois intrigues were equal to the task. When both sides showed their hands, there was enough to do in the east.

The New Englanders had long been familiar with the Nova Scotia coasts, and it had been a frequent complaint of Meules, the intendant, that the Boston fishermen dared to make the Acadian fisheries their own, while there was hardly a pilot or sailor in all Canada. The time had come for a firmer grasp.

1690. Sir William Phips's expeditions to Port Royal; to Quebec. The spring of 1690 was a busy one in Massachusetts Bay, in fitting out the armament which Sir William Phips led against Port Royal (Annapolis), and in May he came back in triumph. He could now enter upon the greater preparation for an attack on Quebec. At the same time a congress at Albany had planned a land attack by Lake Champlain under Fitz-John Winthrop, who was commissioned by Leisler, on July 31, 1690. The two expeditions were to act in conjunction, and Phips sailed from Boston with thirty-two vessels in August. Colonel Church was sent to the eastward along the Maine coast, to divert attention, and he accomplished enough for this purpose; but Winthrop's effort was a failure from the beginning, so that Phips approached Quebec with no prospect of the expected coöperation. His miscarriage was worse than Winthrop's, in that he blustered and retreated. Frontenac put on a bolder front than his strength warranted, and Phips was deceived. The New England ships straggled down the river, and did little but burn, on Anticosti Island, the establishment with which the government had rewarded Joliet for his services in discovery. The baffled New Englanders also managed later to intercept some of the supply ships, which Quebec could ill spare, but Iberville, who was returning with some plunder from a renewed attack on the English at Hudson's Bay, eluded the English ships and escaped to France.

Phips's failure was every way dispiriting. The merchants of New England and New York had counted on his success to control the Indian trade of the west, for the monopoly of the Hudson Bay Company was diminish-

Fur trade north and south.

ing this western trade too much to make a division of it between the French and the English profitable to both. The Carolinians were already opening the channels of trade in the valley of the Tennessee. In this same spring London merchants, trading in these colonies, had urged a protest in the Lords against the Commons being allowed to give new force to the charter which Charles II. had bestowed upon the Hudson Bay Company. They represented that, under color of pushing the search for a northwest passage, the company was both engrossing the trade of the far west, and driving the French to an interference with the trade of other English farther south, upon whose prosperity that of England depended.

Frontenac had never shown himself more signally equal to a trying emergency than when he hurried to Quebec and defied the English fleet. When he saw it disappear behind the island of Orleans, he experienced a relief which he could hardly have anticipated. His good fortune did not consist in the discomfiture of Phips alone. He had succeeded in running down to Montreal the first flotilla of fur-laden canoes which the merchants of that town had seen for a long time. There were a hundred and ten of these little cargoes of peltry to reanimate trade. Frontenac, seventy years old as he was, was joyful enough to dance a war-dance with the Indian boatmen.

In November, Frontenac wrote out his dispatches upon his success. He somewhat exuberantly told the minister that if he would take care of the English for the future, he could deal with the Iroquois. He sent his letters by a young Gascon, who had come to Canada six or seven years before, and had made his way into Frontenac's favor. He was an imaginative, if not audacious, story-teller, La Hontan by name, and what he claimed to have seen in the far west, beyond the Mississippi, along a river by which one could ascend to the mountains, and thence reach by another stream the Pacific, passed into current belief some years later, when he published his book. His story began to be doubted by 1716 ; but it continued to have a fitful existence, accepted wholly by some, in a qualified way by others, and discarded entirely by the warier, till its last defenders disappeared in the early part of the present century. The Long or Dead River, as he calls it, — the last name fitting its sluggish current,

1690, November. Frontenac's dispatches.

La Hontan.

LA HONTAN'S

CANADA.

— came and went on the maps, and was now identified with this or the other stream of the modern geography till the later discoverers found it difficult to place it anywhere.

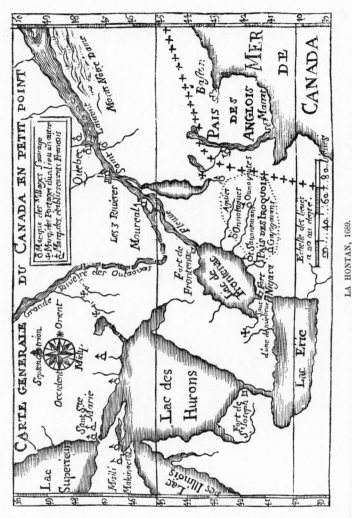

LA HONTAN, 1689.

[The line of crosses indicates the French view of the English limits.]

Frontenac lost no time in sending the tidings of his successes to the western tribes, hoping to stay their defection, but the defeat of Phips and the discouragement of Winthrop had little effect on the Iroquois. They still prowled and attacked, and it was thought necessary to palisade the Jesuit mission The Iroquois
still active. at Mackinac.

The government in London was little inclined to risk another armament in the St. Lawrence. In November, 1691, Phips was in London suggesting it, but he did not press the subject.

The colonists were soon using their influence to bring the Iroquois and the Shawnees into terms of agreement. The result was to relieve the confederates of an enmity which distracted them, and it left them freer to renew their raids along the St. Lawrence. So it happened that it was not till 1693 1693. that the French succeeded in getting through to Montreal another flotilla of canoes, when two hundred of them, under escort of a force which Frontenac put at the disposal of Louvigny, now the commandant at Mackinac, relieved the storehouses at the straits, and brought trade once more to the St. Lawrence.

There were rumors of another attack on Quebec from Boston, to be aided this time by a naval contingent from England, and Frontenac set vigorously to work to strengthen the defenses of his capital, and kept the confederates occupied by new irruptions among them. Governor Fletcher, then in authority in New York, had received enlarged powers, particularly in relation to the militia of the neighboring colonies, in order that he might command a dangerous force, if invasion was 1694. intended. In 1694, the Iroquois showed signs of faltering. They told the English that they must have more active help if they were still to press the French. At the same time they sent a deputation to Quebec. In May, and again in September, they urged their diplomacy with Frontenac, but he was firm in his rejection of any offer that did not include the western allies of the French, and which did include the English. The Iroquois were not quite ready to abandon their white neighbors, or forego their hope of eating the Illinois, as they always expressed it. So the negotiations failed.

Frontenac's sense of duty towards these western allies was not acceptable either to the bishop or to the home government. It meant too much interference with plans, to please the Jesuits, and the king was easily persuaded by that body. When

Louis tried, a little later, to force Frontenac to make terms with
Frontenac   the Iroquois on conditions that broke faith with the
and the   western tribes, the courage and obstinacy of the gov-
western
tribes.   ernor were put to the test, but he carried his point.
He knew there was one, in his ardent lieutenant on the Illinois,
who was ready to make a new effort for the occupation of the
Mississippi.   Tonty hoped for an attack on Mexico from such
a base; he hoped to develop the lead mines and augment the
trade in peltries; and above all, he hoped in this way to prevent
the threatening advent of the English.   It was to warn the
government of this danger that Le Sueur went to Paris the
next year (1695).   This adventurer was now given a trade
monopoly for ten years of the upper Mississippi, to make good
the French hold on that part of it; but the English captured
him on his way back.

With the return flotilla in September, 1694, Frontenac sent
1694. La   La Mothe Cadillac to govern at Mackinac and be-
Mothe at   yond.   This lieutenant soon informed Frontenac that
Mackinac.
he found the Ottawas despairing of the French protection, as the governor was too well aware that they must be, considering what kind of lessons the Jesuit spirit was inculcating.
That liquor was no longer sold to them was one of the enforced
deprivations which the Indians laid to the Jesuits.   If this
deprivation had in many ways proved salutary, Cadillac saw
The English   that it had also a bad effect on French domination,
and the   since it induced communication with the English,
liquor traf-
fic.   where the savages had little difficulty in obtaining
what they desired.   This longing for liquor was always strong
enough to counteract the purposes of the French trader, who
aimed to keep the Indian sufficiently in his debt to leave him
little occasion to seek the English for trade.   Communication
with these rivals of the French could only mean a weakening
of their allegiance, and there was enough of it to cause no small
disquiet to Cadillac.   This officer soon found that the most
stubborn pagan would receive any amount of baptism for
an equal amount of brandy, and would make little distinction
between brandy with and without the sacred rites.

Cadillac soon informed Frontenac that there could be no
peace with the Iroquois till the English were eliminated from
the problem, and there was no effectual way of doing it but

to capture and hold the English posts at Albany and New York.

[From La Hontan's *Nouveaux Voyages.*]

Cadillac, in his fort at Mackinac, — it had a garrison of two hundred men, — was in every way situated to know the conditions of the problem. His was an active mind, and it mattered little

THE LARGER

HENNEPIN MAP, 1697.

to him whether he had the mischievous Huron or the ungodly bushranger to control. He liked most to thwart the Jesuits, Mackinac post. and his purposes were all that Frontenac could wish in this respect. A pistol-shot away from the French post at Mackinac there was a permanent Indian village of six or seven thousand souls ; and not a tribe of the northwest but had all the time more or less straggling representatives hanging about the spot. The little place had some attractions for wide-eyed wonder. It was as fine a village as there was in Canada, as Cadillac describes it, with its sixty houses in a straight street, and the land, which the Indians cultivated for supplying the settlement with corn, cleared for three leagues around.

Frontenac, in forcing his policy, had other steadfast abettors Perrot and Le Sueur. in the west beside Cadillac. Perrot was a man to be trusted. The Sieur Juchereau was starting the first industry on the Mississippi in a tannery at the mouth of the Ohio. Le Sueur was building forts on the upper Mississippi to hold all hostile tribes in check. It was he who, in 1695, took the first Sioux to Montreal that had been seen on the St. Lawrence, — a chief, who did not survive the winter in his unwonted environment. That same year, as we have seen, this trader went to France to get new privileges.

In 1696, Frontenac was ready once more to try, on the Mo- 1696. Frontenac attacks the Iroquois. hawk, to settle this vexed question of the west. Early in the summer, the Iroquois were again making trouble, and the governor determined to deliver a heavy blow. He had recently received three hundred soldiers from France, and he sent a party to put Fort Frontenac in repair. He made the work move briskly for fear his intention would be checked by orders to desist. The confederates took the movement as a menace, and moved as rapidly. Early in July (1696), Frontenac was ready, and left Montreal with twenty-two hundred men. He went to Cataraqui, and then, crossing to Oswego, was at Lake Onondaga on the 1st of August. Here he saw the light of the village, which the Onondagas were burning as they retired before the French advance. A detachment was sent to destroy an Oneida town, while the main body did all the mischief they hurriedly could. This end accomplished, they were off for Fort Frontenac before the English at Albany knew

what had happened. The occurrence readily suggested arguments to those who were at this time urging, in the Board of
Trade at London, that the English power should be centralized
in a captain-general; and it gave force to the demand of William Penn that the English colonies could more effectively act
if they only had an annual congress.

It seemed, for a while, as if the vigor of Frontenac's campaign had unnerved the Iroquois. The English sent corn to
their desolated villages, but it did not prevent the The Iroquois
confederates sending messengers to Quebec to pro- ask for
peace, but
pose a peace. Their incessant wars had told on their are refused.
strength, notwithstanding their custom of adopting prisoners.
Fletcher, the English governor, reckoned that they had been
reduced from twenty-five hundred warriors to less than thirteen hundred, and that they numbered perhaps fifteen thousand
souls in all. They had not, however, been reduced enough
to abandon their old grudge against the western Indians, and
Frontenac was not disposed to listen, unless they would include
in their peace the Ottawas and the other distant allies of the
French. The Iroquois would not yield, and the negotiations
fell through.

The French were now seriously considering an attack on
Boston, and we have the plans which were made for them
(January, 1697) and put in shape by their cartographer, Franquelin, to guide them up the harbor of that New England town;
but the Peace of Ryswick, in the autumn (September 1697. Peace
30, 1697), prevented action and brought a five years' of Ryswick.
truce with the English, and stayed the latter's purpose of seizing the mouths of the Mississippi. The news of the treaty
reached New York before it came to Quebec, and Frontenac
heard of it from this source in February, 1698; while 1698. Known
no confirmation came from his own government till in Canada.
July. This delay illustrated anew the disadvantages of an ice-
bound river, and brought a fresh reminder of the desirableness
of a more salubrious ingress to Canada. The Quebec government had long been aware of the maritime supremacy which
the open seaboard of the English colonies gave to their rivals,
and the English government had of late begun the construction
of ships of war in Massachusetts Bay, the "Falkland," a frig-
ate of fifty-four guns, having just been finished at Portsmouth.
This act was of itself ominous.

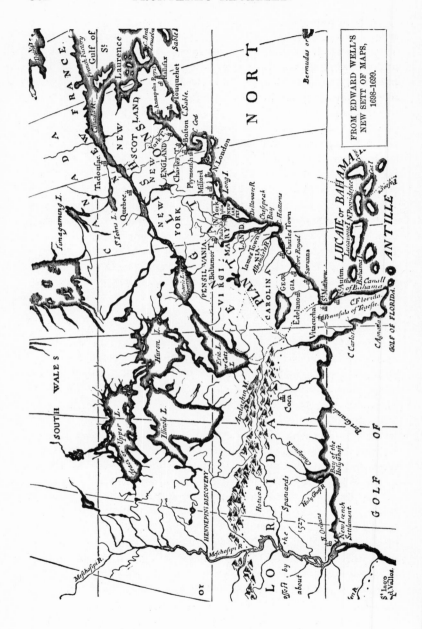

Lord Bellomont was now in command in New York. He had arrived April 2, 1698, and his authority covered also Massachusetts and New Hampshire. He soon undertook to arrange an exchange of prisoners with Frontenac, and demanded the return of some Iroquois whom the French had taken. To have acceded would have been to recognize the English sovereignty over those confederates, and Frontenac was too wary to be caught. As the summer went on, Bellomont (August 22) gave a more forcible expression of the English position in a warning to Frontenac that if the French attempted another invasion of the Iroquois country he was prepared to resist it. Frontenac received the intimation in his usual defiant spirit. *August. Bellomont warns Frontenac.*

A man of seventy-seven, as Frontenac now was, with all his rugged and blunt determination rendered bolder by a sort of barbarous pride, had not lived a life of turmoil without some

CHÂTEAU DE ST. LOUIS, 1698.
[From Sulte's *Canadiens-Français*, vii.]

inroads upon a naturally robust constitution. In December, word came to Boston from Champigny, his associate in the government, that the old soldier had at last succumbed, on the 25th of November (1698). A frozen river had again brought the necessity of communicating with France through a rival province. Champigny's messenger, Vincelot, sailed for Europe from Boston; but another messenger reached Paris a few hours ahead. This was Courtemanche, whom Callières had secretly dispatched ahead of Vincelot. This other messenger had ascended the Sorel, and reached New York by the Hudson. His earlier appearance in Paris very likely helped assure the appointment of Callières as the successor of Frontenac. *1698, Nov. 25. Frontenac dies.*

The death of Frontenac left France with many difficult problems yet unsolved. Notwithstanding the exclusive trade which the government preserved to itself at Tadoussac and elsewhere, Canada had not been able to *English and French rivalry.*

yield a revenue equal to the charges. The English and the Iroquois were a constant danger to the French occupation of the great valleys. The Iroquois still hovered along the St. Lawrence, and both they and their English allies were feared on the Mississippi. Adventurous traders were already crossing the Alleghanies from the seaboard colonies, and their huts were becoming permanently fixed along the Ohio. The government

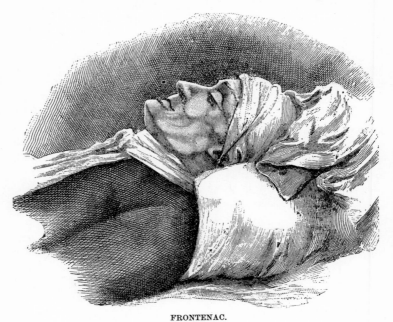

FRONTENAC.

[From Sulte's *Canadiens-Français*, vol. ii.]

at Paris, aware of this, and having no occasion of their own as yet to take possession of the region towards which these English were heading, felt the necessity of occupying the great valley of the west, merely to keep their rivals out. An expedition under Montigny and St. Cosme had started along Lake Michigan in the later months of 1698. It was the advance of the church to make good the prophecy of Marquette. They passed up the western shores of that lake; they stopped at Melwarik (Milwaukee); they crossed the Chicago portage early in November, and on

1698–1700.
Montigny,
St. Cosme,
Tonty,
Gravier,
La Sueur.

December 6 they reached the Mississippi. They had picked up Tonty at his post, and he guided them on as far as the Arkansas, when he was obliged to return. The missionaries, in their narrative, speak of this old companion of La Salle as the man who best knew the country, where he was both loved and feared by all the tribes. The next year (1700), Father Gravier made his descent of the Mississippi for the same purpose, and we have his additional account of experiences along its course. We learn from him how the English forerunners were active along the lines of the Tennessee, where some scattering Mohegans, remnants probably of those outcasts from New England whom La Salle had found so serviceable, were trading with adventurers from over the Appalachians. On the lower Mississippi, Gravier reports finding English guns in the hands of the savages. It is evident that Gravier was by no means sure that these English were destined to be seriously opposed. "I do not know what our court will decide about the Mississippi," he says, "if no silver mines are found, for our government does not seek land to cultivate. They care very little for mines of lead, which are very abundant near the Illinois." The previous year (1699), Le Sueur had passed up the Mississippi from its mouth, in charge of a band of miners.

The friendship of the Iroquois was still the key to the situation between the English and the French, not only along the St. Lawrence, but at the remotest western posts. Towards the close of Frontenac's life, the colonists on the Hudson were renewing their efforts to make it appear by deposition and memorial that they held the confederates as subjects of the English crown. Callières, while yet in tempo- Callières and the rary authority by the death of Frontenac, and before Iroquois. he was confirmed in his power, had assumed the same air of confident indifference toward these savages which Frontenac had borne. He refused to entertain any proposition for the exchange of prisoners which could be thought to constitute the slightest recognition of their dependence on the English. William III. had sent orders to Bellomont to unite with the powers in Canada in making the Iroquois keep a peace. Callières revealed this fact to the confederates, and in July, 1700, they thought it prudent to send mesengers to Quebec. Bellomont, on his part, tried to prevent any pact of the tribes with the French, and the Iroquois determined to treat with the French first and with the English next. The Onondagas even

1700, September 8. Peace with the Iroquois.
seemed inclined to break with the English, and on September 8, 1700, Callières concluded a treaty with the Iroquois deputies at Montreal, by which the confederates, the Hurons, the Ottawas, and the Abenakis were embraced in the terms of peace.

Meanwhile, the French and English were scheming to attain

1699-1700. Detroit.
a position at Detroit. Robert Livingston had urged Bellomont to take possession of that point, and secure control through it of the Miamis, Illinois, and Shawnees. It was hoped in this way to keep the Iroquois in subjection to the purposes of the authorities at Albany, by making them friends of the more distant tribes, and so to secure their trade. The English plan was delayed, and this hesitation gave Callières his opportunity. After he had made his treaty at Montreal, he planned to occupy Detroit, and in order not to attract the attention of the Iroquois, his purpose was to let Cadillac and Tonty approach it from the side of Lake Huron, and begin a fort there. It was Cadillac's notion to make it the chief western post for trade, and to discontinue the establishments at Mackinac and other points on the upper lakes. This plan raised great opposition both in Montreal and Mackinac, as tending to destroy or weaken their business prospects. The Jesuits, too, were aroused because Cadillac intimated a preference for Recollects in the missionary work, and had proposed to instruct the tribes in French, thereby diminishing the influence of the Jesuit interpreters.

To push his views, Cadillac went in the autumn of 1700 to France, to urge the scheme upon the Comte de Maurepas. He succeeded in bringing Pontchartrain over to his interests, and the way was opened to other movements, which took the active interest of France from the St. Lawrence and the lakes to the mouths of the Mississippi. This is another theme, beyond the scope of the present book.

INDEX.